"Impassioned insight. . . . By turns comic and elegiac, respectful and blasphemous, the book serves to broaden our concept of 'the sphinx who helped us to stage-manage chaos.'. . . Koestenbaum is an obsessive's obsessive. Little or nothing escapes his gaze."
—*Newsday*

"A series of very eccentric takes on the Jackie Kennedy of our dreams."
—*New York Times Book Review*

"Why are we fascinated with Jackie? What made her a public icon, an object of pity, envy, scorn, admiration? Audacious and brilliant . . . Koestenbaum provides answers that promise you'll never look at Jackie the same way again."
—*Hartford Courant*

WAYNE KOESTENBAUM, an associate professor of English at Yale, is the author of the National Book Critics Circle Award nominee *The Queen's Throat: Opera, Homosexuality, and the Mystery of Desire*, as well as two volumes of poetry. The recipient of a 1994 Whiting Writer's Award, he lives in New Haven, Connecticut.

"A rapturous experience for all Jackie junkies. Wayne Koestenbaum reads the sacred icon with a shrewd yet delicate sensibility."   —Avital Ronell

"Brilliant . . . Koestenbaum's steely finger never leaves the quickening pulse of American mythology. . . . Read this book."
                                        —*Memphis Commercial Appeal*

"A very funny portrait and . . . a great deal of truth."   —*Tampa Tribune-Times*

"Some of the most entertaining prose in years . . . a thoughtful and unexpectedly moving book."
                                        —*Atlanta Journal-Constitution*

"Buoyant, witty . . . daring, truthful, and fun."
                                        —*Literary Review*

Also by Wayne Koestenbaum

The Queen's Throat:
Opera, Homosexuality, and the Mystery of Desire

Ode to Anna Moffo and Other Poems

Rhapsodies of a Repeat Offender

Double Talk:
The Erotics of Male Literary Collaboration

Jackie
Under My Skin

INTERPRETING

AN ICON

•

WAYNE

KOESTENBAUM

A PLUME BOOK

PLUME
Published by the Penguin Group
Penguin Books USA Inc., 375 Hudson Street,
New York, New York 10014, U.S.A.
Penguin Books Ltd, 27 Wrights Lane, London W8 5TZ, England
Penguin Books Australia Ltd, Ringwood, Victoria, Australia
Penguin Books Canada Ltd, 10 Alcorn Avenue,
Toronto, Ontario, Canada M4V 3B2
Penguin Books (N.Z.) Ltd, 182–190 Wairau Road,
Auckland 10, New Zealand

Penguin Books Ltd, Registered Offices:
Harmondsworth, Middlesex, England

Published by Plume, an imprint of Dutton Signet,
a division of Penguin Books USA Inc.
This is an authorized reprint of a hardcover edition
published by Farrar, Straus and Giroux. For information
address Farrar, Straus and Giroux, 19 Union Square West,
New York, New York 10003.

First Plume Printing, May, 1996
10 9 8 7 6 5 4 3 2 1

Picture research by Natalie Goldstein. Picture credits: [25], AP/Wide World;
[33], Eric Weiss/WWD; [39, 45, 55 (l & r), 87, 121, 149, 157, 163, 169, 191,
212], UPI/Bettmann; [63, 235], Archive Photos; [69, 70], © 1962, 1963
MacFadden/Bartell; [75], The Kobal Collection; [85] Paul Shutzer,
Life magazine © Time Inc.; [101], Archive Photos/Archive France;
[103], Art Rickerby, *Life* magazine © Time Inc.; [111] CBS Photo-Warnecke;
[127], Archive Photos/Wargacki; [131] *Sixteen Jackies*, 1964. © The Andy
Warhol Foundation, Inc./ARS NY; [217], Ideal Publishing Corp., Inc.;
[235], Camera Press, London; [243], John F. Kennedy Library. Photo:
Arnold Sachs

 REGISTERED TRADEMARK — MARCA REGISTRADA

CIP data available

Printed in the United States of America

for Steven Marchetti

Acknowledgments

I especially wish to thank Jonathan Galassi, my magical editor; Faith Hornby Hamlin, my peerless agent, who gave this project the benefit of her enthusiasm and energy; and Elaine Pfefferblit, who inspired me to write this book, and passionately followed its progress.

For commenting on early drafts, I am grateful to Gary Luke, Jeanne Schinto, and Jacqueline Osherow. For providing the clarity that makes composition possible, I thank Lisa S. Rubinstein.

Clifford Chase, Lynn Enterline, Joseph Gordon, Kevin Kopelson, and Glenn Ligon extended precious solidarity. Julie Bertles and Paul Elie at FSG expertly handled countless details. Natalie Goldstein indefatigably tracked down the photographs. A fellowship from Yale University gave me time to write.

And I could not have completed this book without the sustaining table talk of Bruce Hainley, my partner in reverie.

Contents

Jackie Under My Skin

INTERPRETING AN ICON

JACKIE'S DEATH

I BEGAN TO WRITE about the allure of icon Jackie in May 1993, while the real Jacqueline Onassis was alive and well. I addressed my sentences toward her, in tranced apostrophe: *Dear Jackie, for a long time I have wanted to tell you about your frequent appearances in my dreams.* I had a mad notion that she would read my book and understand my desire; that she would acknowledge the legitimacy of public curiosity; that we might become friends. It was a hopeless quest, doomed to fail. Brashly, I wanted to effect a truce between Jacqueline Onassis and icon Jackie. I wanted to find—to liberate—my "inner Jackie"; somewhere in my body was trapped a mimic Jackie O, and I wanted to afford her some room to breathe. But my plans to scale Mount Jackie—to give voice to Jackie's charisma—were foiled. Her cancer was announced; with sad suddenness, she died. I can't address Jacqueline Onassis anymore. But icon Jackie remains, a baffling array of images still requiring interpretation—not because interpretation is a panacea for loss, but because Jackie darkly captivates, and captivation fumbles for a foothold in speech. Dare I find words for why Jackie mesmerizes? Even while Jacqueline Onassis was alive, icon Jackie had a life of her own, obeying comic-book laws; we could no more explain the icon than we could avert war, bewitch our neighbors, or reverse time.

The real Jackie may have been impatient with her icon; she may have wished her icon, her troublesome twin, would go away. But the icon refused to vanish. Millions felt that the icon was virtually part of their own flesh, indispensable as an artery. Millions felt warmly toward Jackie, not because they'd met her, but because her face and story had become part of mass consciousness, and had shed illumination helter-skelter across the globe.

We called Jackie an icon because she glowed, because she seemed ceaseless, because she resided in a wor-shipped, aura-filled niche. We called Jackie an icon because her image was frequently and influentially re-produced, and because, even when she was alive, she seemed more mythic than real. We called Jackie an icon because her story provided a foundation for our own stories, and because her face, and the sometimes glam-orous, sometimes tragic turns her life took, were lodged in our systems of thought and reference, as if she were a concept, a numeral, a virtue, or a universal tendency, like rainfall or drought.

It is easy, and tempting, to forget that an icon is an idea, not a person. Sometimes the two—icon, person—converged; most often they diverged. Say, once, that the real Jackie smiled, and that someone took a picture of Jackie smiling. The real smile, and the photo of the smile, occupy two separate spheres. The photo contributes to the formation of the icon, the colossus; the photo gives us a paper smile, a likeness, a representation, which necessarily deviates from its source. To those of us who never met Jackie, she remains mostly a figment; we may have wished that Jackie would grow more substantial, that she would step out of the photograph and intervene in our quotidian lives—but even to daydream about "the real Jackie" meant that we were deep in the throes of the icon.

When I began to dream about Jackie, years ago, she seemed public property, a shared figure, everyone's: a universal entity. What a safe celebrity to contemplate! She'd never contradict me. She'd never materialize, to prove my fantasy invalid. Then, with her death, the space of Jackie contemplation—which had seemed large as a carnival—shrank again to the size of a single, mortified body. Where I had previously felt great freedom contemplating Jackie—where, previously, "Jackie" had represented a zone of prairie space and unchecked rumination—suddenly Jackie was once again real, dying, dead, personal, absolute, her own. Thus I felt ejected from the premises on which I'd tried to build a dreamer's shaky home: the grounds of icon Jackie, which had seemed the most anonymous and grand of any public space I'd known, were suddenly, once again, off-limits. I write these sentences from an ambiguous moment in the history of Jackie: her size always changes, and it's difficult to know what size she is right now. Soon she may expand again. I cannot control the ebb and swell of Jackie's spectral media body, even though it is a body in which I have a considerable investment.

Despite the intense media coverage of Jackie's death, the fulsome tributes, the commemorative issues, she resists language. To speak about her has always seemed either tasteless or trivial. During her life, Jacqueline Onassis enforced silence: friends and family never spoke about her to the press, for they knew the consequence would be banishment. The night after her death, however, Brooke Astor and George Plimpton, among others, appeared on TV, offering reminiscences, braving the disapproval of Jackie's shade. About Jackie, all speech is unauthorized—including, of course, these words.

Jackie's funeral in St. Ignatius Loyola, the church where she'd been baptized sixty-four years before, was private, so with other fans I stood across the street on the corner of Park Avenue and Eighty-fourth Street in Manhattan, behind a police cordon. We Jackie lovers were pressed together behind sawhorses; police presence made us seem like revolutionaries or radicals, needing containment. I thought, "What do I want to see? Jackie is dead." But I needed to be present, to glimpse, at least, the casket; to experience an atmosphere that was, though generically sepulchral, also Jackie-specific.

We were many and restless, a crowd stirred by vague emotions. Next to me a black woman my age sipped a Coke while she listened to the funeral on a Walkman. Another black woman, middle-aged, addled, but with the charming gregariousness of New Yorkers unafraid to display their eccentricities, said to her, "Can't drink while you hold a radio. You'll be electrocuted." "Lay off," the Coke-sipping woman barked. This altercation might have been going on for some time.

As if on a crowded subway, I couldn't help but lean into the Coke-sipping woman. The older woman said to me, "You're touching her! You'll get electrocuted!" When a maid or mother emerged from a Park Avenue apartment house, wheeling a baby in a stroller (she tried to make her way through our throng, without success), a gay man with a fashionable goatee said, "Choose another morning to take a walk, lady." How easily we mourners expressed pique! An argument ensued between two pale women with stiff hair and an ineffable air of wealth. One of them—the more elegant—said, "Fuck you," or "Move the fuck out of my way," to the other, and attempted to enlist the intervention of a nearby policeman. In response to the obscenity, the electricity-fearing woman scolded, "Jackie O wouldn't approve of your mouth!" Meanwhile I heard a crazy derelict wandering through the crowd, yelling, "Jackie was a slut! She slept her way to the top!" For the first time I comprehended Jackie's dread of the public; I understood the not so latent hostility of fans.

Why were we angry? Because we were crowded; because we couldn't see the famous mourners gathering on the steps of St. Ignatius. Those with press passes, stationed on the traffic island in the middle of Park Avenue, obscured our view. Jackie watchers shouted, "Down with the press!" We weren't making a moral or political judgment; we just wanted to see. Someone said, "There's John-John. John-John is so handsome." The anti-electricity woman said, "He's a grown man! He's too old to be called John-John. I hate when people call him John-John." A limo drove past us; though our crowd shouted with delight, I couldn't see who was inside. Then, through the glass, Lee Radziwill smiled and waved. I thought, "Lee is all we have left."

When Jackie's casket appeared, carried up the church steps, our motley congregation applauded. I applauded, too, though later I read a disapproving editorial about how crass we were to clap. I clapped instinctively; I wished to exclaim, to shout, to turn grief into noise. For we were a long street away from the casket; applause was homage, but it was also protest against our distance from the proceedings, and against our inability to show evanescent Jackie our complicated, serious regard. About these feelings there was nothing to do, nothing to say.

Through no rituals—except reading the paper and saying "Poor Jackie"—could we build a sympathetic bridge between our condition and hers. And so we applauded, as if the funeral were a performance, and Jackie's casket were a final, astounding *coup de théâtre*.

A man in a business suit stood near me; he held a rose. Had he intended to leave it on the church steps? Or perhaps he'd meant to stop by 1040 Fifth Avenue, Jackie's apartment building, and deposit it there. Later I saw him on the subway; he was still holding the rose, drooped now. I knew the gift's futility—the uselessness of tribute to a dead woman who, even in life, refused her public.

When a star dies, a person with whom one had no relation, a person one never had the luck to meet, one feels a disembodied variety of grief, allied to dehydration. About lost friends, one may justifiably feel bereft; one has not quite the right to mourn Jackie as if she were kin, so one experiences, instead, foreclosure. One was never the appropriate proprietor of love for Jackie; it was always an illegitimate alliance, without grounding in law or ceremony. Lacking arenas in which to celebrate or acknowledge affection for Jackie, one was left stranded, after her death, with unspeakable nostalgias. Despite the pretense of communal mourning for Jackie, icon shared by millions, there returned the contemplative solitude in which we who harbor relationships with imaginary figures must dwell. The solitude deepened, after Jackie died; Fifth Avenue seemed deprived of its preeminent resident, Grand Central Station of its savior patron, Central Park of its sprite, Manhattan of its motivation. For me, Gotham had become a marionette collapsed on the ground, its secret puppeteer having abdicated her serene position behind the screen.

It is difficult, writing about Jackie's death, to avoid sentimentality; I hear in my voice the suspect, maudlin tones that journalists summoned to describe the ambiguous power of Jackie's passing. She dominated the media at the moment of her death more than ever before in her starry career. But the coverage was bland, conformist. Indeed, the press collaborated on a revision—rehabilitation—of Jacqueline Onassis, restoring her to sainthood. Her role as model mother was emphasized; her marriage to Onassis was erased with the absoluteness of Soviet regimes banishing dissidents from the historical record. Many TV anchors referred to her as "Mrs. Kennedy." Such stalwart barometers of public emotion as *Time*, *Newsweek*, *U.S. News & World Report*, *New York*, and *Life* put on their covers, as memorial image, photographs of Jackie in the early years of the Kennedy administration—photos not of Jackie in strapless gown and brioche hairdo beside the Shah, nor of Jackie with memorably opulent and royalist hairdo in Paris, a coif so elaborate it had a special name ("Fontanges 1961"), but of Jackie in such outfits as simple pearls and day dress with bateau neckline. In these photos, she did not display the signature Jackie O smile—wide beam, glazed eyes —but looked ordinary and untraumatized, as if fame had not yet caused her to suffer. Only *Vanity Fair*, among the major periodicals, featured a photo of Jackie *Onassis*; here, Jackie in shoulderless black dress, baroque diamond earrings, her open mouth seeming to say, "Oh!" or "I dare you to stop me!" or "I've caught you!," was swiveled around in her seat (outrageous Jackie O is often photographed in the moment of *turning around*). Smiling archly and wickedly, eyebrows angled, pupils swerved to the far leftmost corner of her eyes, she seems a woman not only unusually photogenic but unusually rapacious.

Because it's a candid, she has not composed her face to be commensurate with a public image (the *Time* and *Newsweek* cover shots, in contrast, were taken while she was a professional political wife). In the candid, she seems frozen in the middle of an indiscreet aside, and the words "VANITY FAIR" above her head seem the photo's caption, a description of her nature. Only *Vanity Fair*'s photo documented the Jackie O whose spirit I adored—a pleasure principle; a woman who migrated from sanctity to scandal, and who demonstrated the secrets of extravagant living; a woman who turned away from one conversation (the proper, obedient colloquy in which she was supposed to be immersed) to deliver, on her other side, an unpredictable and unsanctioned exclamation. In this cover photo, Jackie seems to have dropped one mode of conduct, and to have, on an instant's whim, picked up another, a course that would surely earn public disapproval and envy.

The media's canonization of Saint Jackie, after her death, produced a time warp. All over newsstands were photographs of Jackie Kennedy in 1960, 1961, 1962—but they were brightly recolored, retouched, so the yellow of her checked dress as she sat on her Cape Cod porch's chintz chaise longue (*People*), or the magenta of her lipstick and her wool dress (*Time*), seemed present hues, not past; like black-and-white classics colorized to seduce contemporary tastes, or like expensive live-action remakes of vintage comix (*Dick Tracy*, *Batman*, *The Shadow*), these photos of Jackie gave the illusion of being sprucer than their originals. These commemorative images of Jackie weren't nostalgic glimpses of a vanished era and of the woman who, at thirty-one, had symbolized promise, or the hype of promise; these photos presented a woman who was realer now than she had ever been before. If Jackie, after her death, preoccupied the media with unprecedented force, and if her pictures seemed not vestiges of a securely remote past, but fragments of present time, this in itself was a familiar sensation. We are accustomed to seeing wars, and personalities, replayed.

In the images of Jackie that circulated after her death she looked relaxed and unselfconscious. On the cover of *Life*'s memorial issue, she slouches in an easy chair, smiling, her head resting on her upheld hand; one can even see faint blond hair along her arm. In this picture we are closer to Jackie than ever before; and she has abandoned good posture, assuming, instead, a rare position of unpremeditated repose. The impression this picture gives the mourning reader is that only now, after Jackie's death, has her real self emerged. Now her duties as icon are over, and she can unwind. This bizarre emphasis on "casual" Jackie reversed the tenor of her public image; if we thought we could never get close enough to her, if we felt that she was glacial, never submitting to interviews, never exposing her true feelings, that impression was posthumously revealed to have been a ruse. Here, before the deluge, was the anterior Jackie, an easier Jackie. And though these glimpses of supine, reposing Jackie, Jackie off her guard, might have been intended to comfort the bereft public—to convince us that Jackie was pleased with her lot—the photos had the opposite effect on me; they made me uncomfortable, uneasy. They persuaded me that another person—a wilder Jackie—had been erased. Alternately, they accused me of having misjudged Jackie; by having refused to notice her lightheartedness, I had betrayed her.

I find myself resorting to hyperbole—to grandiosity.

Betrayal? How could *I* betray Jackie? Note that I can't speak about Jackie without falling into lavish unwise exaggeration—for only photos, and the uncaged fantasies they inspire, ground my sense of her.

Part of the uncanniness surrounding Jackie's death was the clear evidence of her hand in the funeral proceedings; she had, after all, chosen to be buried beside JFK at Arlington, even though for over two decades she'd gone by the name of Mrs. Onassis. To be buried near the eternal flame that she herself had lit in 1963 was a posthumous public relations coup; clearly she cared about her preservation as symbol and wished for immortality as a Kennedy. Prime architect of the Camelot myth, she consummated the process of legend-making by choosing Arlington for her own grave. That gesture made her seem more aware of the effects of her actions on public consciousness—more interested in how she would be perceived by history—than she had professed, in life, to be.

Her burial at Arlington, a public event, televised, was inevitably political, given the presence of President Clinton and his wife, Hillary. The President gave a funeral oration; Hillary Clinton had earlier made a statement, saying that Jackie had shown her, by example, how to provide a modicum of privacy to children raised in the political limelight. Whatever the extent of the Clintons' personal grief at Jackie's death, it was transparent that they were using the occasion to shore up their own uncertain political fortunes—the President reinforcing his reputation as JFK's successor, and Mrs. Clinton deflecting critical attention from her own controversial activism in health care legislation and her own eschewal of the traditionally subordinate position of First Lady. Even Teddy Kennedy, who made a self-conscious reference in his eulogy to his own reelection campaign, relied, for most of his anecdotes about Jackie, on information already long part of the public record—such lines as her famous "If you bungle raising your children, I don't think whatever else you do matters very much," an oft-quoted Jackie-ism that Ted misrendered as "If you bungle raising your children, nothing else much matters in life." Couldn't he have used, instead, a line he'd heard directly from Jackie in private conversation, instead of this statement from the 1962 TV special *The World of Jacqueline Kennedy*? Only Maurice Tempelsman, Jackie's companion (*People* magazine flamboyantly referred to him, in a follow-up story, as "Jackie's Last Love"), struck a note that recalled the Jackie O who had originally captured my affection: reading the C. P. Cavafy poem "Ithaka," he artfully resummoned her years in Greece with Ari. It was wonderfully contrary to the spirit of the mawkish and idealizing media coverage that Jackie's Jewish companion should have chosen a poem celebrating the louche and sybaritic virtues for which Jackie O, in the tabloids, had long been recognized. Of particular interest were the lines: "may you stop at Phoenician trading stations / to buy fine things, / mother of pearl and coral, amber and ebony, / sensual perfume of every kind"—a passage confirming and blessing those acquisitive aspects of Jackie's reputation that the media momentarily neglected. For a modest charge I called a *Connecticut Post* information line (203-333-3900) and heard Jackie's voice (her address to the nation in 1964, thanking the people for the nearly 800,000 condolence letters she'd received); but I despaired at not being able to hear Tempelsman—the companion with whom she'd lived out of wedlock—read "Ithaka" over the telephone wires.

I emphasize the media's rehabilitation of the errant

Jackie O in order to express the divergence I felt between my own dream Jackie and the images greeting me from TV, newspapers, and magazines. The Jackie who dwelled under my skin—the Jackie I'd absorbed into my private system of meanings and myths—was more extravagant and grandiose than the splendid Jackie being posthumously glorified. Here I wish to give voice to this other—this different—this *dream* Jackie. Any Jackie we privately harbor in our imaginations will be a perverse Jackie—for it is necessarily *perverse*, even if it is also *pervasive*, to take a public figure into your own flesh and fancy.

Doubtless Jackie would not have approved of my mouth. Writing about Jackie, I enter a terrain of embarrassment, error, and excess. I risk sacrilege. Or I risk sentimentality—idealizing a figure who may have been insubstantial. Even after her death, I feel the power of Jackie's image to make me uncomfortable, curious; the power of icon Jackie to incite speech, and then to cast doubt on that speech's veracity and authenticity.

JACKIE WATCHERS,
JACKIE LOVERS

WHEN I SPEAK about Jackie, who do I become? A weirdo? A stalker? A fan? A mourner? A gossip? A historian? Does speaking about Jackie feminize me? Does it Americanize me? To contemplate Jackie is permitted: millions do. One cannot be arrested for it. But on some archaic level, Jackie watching is a prohibited activity, and not merely because Jackie Onassis sued Ron Galella, the paparazzo, for intruding on her personal space. It is forbidden to speak about Jackie because she is surrounded, Brünnhilde, by a ring of flame (her "O"?), a command not to reveal. This prohibition, clearly, has stopped no one, though it renders the speaker declassé or perverse. Rumor: Jackie, passing a bookstore's stack of novels by Jacqueline Susann (author of a roman à clef about Jackie O), held her nose, as if against some foul-smelling object. Discourse about Jackie stinks. Even Jackie thought so.

Contemplation and *Jackie O* bear some relation to each other, as do *speaking* and *Jackie O*. Jackie did not like to be written about. Jackie did not appear to enjoy being famous. And yet one contemplates her; one speaks about her. Even to recognize the sobriquet "Jackie O" is to confess her unwilled presence in one's system.

I speak as representative of those who loved Jackie from afar. A Jackie watcher, a Jackie lover—it is not exactly an identity. Nor is it a club, a community, a religion. And yet I belong to this strange fellowship.

Do men who dream about Jackie differ from women who dream about Jackie? Why has Jackie appeared principally in women's magazines (*The Ladies' Home Journal, McCall's*)? Is she mostly of interest to other women? Does the man who identifies with Jackie, or seeks consolation and stimulation in her image, participate in a female cult? Certainly I have a male relation to Jackie. Looking at Jackie, interpreting her resonances, I use her image to confirm my vision, to bolster my place in the world, even if the route I take toward confirmation is the momentary detour of disorganization and fragmentation. Even if it seems that Jackie disorganizes me, it is actually I who disorganize Jackie, only to reorganize her in my own image. And yet since it's likely that more women than men think about Jackie, the quest for self-realization via Jackie contemplation isn't a standard male route. But it is a customary American mode. In fact, when I think about Jackie, I consider myself to be acting at my most collective and communal; I become part of a larger world—the world of those who use Jackie as historical marker or as index of stylishness. Thinking about Jackie, I join a "we," a group.

Is Jackie to be taken straight—seriously, at face value? Or does her image shift when seen from different vantage points? Is she a camp figure, and, if so, at what point in history did she become camp? I suggest that there were two moments when Jackie became susceptible to a greater freedom of interpretation, two moments when her potential as a fantasy agent grew virtually unlimited: the first was November 22, 1963, when she survived the assassin's bullet; the second was October 20, 1968, when she married Aristotle Onassis, and became tarnished Jackie O.

Her political significances resist easy circumscription. Although she can function as a subversive figure (an instrument of longings we can't name), she more frequently is portrayed as a reactionary figure—a cautionary symbol, primarily for women of her generation, of the proper way to behave (how to obey one's husband, how to limit one's accomplishments to the domestic sphere or to the appropriately feminine realm of the arts). And yet Jackie didn't exactly perform as expected. Not only did she offer an alternative to the Marilyn Monroe/Jayne Mansfield body image then dominant in popular culture, but, by refusing to behave like an ordinary 1950s political wife, she subtly broadcast shifts in female protocol and possibility.

Some people—including a few of my friends—profess indifference to Jackie, saying, "I've never been a Jackie fan," or "I think she's overrated," or "I never understood why everyone made such a fuss about her." Even those who abstain from the cult of Jackie, to which millions belong, are setting themselves up *in relation* to a cult whose importance or centrality they acknowledge even while they dismiss it.

Do I seek out Jackie? Or does her image seek out me? Am I, in fact, the object of her image? Imagine that Jackie O is a trajectory, and that I'm one of the destinations the arrow flies toward. Or imagine that she is a circle, and that I am one of the points within her circumference. To the extent that I did not invent Jackie, I cannot rewrite, from scratch, her premises. She comes to me already formulated. I was born into the world of Jackie; I did not create it. But it is a world I perpetuate by choosing to speak about it.

To speak about Jackie: it's not exactly romantic address.

But it presupposes amorousness, even of an asexual variety. It assumes that I am fervently interested in her, if only for the sake of abstract commentary. Fact is, she's a sort of pinup: an image posted everywhere, inspiring curiosity and fabrication.

All of this is true about many stars. But most stars *do* things (act, sing, preach, commit crimes, govern) to earn stardom. Jackie was unique in doing little or nothing to justify speculation. And so Jackie is a pure case of the star *qua* star, without the utilitarianism of art or politics.

If she governed, it was an imaginary kingdom over which she held and continues to hold sway; and of her subjects she demanded nothing.

Of course, with every sentence I am striving retroactively to set up a relation with Jackie, and trying to avoid the besmirching aura of he-who-appropriates. For I am violating Jackie's silence, and Jackie's evident wish to be left alone, to let her fame fizzle away. It is morally ambiguous to ascribe symbolic status to an individual, to use Jackie as if she were a theorem or a metaphor. She represents nothing but herself; and yet she set off unintended frequencies, including this wish, under whose force I now labor—the desire to make Jackie signify.

She was one of the most philosophical and abstract foundations of American life and she was never given credit for the degree to which her presence irradiated us with sensation—intimations that resist naming.

She functioned both as anesthetic and as stimulant. Anesthetic: she was an opiate, a numbing agent. She stupefied us. She mystified. By contemplating her, by dreaming about her, by reading about her and looking at her image and holding her up as lodestar and point-of-no-return, we grew dead to parts of ourselves. If she was ether, what operations and alchemies did she permit us to remain insensitive to? Alternately, she was a stimulant: she annunciated parts of ourselves to which, otherwise, we might not have had access. She awoke rapture in us; or she awoke nostalgia; or she awoke longing for a different life. It was difficult to speculate on the contours of that life—only that Jackie seemed the key to it, and her silence was an indication of how hard it would be to discover how to get there.

Perversely, I'm ascribing agency to Jackie. Though she was silent and didn't seem to do anything to merit fame or to perpetuate notoriety, her image actively worked in us, like a potion or propaganda. We didn't fabricate her from thin air; she must have collaborated with the media, however unconsciously, to form her image and to preserve it (always the same smile, the same hairdo). Because we didn't willfully make her up, but accepted her as part of our landscape, we may consider ourselves her beneficiaries and her audience, and we may consider her appearances—captured in photographs, whether authorized or unauthorized—to be a slow, serial, fragmented performance piece, drawn out over more than thirty years, and highly conceptual, its premises never articulated or codified. Jackie was a show—the Jackie O Show—but its plot was buried, its backers were invisible, and its spectacular special effects seemed unpremeditated, thoroughly natural.

Doubtless Jackie's image compelled radically different emotions in different people; she revealed the nature of the mind she permeated. The fantasies and emotions I describe in the pages that follow may therefore be solely my own; I wonder, however, if my Jackie overlaps with other people's—or if, instead, Jackie was so pliable and protean, as a catalyst of fantasy, that she could mean anything to anyone, her significance sheerly relative.

Writing about Jackie, after her death, I am besieged by melancholy. I wonder whether this melancholy is a sign of my integrity or of my lack of integrity; a sign of my fealty to Jackie, or of my cravenness.

DREAM JACKIE

HAS JACKIE EVER appeared in your dreams? If so, what does her appearance there signify? If one were to compile a new *Interpretation of Dreams*, and were to align stars with symbolic properties, what would Jackie mean? (What would Tony Curtis? Mia Farrow? Ringo?)

In the last fifteen years, Jackie has appeared over two dozen times in my dreams. She has approached me in greasy spoons; we have swum together in strange oceans; we have flown on airplanes; we have shared a Christmas celebration (she gave me a twenty-five-dollar check); she has advised me on how to cook; we have taken a bus from Baltimore to Manhattan, a ride during which she observed to her companion, "One never knows when Wayne is going to tell a dirty joke"; from an adjacent apartment she has yelled "Jew-boy!" at me; she has con-fessed, at a dinner party given by Ronald Reagan, that she never carries cash (about her checkbook, she said, "How pretty!"); we have met on street corners, on sub-ways, on yachts, in fancy French restaurants, at a bar-and-grill on Martha's Vineyard; she has assisted me with the composition of a book called *The Soul of Jackie O*; she has described me to her sister Lee as a dandy. The dreams prove nothing conclusive about my character or my prospects. About Jackie, they prove even less: only that I perceive her to be rich, mobile, and selectively attentive—that in the dream realm of Jackie O, the rules governing matter have been suspended, and she is capable of moving anywhere and encountering anyone. It has been my good fortune that Jackie, in my dreams, always knows who I am, even if only for a few seconds. She doesn't have much time for me. But I'm grateful for her momentary condescensions. In my dreams, she is rarely busy or preoccupied. She drifts through rooms, restaurants—en route to glamorous elsewheres.

The keynote of Jackie O in my dreams—in your dreams, too?—is *imaginary complicity*. Often, Jackie and I are huddled together in conspiratorial conversation. She has gossiped with me about LBJ; she has recognized that she and I share a vampish cosmopolitanism; she knows that we love the fine arts, that we are secretive and bookish and aloof. The purpose of Jackie entering a dream may be to restore equilibrium. Her cameo appearance indicates my grandiosity; or my need to be uplifted; or my fear of catastrophe.

I wake from dreams of Jackie with a sensation of having been blessed; her visitations aren't ordinary, aren't to be taken for granted. I can't predict when they will occur again.

JACKIE AND

TRANSPORTATION

JACKIE SEEMED to have surreal powers of movement and metamorphosis. She was a figure of transportation. She sailed away on the *Christina*. She rode in motorcades. She flew on Air Force One. She appeared at a gala and then disappeared—for how many months, before she'd be seen again, at a performance of *Company*, or *Hair*, or a dinner at the Metropolitan Museum of Art? Photographs of Jackie catch her *en passant*, moving quickly from one site to another, from Onassis's apartment on the Avenue Foch in Paris to their villa in Glifádha; from a bullfight in Seville to the ruins in Angkor Wat. She transports herself magically from one identity to another; she vanishes as Mrs. Kennedy and resurfaces as Mrs. Onassis. Her name remains Mrs. Aristotle Onassis but her identity shifts again: she has become someone else. We catch her at the moment of reemergence. She appears in the ocean—paparazzi snap her picture—and then she swims away, in the opposite direction from land.

In one of my favorite Jackie Kennedy pictures, she is walking away from a black car. She wears black sunglasses, white gloves, a white scarf tied under the chin. Her face is expressionless. Is she guilty, innocent? Is she approaching a church or a courtroom? JFK stands a few feet behind her; clearly she is First Lady, an official person. Her lanky, athletic arm describes a pure line (a balletomane's delight). The dress is so severe, its cut so absolute, so devoid of ornament, that she also resembles Audrey Hepburn prepping for *The Nun's Story*: Jackie looks like a sanctified woman, but also like a woman in a hurry—a woman with nasty (Mafia?) business to transact, beyond the photo's borders. Is she a gun moll? Is she the Pope's confidante? Crowds gather in the distance behind her, but they seem scenery—background peasants in a Renaissance religious painting. Or is Jackie the fake? What attracts me to this image is Jackie's seriousness: spy on a dangerous mission, she's intent to escape, to reveal nothing. She must preserve the Iron Curtain with her own well-ironed dress and well-ironed manners; she must not give away the code. She's caught in the midst of flying away from inspection. She can't be held accountable to one identity; see, she's walking briskly toward another identity, much faster than JFK, who must always remain JFK. That's why he seems to move more slowly, always struggling against back pain and the leadenness of a steady self.

From a distance, in pictures, she appears motionless, always smiling, groomed, rich. But readers of gossip scoops know that she was, at least in myth, always on the verge of a potentially disastrous transformation: about to lose her husband; about to lose her money. Just as she was transported from one mode of existence to another, she filled her fans with semireligious transports. In imagination we may have been lifted to a higher echelon, bumped from Coach to First Class on our imaginary Olympic Airlines flight with Jackie O.

Her feats of transportation were not always literal. The primary transportation she underwent was a movement

"Elegance is refusal": she can't be held
accountable to one identity.

in moral register—from sacred to profane, when Mrs. Kennedy became Jackie O. Coverage of her, during the heyday of public fascination with the incongruous marriage ("America Has Lost a Saint!" said one headline), was increasingly salacious—culminating in photos of a nude, sunbathing Jackie, published in *Screw*. At this moment, Jackie had been definitively transported; a sacred icon had been forcibly translated to a pornographic context.

Remarkable, the speed and suddenness of her passage through cultural arenas. Her appearances were brief: a one-minute speech thanking the nation for its condolence letters, a quick photo opportunity outside an art opening.

The speed itself seemed a form of insouciance, arrogance. Jackie making another appearance, another exit, was liable to provoke envious wisecracks or awestruck silence. *How does she get away with it?* we asked, in the wake of her transitory appearances, though it was never clear what specific transgression or immunity she was getting away with. Her speedy movement in and out of sight constituted a type of heroism—heroic, to escape quickly, unscathed; heroic, to leave no trace but a photograph; heroic, to make so indelible an imprint with so little apparent effort—to achieve immortality without even wanting it or doing anything to merit it (unless speed and evanescence are forms of action, effects that must be willed, and do not happen accidentally).

She fled milieux. She fled Newport, she fled the Kennedys, she fled touch football. She fled Rose, she fled Skorpios. She fled the United States, she fled photographers. She fled interviews, she fled parties, she fled her childhood. Her friend and collaborator Diana Vreeland famously said, "Elegance is refusal." Jackie refused, abstained—she refused *us*. And refusal occurred instantaneously: the instant the paparazzo caught on film— Jackie in flight, Jackie smiling—was the duration of her cameo appearance ("This is how much I will give my public, this instant and no more") and it was the duration of her refusal ("I will be gone by the time you put down your camera"). Each photograph, then, records an acquiescence, a performance, as well as a snub; to us, she says a firm, final "no."

And yet one could spot her. Jackie watching flourished because, though inaccessible, though an artist of refusal, she *did* occasionally appear. Few supernatural entities were as generous in their visitations as Jackie O. Think of all the people who can say, "Once, I saw Jackie O, in person!"

I saw her four times in person. The first time was at the opening of a new building at the John F. Kennedy School of Government at Harvard. I stood as close to the ceremony as security allowed. From that event I remember only that Jackie managed to continue a conversation with her companion (some relative) while she walked from behind the concealing screen to the folding chairs gathered on a platform or on the grass. I remember her reddish hair, and my sense of luck and caravansary—there I stood, witnessing one of the world's floating, elusive foundations! The second time I saw her was at my Harvard graduation. She was sitting at a table with Caroline, under a tree, in the Yard; as I walked past them, I slowed down to observe more closely. I wish I could report more particulars, details that don't register in photos. All I remember is a large beautiful face, and the knowledge that an abstraction (historic Jackie O) was coinciding with a presence (Mrs. Onassis on the lawn); the instant of coincidence, of convergence, made, in my brain, a mild sound—the sound of *proof*. For, seeing Jackie, I'd proven something—that she existed. All I could say to myself was "That's really Jackie O," as if a vexing metaphysical problem had been solved, and I could place a check mark in the column beside it, and proceed to the next conundrum.

I heard the same sound in my brain when I saw Elizabeth Taylor, in 1976, riding in an open car in a parade (she'd been chosen as the Hasty Pudding Club's "Woman of the Year"); I remember that her turban was the same violet color as her eyes. I don't know if I could truly *see* her eyes, from the distance at which I was standing; but

I remember a gratifying sensation of two contradictory realms of experience (a star on a movie screen, a woman in a real parade) dissolving into consonance. The turban's color confirmed the color of Liz's eyes, just as the actual presence of Liz in the parade confirmed my experience of having seen her in *Cleopatra* and *Elephant Walk*.

In retrospect I'm muting the emotional force of these sightings; I'm rendering them with deliberate blandness, as if these instants of convergence meant little. It's more likely that, seeing Jackie and Liz, I felt as transported as the woman in San Antonio, in 1963, who said, upon seeing Jackie (as reported by William Manchester): "Mrs. Kennedy, Mrs. Kennedy, please touch my hand!" And then: "Oh, my God! She really did touch me! She really did!" Jackie *really did touch me*, without physically doing so; she appeared, in person, before me, and rendered me proven, beyond a shade of doubt, and rendered herself equally located, a true solid entity on Earth's ambiguous surface.

The third time I saw Jackie in person was at the movies in Manhattan—the Paris Theater, by the Plaza Hotel. With my mother and my boyfriend I was there to see *A Sunday in the Country*, a French film by Bertrand Tavernier. I remember wondering whether Jackie had ever met the filmmaker, or whether an interest in French-style pastoral outings and tranquillities had prompted her to see *Sunday*. At this Jackie sighting I was aware of divergence rather than convergence: as I realized that the woman waiting in the ticket line was actually Jackie Onassis, I found it difficult to reconcile one fact of her face—the jutting chin—with the archetypally boxy face I knew from photographs. The woman in line seemed a not very successful Jackie impostor. A second divergence between real Jackie and icon Jackie emerged when, once the lights dimmed and the film started, she put on glasses, slumped, pressed her knees against the seat in front of her, and fed asides to her companion (Tempelsman?). She was not living up to my definitions of decorum. Observing Jackie's persistent attentions to Tempelsman, my mother quipped, "That's how she keeps a man! I should pick up some pointers." The irony of my mother's statement seemed palpable: Jackie doesn't keep men, she loses them (Black Jack, JFK, Ari).

The last time I saw Jackie was the winter of 1993. Already her cancer had been diagnosed, I understand in retrospect, but it had not yet been publicly announced. The occasion was a party for a book Jackie had edited about India's healing plants. A few days before the event, according to the tabloids, Jackie had fallen off a horse and been knocked unconscious.

From this sighting I primarily recall details of Jackie's appearance—details I mentally compiled, while the event unfolded, as a dossier of *proof*, evidence of Jackie's uncanny extraordinariness. I noticed that her head was unusually large—out of proportion to her body—and I remember thinking, "Stars have large heads, that's why they are stars." I noticed that she didn't drink, and I thought, "Jackie never drinks in public, she might lose control, and that would be disastrous." I noticed that she held her clutch purse with unusual firmness, and that her fingers were large and stiff, as if with arthritis, and I thought, "Jackie's anxiety centers in the fierce hand clutching the purse. Being an icon makes Jackie nervous, and panic must find some egress, some manifestation, in body language." She never rubbernecked; in fact, she kept her head still, which struck me as a further piece of proof—that she was equal to the demands of her fame, or that she had *earned* icon status through unusual composure, a poise I was now witnessing. Admiring her microfiber pants suit and her fashionably chunky black suede platform shoes, I privately exulted: "Jackie is still on top of fashion!" On her lapel she wore a folk-art cross, a humble ornament for someone so grand. Again, I felt the pleasing zing of confirmation. This event confirmed Jackie's right to be an icon. And I remember feeling, sentimentally, that JFK had been a boor and an idiot to philander. How, I wondered, could he have cheated on a woman so splendid? At this moment, Jackie's survival and her continuing attractiveness rebuked JFK's inconstancy, as if, with her formidable beauty, she were demonstrating that he'd been a fool to betray her and that she was having the last laugh.

At this book party, I noticed Jackie conversing with socialite Chessy Rayner, and I felt "out of it" (a nobody) but also glad that constellations were intact, glad that luminaries were doing business. Even from some distance I could see Jackie's mouth enunciating words on a large scale, as if for lip-readers. I took the deliberateness of Jackie's enunciation as further proof that she operated on a different—a larger, more epic—scale than the rest of us. Also, I noticed that she frequently licked her lips, and I wondered if this was a nervous tic or else a side effect from some medication not documented by the press.

This event was abstract, but also particular; unfortunately, the details are surrounded, in retrospect, by a haze compounded of two clashing sensations. The first was tranquillity: I thought, "Jackie Onassis is here at last, I don't have to conjure her." The second was defeat: I thought, "Jackie will soon vanish, I'm an interloper, this may be the last time I ever see Jackie, and I can do nothing concrete with this fascination. I cannot sublimate it into any sane course of conduct or philosophy. It is an utterly useless emotion and yet it gives the illusion of engineering and justifying my life."

At 6:45 she moved toward the door—and then unexpectedly veered toward a young editor with whom I was speaking. Jackie's face lit up. She said the editor's name. Had I wanted to speak to Jackie, this would have been my chance, though I had nothing appropriate to say, only a gushy desire to praise her magnificence. I understood how unwanted such a statement would be, and therefore kept silent. Why can't I remember more than a dizzy, drunk sense of my own unimportance and the futility of telling Jackie that she was supernaturally beautiful? The one concrete sentence of Jackie's I can offer you is this: upon parting, she said to the young editor, "Keep in touch." Jackie granted the word "touch" an extra, aristocratic sibilance, as if she were saying "hush" or "shush." While she said "Keep in touch," she was already turning around to leave. Here, then, was evidence of Jackie's transitoriness: she wasn't even standing still long enough to say "Keep in touch." Shouldn't she have waited to finish saying goodbye before she swerved away? ("Swerve" is the wrong word; her every motion was stately. But "swerve" conveys the sense of accident and retraction—of being suddenly *banished* from her presence.) Everyone nearby seemed suspended in the amber of her mystic "Keep in touch," an envoi sent out into the recumbent air. Then she left the reception room, and I followed her to the stairwell to see her descend. She looked down at her feet as she walked, just as I'd seen in newsreels: I suppose this was a pre-caution against tripping.

A photo of Jackie at this book party was published in W: Jackie in conversation with C. Z. Guest. The photo proves that the party happened; that Jackie attended it; that her folk-art cross was indeed as large as I remembered; that her head does dwarf her body (a consequence of her hairdo's size). The picture proves that Jackie seemed, as I remembered, attentive to her companion. But this is one of the only Jackie photos in which her aura seems missing. One learns aura from photographs; and then applies it to real-life situations; and then discovers, look-ing again at the photographs, that the aura has migrated out of them. I still do not know whether Jackie's aura originated in photos, or whether photos recorded a prior, actual incandescence, evident to anyone who actually *saw* Jackie in person.

I'm reminded of a story that Paul Horgan tells, in *Tracings: A Book of Partial Portraits*, about surreptitiously watching Greta Garbo perform a scene from *Conquest* on an M-G-M soundstage. Later, when he sees the fin-ished movie, he finds that her performance of this scene pales in comparison to his memory of the actual filming. He concludes that "the impact created by a temperament physically present" exceeds the impact of "a photograph of a temperament." It shocks me to consider that Garbo in person might have been more electric than Garbo on the screen—and that, therefore, Jackie in person too might have been more scintillant than in photos, that Jackie's aura actually *exists*, and that photography can only feebly produce its replica.

Jackie spotting: she enters a room, leaves it, and de-posits fantasies in her wake. Where does she go, after

"Keep in touch."

quitting this room, this cameo appearance? The brevity and rarity of her visits create a space for awe; do little to interfere with expectation; give the illusion that her life consisted solely of instants of vanishing, instants which were anticlimactic (they proved nothing, they only confirmed that Jackie was Jackie) and epiphanic (moments when a hypothesized star suddenly becomes flesh confirm the vocation of wishing, and confirm that gods and goddesses still walk the earth and are not merely media-manufactured fumes).

As a figure of transportation, Jackie seemed magical. In photos of Jackie walking through crowds, she seems transported by a flying carpet or seven-league boots. Many people have reported Jackie's ability to stare straight through them. This is a self-protective device: the star, walking in public, can't establish eye contact, because everyone knows her, and so she must stare ahead into nowhere. This variety of starsight, however, contributes to the aura Jackie projects, in photos, of intending to mesmerize the viewer, to cast a spell. Her friend Bunny Mellon called her a "witch" with "supernatural powers" (so Kitty Kelley reported). Jackie-as-witch: a tabloid headline dubbed Jackie "THE QUEEN WHO DESTROYED CAMELOT" (neglecting to say that she also invented Camelot). Alexander Onassis, her stepson, said that she had the power to "jeopardize a whole epoch," as if she were a Lady Bluebeard disposing of husbands, or else a Helen of Troy, passively altering the temperature of her time. The compulsion to see Jackie as magical—a Circean figure with the ability to vanish and appear, to destroy and to deceive—is not simply a misogynist cliché (powerful women have throughout patriarchal history been condemned as witches); rather, the vision of Jackie as sorceress or sprite, an icon with the will to transport herself and to transport viewers, testifies to the strength of our imaginary identification with her. We think she's magical because she can enter our minds and then quickly leave them. She encourages ESP, or tempts us to read *her* Atlantis mind: looking at photos of Jackie, reading stories of her life, we invest her with our own complexities, streams of fancy that we could never ford without her image to assist us.

IN IMAGES OF JACKIE O, her eyes look at once astonished by the flashbulbs and equal to the camera's demands. Looking at these images, I identify with her spellbound stare, an astonishment that contains catatonia, irreverence, and rage. Her eyes open wide; she smiles; the smile is genuine but also fixed, frozen, repeated from earlier photographs. Her face is as big as the camera's wish, and so she takes on equivalence to the camera: she becomes a flashbulb detonating in the viewer's face, or a lens seeing *us*. In response, I freeze. I'm "astonied"—the antique form of "astonished": to be astonished is to be turned into stone.

In photographs, Jackie refuses to express herself, refuses to express anything. And so the photos render the viewer—me—inexpressive. I identify with Jackie's inexpressivity. And this astonishment—Jackie's appearance of being *fascinated* by the lens that sees her—is not a state amenable to speech. That is why all the commentary on Jackie is about her life rather than about the pleasure or discomfort of looking at her. What can one say about the state of being frozen, being arrested?

One can only say: *I am fascinated by Jackie O because she herself is frozen in a posture of fascination, a mood I mimic.*

Jackie's face *fascinates* the public: the public is arrested in a gelid condition of being unable to comment, unable to explain. She induces, in the viewer, a state of trance, because she herself seems entranced. Someone once said that Jackie seemed dazed or drugged; it's equally the case that she drugs *us*.

Freud's infamous explanation for this state of fascination is castration anxiety: in his essay on the Medusa's head, he describes how a boy-child's glimpse of female genitalia, and his subsequent misconception that the woman has lost a penis, turns him to stone, as if he were facing the Medusa. Loosely applying this flawed theory to Jackie watching, I'll suggest that Jackie's face, like the Medusa's, partly fascinates because JFK's missing head lurked behind it. Jackie, frozen or "astonied" (turned to stone) by JFK's assassination/decapitation, in turn astonishes us: in a chain reaction of astonishments, we're frozen at the notion that the leader's head might disappear, collapse, explode. A simmering anxiety or terror over JFK's death may have caused a populace to regard Jackie's frozen and fame-blinded gaze as a permanent look of astonishment at JFK's sudden departure, and as a totemic replacement of his absent head. Jackie, as fetish, reminds us of something missing. For there are catastrophes to which we need, for our sanity, to remain blind.

Is Jackie the Medusa? Or is she herself a heroine turned to stone by JFK's death? In either case, Jackie's astonishment protects us, even while it superficially immobilizes us in a delighted trance. We need to be motionless, lest we collapse at the news of the figurehead's absence. Jackie's face, like a shield held up to the Medusa, may have prevented an ill-defined populace from dissolving.

Long before Jackie's time, Wordsworth described this

sensation of a face or a landscape or a flower evoking offstage, missing experiences:

> —But there's a Tree, of many, one,
> A single Field which I have looked upon,
> Both of them speak of something that is gone:
>   The Pansy at my feet
>   Doth the same tale repeat . . .

Like the Pansy at the poet's feet, Jackie's visage seems redolent of missing glories. Are these glories JFK? Not entirely. I don't idealize him, and don't thank him for Jackie's aura. But her face, in photographs, *does* derive power from something latent or unexpressed (her visage mesmerizes because the glory it conceals is forever gone, and JFK's permanent absence is one billow of this glory-cloud trailing behind her): that's why we need so many pictures of her, no matter how repetitious.

Jackie never completes the action she's photographed in the midst of—exiting a taxi, entering a restaurant. Because she can't complete the gesture (she's ensorcelled in the photo's box) we can't finish our process of contemplation either; we hang in suspended animation, wondering where Jackie will go, what adventure she will next seek.

One sense-analogy for the trance condition that Jackie photos induce is *shininess*. Think of numb fingertips, their prints gone: that is shiny skin. Such skin slides across whatever surface it touches, unable to establish traction. Think, too, of a car skidding on a frozen road. Think of a photo of Jackie Onassis against a dark background, the flashbulb so bright in her eyes that she looks dazed, uncomprehending. Note the peculiar glaze or shine that

Astonished Jackie: shininess; slippage;
skidding; frost.

adheres to her cheek, as if her face had been waxed,
glossed, or airbrushed. Her soul has been evacuated, her
location lost, so she slides away from her identity; she
skids down an icy slope away from herself. This gesture
of *skidding* or *slippage*—Jackie slipping away from herself—is replicated by the shininess of the glossy magazine
page containing Jackie photos, and by the shininess or
slipperiness of the viewer's soul, as if the viewer, too (in
this case, I), were sliding into another identity—or as if

the viewer were stuck in the wrong body or the wrong incarnation and could, by virtue of a magic spell, slide into a new identity. Photos capture Jackie eerily sliding away from herself, and so the viewer can slide *into* imaginary identification with her; these photos create the illusion that she has generously left her soul empty so that the viewer can enter it. The name "Jackie Onassis" beside her photo pretends to function as an ID tag saying, "This is a photo of Jackie Onassis." But really the name "Jackie Onassis" can't seal off the photo, which spills directly into your desire for it, and becomes a map of your rapture. Looking at a photo of Jackie, my "I" slides on top of her lacquered image, as if I were a checker and Jackie were a checkerboard and I were sliding off it.

A second sense-analogy for the effect of Jackie photos is *frost*. Think of cold hands, sensation lost. Hypothermia is supposedly pleasant: though freezing to death, one feels sleepy and warm. Though Jackie smiles, she is cold to the viewer; and it is a religious coldness, the chill of otherworldly contemplation and of someone too busy with her own godhead to notice petty particulars. A masseuse once commented that Jackie's was the "coolest skin she had ever touched"; coolness is an appropriate attribute for a woman who keeps her cool and is "cool" (chic) and seems, also, frosty. (She liked to keep the White House at 65 degrees, which is, by my standards, on the cool side.) An acupuncturist reported that Jackie had a high pain threshold: this, too, whether fact or fiction, fits the image of frosty Jackie. Looking at Jackie, we're not fully sentient; nor is she. Gazing, we acquire the cold granular texture of a frozen slushy drink (I am thinking of a blue Slurpie). In photos she mimics laminated surfaces like Formica. Unnervingly still, zombie, she seems to be holding her breath, and we, in sympathy, hold ours, imitating the wide Sargasso Sea of her composed face.

Jackie watching induces "you"/"I" vertigo, a slipping and sliding between "you" and "I"; the viewer loses his or her "I" location, and borrows Jackie's. Jackie's "Thou" possibilities—her ability to seem a looming Other that we wish to apprehend or greet, as if in exclamation, protest, or prayer—explains why I've always been tempted to address her directly, to reverse her nickname and say *O Jackie*; but she is so mute that the exercise has always seemed futile, and I relapse into silence, imitating her.

SILENT JACKIE

JACKIE'S SILENCE was profound, proverbial, virtually unbroken. Did we love her silence or resent it? Was the silence, like Garbo's, a willed refusal, or was it self-sacrifice, a pathetic capitulation to the misogynist dictate that women be seen but not heard? A speaking Jackie could not have remained the demure and enigmatic repository of our projections.

There were two varieties of Jackie silence: her absence of public statements and the intrinsic silence of photographs.

Even when she spoke, her voice was notoriously soft —so breathless and whispery it seemed a put-on. Her rival Maria Callas said that Jackie spoke like Marilyn Monroe playing Ophelia. "Speak up," a TV technocrat told Jackie, and she replied, "I am speaking up. I don't talk any louder than this." Her in-laws made fun of her "babykins" voice. But others have claimed that beneath the wispy façade there lay biting, authoritative tones, remote from the voice spoofed on the Vaughn Meader *First Family* album. Of course, the notion that a different, nuanced voice, available only to her intimates, lurked behind the Ophelia voice of the White House Tour reinforced the attractive myth that Jackie's personality, which few were privileged to experience, held reservoirs of depth and vivacity.

Whatever her voice sounded like, her photos never spoke, and photos were our primary connection to Jackie. If Jackie was a star, she was a silent-era divinity in the style of Mary Pickford, Clara Bow, Norma Talmadge, Edna Purviance, Mabel Normand, Lillian Gish, ZaSu Pitts, Gloria Swanson, and Theda Bara. Jackie's smile often seemed exaggerated, much as silent-screen actors, faces pale, lips dark as plums, seemed Pierrots or mimes. Jackie's silence communicated; it hypnotized, without supplementary words. Like Pola Negri's face in melo-dramatic close-up, Jackie's huge face—its attitude of imploration—seemed fuller than speech.

Silence fertilizes fantasy; had Jackie hosted a talk show, she would doubtless have lost cachet. And yet I like hearing Jackie's voice, if only because there are so few extant samples, and because in her sentences I try to decode aspects of her upbringing and her psyche that remain buried from the public record. Listening to Jackie speak (primarily on the White House Tour, which I saw at New York's Museum of Broadcasting), I imagine that secrets of her temperament and milieu are revealed. As Henry James wrote in *The Princess Casamassima* (he might as well have been describing Jackie, or a certain infatuated and fetishistic attention to the way Jackie spoke): "The Princess's voice was low and rather deep, and her tone very quick; her manner of speaking was altogether new to her listener, for whom the pronunci-ation of her words and the very punctuation of her sen-tences were a kind of revelation of 'society.' " Jackie didn't say much that was quotable. When she christened the Polaris submarine in Groton, Connecticut, she whis-pered, "Je te baptise le Lafayette." On the White House Tour, she said, "I hate to make changes": it's a funny line—mostly because she seemed to adore making changes. I like, on the tour, her use of such interior decorator words as "eglomise," "Morris velvet," "candelabra," and "vermeil"; I like the way she pronounces "candelabra" ("can-de-*laaaah*-bra"); I like when she says, thanking women (including the oddly named Mrs. Noun) for donating furniture and art to the White House, "I wish there were more people like Mrs. Noun." Is Jackie a second Mrs. Noun? Jackie seemed a noun: she liked objects, and had the reified dearness of eglomise or vermeil.

Jackie had an accent: it was not a generic voice, but a voice located in a class, a region. She dropped her *r*'s. Her *a* sounds were drawled and flat: she pronounced the *a* in "Pablo" like the *a* in "pablum"—Pablum Casals.

Jackie had an eerie voice, and one never heard enough of it. An uncharitable critic, like Norman Mailer in his essay "The Existential Heroine," might knock Jackie for the zonked-out quality of her voice on the White House Tour (she does sound, at times, like a docent on drugs, leading tourists through a vast and drafty property); and yet when I read that Jackie went to bed in tears after seeing the tour on TV, and when I remember that her last words on the show were inaudible (she says, "Thank you," but JFK has entered the room already, and Jackie's quiet voice has become even quieter), I must, if not pity her, at least acknowledge the circumstances that dictated and reinforced her silence. In light of her elite yet straitened plight (professional wife and widow), I may wish her to howl. In the midst of luxury she seemed abandoned (her seeming dependence on powerful, ruthless men cast her as martyr); her silence reinforced the aura of hurt, as if any speech, if it came out, would be an inchoate whimper.

Silence.

Her silence, in two disparate photographs, seems emblematic of pain. In the famous photograph of Jackie on Air Force One, after JFK has been shot, Jackie's thick hair covers her eyes, and she gazes solemnly downward (or is she looking into the eyes of Judge Sarah Hughes, who swears LBJ into his presidency?). Everyone—judge, LBJ, Lady Bird—is silent in this picture; all photos are, perforce, silent. But Jackie's silence leads us into her sorrow. And her subsequent refusal to comment on the assassination makes these 1963 photos seem, in retrospect, more silent—*intentionally* silent, wordless because that's how Jackie planned it.

Five years later, in the Skorpios wedding photo (short Ari, tall Jackie), Ari's lips are slightly apart, as if he's speaking, but Jackie's are shut; she wears a dulled half-smile. Her silence in this picture is protest—against the Fates, against the paparazzi. The viewer may imagine: "Jackie is not thrilled about this marriage but she must go through with it." Here is an activity with which I've long been familiar: staring at wedding photos and imagining that the bride is secretly miserable. Looking at a photo of Jackie, silent on Skorpios, I imagine her reluctance, I forecast trouble, and my own astonished gaze says, "Turn back now, Jackie, before it is too late."

JACKIE'S WEALTH

JACKIE WAS RICH and wanted to be richer. Recall this series of mythic sums: the $26 million she bargained from Christina after Ari's death; the $175,000 a year she received from the Kennedy Trust; the $200,000 she paid for the Fifth Avenue apartment; the $200 million she accumulated by the time of her death. These figures might not be accurate. To most of us, these sums are abstract, surreal. They create the picture of a woman whose wealth isolated her from customary, plebeian modes.

But it was a shifting fortune. It tended to expand and deplete and then billow again. So Jackie seemed, alternately, filthy rich and a little match girl. It's not necessary to quantify *how much* Jackie actually had at any period of her life; focus, rather, on the impression of securities in oscillation. She was born to privilege but the fortunes of her father, Black Jack, plummetted—and so Jackie was raised *as if* rich but without secure funds. Her mother remarried—this time, to a genuinely rich man. After college Jackie went to work, as Inquiring Camera Girl for the *Washington Times-Herald*. Her salary ($42.50 a week) is often reported, as if it were a wage on which she actually depended. Marrying JFK, she attained wealth (again), but he fought with her over clothing bills, and she posed, before the American public, as someone in need (she asked for donations to the White House restoration). After JFK's death, she behaved and dressed like a rich woman, but apparently the funds had to be extricated from the Kennedys (with consequent obligatory appearances at political functions), and her own coffers were limited. Marrying Ari, she became definitively, securely rich—until he disinherited her. Then she wrested $26 million from Christina (a huge sum, and yet peanuts compared with what Ari had promised). Then the sum swelled to its proper $200 million, and the story ended. Its moral? Contradictory: Jackie had too much; Jackie never had enough. The "O" of Jackie O stands for zero or for all the zeros that make up millions or billions of dollars: you can imagine that Jackie had zero money or that her fortune perpetually ballooned. Marrying Ari, she had married "a blank check," a headline announced. A blank check is inviting and generous (you can inscribe any figure on it), but it is also unresponsive and null. Who wants to marry blankness? Think of Jackie's blankly beautiful countenance. The O and the blank check imply a hollow soul, an absence of spiritual resources.

It was impossible to be indifferent to Jackie's wealth. We may have believed that she deserved her money for having endured JFK's death; or that she didn't deserve her money. Contemplating Jackie, we must face unearned wealth, a fortune that doesn't proceed directly from labor. If we loved Jackie, it was because of her wealth; if we disliked or disparaged Jackie, it was also because of her wealth. Disparagement: C. David Heymann reports that a stranger accosted Jackie and said, "Why don't you try sharing your money with all of us?" And as early as 1966, some anonymous crackpot complained, "I don't think that you can have deep, deep sympathy for a grieving widow who spends half her time at Ondine's and other places and appears in a miniskirt and then expects privacy for herself and her children." (Here, Jackie is criticized for pleasure as well as for the wealth that facilitates it.) It was impossible ever to forget her wealth, even though many supporters have claimed that her fortune was overestimated, or that her desire for money was exaggerated and that she actually liked simple pleasures. Looking at a recently published candid of Jackie at a Kennedy clambake, I think, "Jackie just wanted to be an ordinary person. Look at her sloppy hair, her common jeans. She almost appears cross-eyed. Maybe she considered herself plain. What an injustice, that she was so often forced to wear fancy clothes and appear at glossy public functions!" Maybe Jackie's wealthy lifestyle was imposed on her, and had she had her druthers, she'd have chosen a bohemian route—painting in garrets, wearing open-toed sandals. Seeing a Skorpios photo of Jackie putting a Band-Aid on Ari's cut foot, I think, "Secretly she was sweet and simple and kind, and we did her a disservice by assuming that her desires were gargantuan." I am never sure, looking at pictures of Jackie in fancy dress, whether her wealth (or the clothes which symbolized wealth) represented her personality's ideal efflorescence or whether fanciness was just another burden, along with tolerating the boisterous Kennedys, surviving JFK's assassination, and enduring the public's curiosity.

The myth: Jackie was secretly simple, secretly Everywoman, and her Empress identity was a grotesque fabrication, one that caused her great suffering, a disguise she would have been delighted to shed, so she could have an ordinary (middle-class?) life. I doubt, however, whether middle-class pleasures would finally have been Jackie's cup of tea.

Jackie as spender: she shopped in a trance, someone

said. JFK "spent" frequently, in the sexual sense of spending. Mythically, Jackie spent, too, her fiscal exorbitance a perverse mimicry of JFK's sexual voraciousness. One of the most famous details used to impugn Jackie's lifestyle—her blank-check mode—was the fact that Ari covered the *Christina*'s barstools with whale testicle skin. Proof of cash, conquest, testosterone? Moby Dick? Jackie's O-ness, her ability to spend Onassis sums, was virtually macho.

The details of Jackie O's spending are no less delightful for being possibly mythical. Exposés like Fred Sparks's *The $20,000,000 Honeymoon: Jackie and Ari's First Year* tell us what we want to know: that she had 72 servants on Skorpios; that she bought 36 pairs of shoes in one binge at Bergdorf's and then returned them the next day; that she charged dresses to Olympic Airlines and then sold them to secondhand shops like Encore for cash; that Ari gave her $5 million worth of jewels during their first year of marriage (every two weeks he'd send her flowers, with a bracelet concealed in the bouquet); that salesclerks needed sedatives after her whirlwind visits. A famous line: "Jackie's face is her charge plate." She didn't need to carry cash or credit cards: she could charge her purchases to Olympic Airlines. Maybe she had a slow-motion nervous breakdown, and collapse took the form of shopping. Maybe she was manic or hypomanic. (See, it's possible to have a sympathetic relation to her shopping: to consider shopping as one of her burdens, a reason to consider her a martyr.) Whether or not the stories were true, we consumed them. Fables of Jackie's spending may have momentarily ruined her reputation, but they also made her seem attractively hungry—always wanting more, and wanting it now.

Even in the Bouvier and Kennedy years, Jackie was notorious for spending money, though she occasionally protested, and though there was contradictory evidence —such as the oft-quoted assertion that the gown she wore to her coming-out ball was an off-the-rack number costing less than $60. During Jack's presidential campaign, Jackie professed that Mrs. Nixon (despite her Republican cloth coat) shopped at high-class boutiques like Elizabeth Arden, while Jackie did not. Jackie said, "I hate a full closet." Contrast *Time*'s 1968 description of her closet: "day suits and evening dresses are segregated, evening dresses arranged by length, all clothing lined up by primary color and shades of color, pairs of shoes catalogued by the hundreds according to color and style." How did *Time* enter Jackie's closet? Odd, that Jackie's closet—or the idea of it—is part of the public record. I suppose the description proves not only that she had an abundance of clothes but that she was well organized. She needed to be, with such variety of, for example, glove lengths— "wrist, above-wrist, elbow, above-elbow." Someone hypothesized that her shoes stayed clean because she threw them away "like Kleenex" after wearing them. Critics called Jackie "too damn snappy"—too damn snappy for a woman who, as First Lady, was not royalty but an ordinary housewife writ large.

Was Jackie a real aristocrat or a fake aristocrat? Or was she secretly progenitor of a populist style? Knockoffs of Jackie Kennedy's look proliferated. Articles in fan magazines advised: "How to Be Your Town's Jacqueline Kennedy." A laudable ambition. One could buy imitations of her pearls for 79 cents, imitations of her alligator purse for $5.00, imitations of her pillbox hat for $3.71. *Life* announced an "outburst" of Jackie look-alikes—even mannequins were formed to resemble Jackie. The Jackie look, as practiced by imitators, was like a *Reader's Digest* condensed book, streamlining the complete artifact's baroque excesses. Legions imitated Jackie's pillbox hat, its shape potentially Maoist (a Chinese scholar's fez?); and yet Jackie was marketed as an aristocrat, even if a simulacral one. At the Inaugural Ball, the band played "I Could Have Danced All Night," which Eliza Doolittle sings after she finally learns proper English and is ready to embark on her career as poseur. "I Could Have Danced All Night" was also Jackie's anthem: *and still have begged for more,* sang Jackie/Eliza, princess impersonator, whose mantra was *more.* (Note how Lerner and Loewe songs, "I Could Have Danced All Night" and "Camelot," frame Jackie's years as official Empress. Who says Jackie wasn't a Broadway star?)

Jackie was often touted as a genuine American aristocrat, but it remains doubtful whether there is such a thing; indeed, if we wish to believe in American aristocracy, perhaps we should look in untraditional places. As James Baldwin wrote in *The Fire Next Time*: "The Negro boys and girls who are facing mobs today come out of a long line of improbable aristocrats—the only genuine aristocrats this country has produced."

I adore Jackie, but not because she was an aristocrat. Maybe she was likable because she seemed a knockoff aristocrat, palpably ungenuine, and always in danger of being found out.

MUCH ABOUT JACKIE seemed ephemeral. Except for her hairdos. They lent her an air of monumentality. Jack might lose an election; Jackie might disappear from public view; but the hair, in pictures, was going nowhere, would prove immune to mutability.

In my favorite of Jackie's hairdos (she sported it in Paris in 1961, but also revisions of it regularly in the late 1960s, notably in 1967, when she visited Cambodia) she seems to be wearing a fall. There's a protuberance above her brow, and the hair is pulled backward over the unseen lump. (Who can inform me if it is or is not a fall? The unverifiability of hair!) These are excessive hairdos. In their artifice, they are nearly obscene: or their monumentality surpasses the "proper" function of a hairdo. So large is the hair, it seems a mission. Looking at photos of Jackie with her hair at its hugest, I marvel at the willpower and audacity implied. Who but Jackie could have carried it off? Jackie had a large face; doubtless she (or her hairstylists) chose coifs to offset the head's hugeness. (She looks odd when wet-haired, in swimming shots; her face requires a generous frame.) But the hairdo has symbolic functions, too: it conveys size of personality, size of wish. It proves her ready to face the world; it proves her preeminence and helps us to recognize her.

Sometimes she wore a "brioche"; sometimes she wore

"slash bangs"; sometimes she wore a "sweeping chignon."
I prefer the chignon, the sense of upsweep, crescendo.
Though I'm tempted to list all her hairdos (I'm sure they
have specific names), instead I'll say what her hairdos
imply.

Because she is silent, we look toward her hairdo for
clues about her personality. From the hairdo we learn
that she is composed and contained; like an armadillo or
a turtle, she carries built-in protection. Hair of a certain
massiveness is not feminine: it is bulbously defensive
armament. Her hairdos remind me of the bubbletop over
the presidential convertible—the bubbletop that *should*
have been lowered in Dallas. Or of a VW Bug. Or
of wide-screen cinematic technologies—VistaVision,
CinemaScope, Todd-AO, Panavision, Cinerama—and
of movies made with such processes, including *The Robe*
and *Around the World in Eighty Days.*

The hairdo seems immobile, stiff; it won't change.
And yet in newsreels one can see that wind often disturbed
her coif, and that she brushed flyaway locks back into
place with her fingers. This was a repeated gesture: shyly
raising her hand to brush fallen hair off her forehead.

The keynote of her hairdo is *lamination*—the plastic
coating placed over an ID card, such as a driver's license,
to keep it firm and to protect it against damage. A
patina—hair spray?—laminates her hair, renders it un-
natural or *intended*. She must be laminated because she
will pass through so many hands, so many contexts.

I suppose that her hairdo is a sexual object, or that I
am treating it like one, though I am not aroused by her
hairdos. I admire them; they blur the distinction between
real hair and wig, an ambiguity that advertises her superior sense of irony, as if she were getting away with
some petty theft.

Hairdo: unverifiability, lamination.

In my first dream about Jackie (June 1978, when I was nineteen), we kissed, and tresses of her bouffant got tangled in my mouth.

I am tempted, watching the progression of Jackie's hairdos, to see them as petite allegories for her movement through life's rigamarole—each hairdo a Station of the Cross. I imagine that the hairdo will hit its zenith, say, in 1966, and the subsequent hairdos will realize their place, will lessen, grow less distinguished, less intimidating. But in fact each year her hair grew larger, reaching its climax in the late 1960s; ever afterward it remained a fortress, inviting us to lionize it. I consider her hairdos to be like Zeppelins or Goodyear blimps. Her hairdos are hyperbolically sized and they encourage, in me, exaggeration.

They are the opposite of the demure, butch haircuts of Mia Farrow, Julie Andrews or Twiggy. Nothing boyish about Jackie's bouffant: it's clearly battle gear of a woman of means.

Jackie may have seemed to lack ego or self. She may have seemed our fantasy's pawn, just as she was the instrument of JFK or Ari. But her hairdo served as ego, as "I": it revised her life's constriction and silence, and seemed the circus tent for feats and menageries. Additionally the hairdo has always seemed to me a chupah, or a pumpkin. Everything else about Jackie's body and self-presentation is refined, bony. But not her hairdo. Isn't glamour simply an engraved shield of Achilles that chic people use to defend against their enemies?

The hairdo reversed Jackie's muteness, and made her a momentary dominatrix, putting opponents (photographers, public, husbands) in their place.

The bouffant eludes photographic rendering. One

can't always see where it ends. In many tabloid photos, images of her face have been cut-and-pasted, by layout artists, onto the page, and sometimes (in sloppier magazines) the photos have been carelessly cropped, not including the entire hairdo, giving Jackie a lopped-off, artificial look, as if she'd just floated in from Alpha Centauri. I can see scissor marks on the border of the bouffant, giveaway traces of decoupage.

During the 1970s and 1980s, a frequently reproduced series of photos showed Jackie in a bare-shouldered evening gown; above her thin long neck and bony, exposed, yet broad shoulders the hairdo seemed an item of apparel, like a cape.

I assume that Jackie chose her hairstyle, that she wanted piled, marmoreal, high-society hair. It's possible that color and treatment thickened the hair shafts. Hair of buttressed ostentation, it made a statement; it provoked, in me, an admiring giggle.

The hairdo lent itself to caricature, hyperbole, metaphor, in part because it seemed the formidable armature of a figure whom one must take seriously, even religiously. The hairdo was the icon's frame. It had no more reality, in a photo, than a Duccio angel's halo.

The hairdo, like her gaze, cleaves space around her; the cartoon bubbleburst of the hairdo, like the flashbulb's, is a mini mushroom cloud that billows in excess of its source.

JACKIE'S HUMILIATION

JACKIE CLIMBED on the car's trunk in Dallas; everyone knows this unhappy fact. When she saw stills from the Zapruder footage, she couldn't remember having climbed backward. But we saw her climb.

The assassination was her moment of humiliation. Her husband was shot; Jackie was also nearly killed (the bullets could easily have hit her). She underwent an intimate agony in public. Everyone saw it—a televised execution. Spectator sports: voyeurs, we watched and continue to watch the killing. Everyone has memorized Jackie's worst moment, its image already banal; everyone has access to Jackie's nightmare. Her dress was bloodstained in front of the entire world. Of course, the principal horror was JFK's death; but a secondary horror was that the world saw Jackie bloodied, the world saw Jackie crawl.

I interpret Jackie crawling as her moment of public humiliation. Two movie scenes come to mind: in *Carrie*, at Sissy Spacek's prom, to ruin this odd, translucent-skinned, demon-possessed girl's moment of vindication, pranksters position a bucket of pig's blood to pour over her head at the instant she is crowned Queen; and in *Hush . . . Hush, Sweet Charlotte*, after someone hacks to death Bette Davis's lover, spilling blood over her dress, Bette, disassociating, takes the blame and believes that she committed the crime. In these two scenes, the innocent girls on the verge of sexual initiation are humiliated by having blood poured on their dresses.

Scene of defilement: the President's interior spilled over the First Lady in public. The President is supposed to be self-contained and boundaried. But his insides opened up, and contaminated his clean wife. A border of propriety was crossed, publicly: we saw the President brought down, and Jackie messed up. Henceforth everyone seeing Jackie would remember that moment; she was most famous for being the woman in the bloodstained dress, the woman whose husband was murdered while she sat beside him. Her fame, therefore, had a gruesome subtext: though in most pictures from her life as icon, Jackie is impeccably groomed and smiling, no one can forget this irregular moment, when she was ungroomed, gore-besmirched, and reduced to flight. All the scenes of clean, contained Jackie are counterpoint to the Dallas moment.

Does the scene prove that Jackie was a bad girl and that she had been punished? Everyone saw her humiliation; doubtless some perversely enjoyed seeing it. Subsequently she would have to undo the shame, get revenge on everyone who'd witnessed it.

Like Tosca seeing her lover Mario killed at the end of Puccini's opera, Jackie passively saw her husband murdered but was symbolically associated with the crime's active staging. Our obsession with Jackie's face, for thirty years after Dallas, is sympathetic identification with a martyr, a woman who went through hell; but it also unconsciously involves wishing to bring Jackie to justice—wishing to pin down her face as *the lady who was there, the lady indirectly implicated*. It's a wish to *find Jackie*, to retrieve her from her state of freedom and immunity from the law, to prosecute her. Photos of Jackie function as "wanted criminal" ads, or (more sympathetically) notices for missing, kidnapped children. The pictures' message: "Where is Jackie? Help us track her down."

Survival is not simple; the survivor does not escape without guilt, without imputation of wrongdoing, even though she was utterly innocent.

Jackie-in-the-car-with-shot-Jack grotesquely rivets because it resembles the iconic Salome and Judith scenes. Jackie tried to keep JFK's head on, after it had been blown away. But doesn't, from a great, unknowing distance, the tableau reduce to this: intact Jackie beside a man who's lost his head? Thus she becomes Salome, Judith—a woman who has custody over a man's head; a woman who (symbolically) beheaded a man.

We know *factually* that Jackie is innocent, a traumatized victim; and yet we also may feel *irrationally* that she is connected to the loss of the Head of State. Of course, Jackie did not kill Jack. And yet her presence, alive, beside his dying body accords her ambiguous, ineradicable, inexplicable power. A living woman next to a dead man (a Pietà) is a uniquely satisfying, if horrifying, icon to contemplate, because the two have been brought to an even level: the man cannot rule now, cannot move mountains, cannot cure lepers. It is the woman's turn to be heroic, to incite worship, and to rule.

It might be in poor taste to give voice to these reflections on Jackie's symbolic complicity with JFK's death, or at least the illusion, in pictures, that Jackie is linked to his beheading; but images of Jackie fascinate us so because her face and the retinue of scenes it conjures evoke shameful, irrational undercurrents: as if Jackie's image, contaminated by JFK's blood, in turn contaminates us.

Just now I took a *Life* photo of Jack and Jackie arriving in Dallas (Jackie clutching red roses) and folded the picture in half, leaving only Jackie visible. How does Jackie look when we remove JFK from the picture? I'm still trying to figure out how much Jack contributed to her mystique—whether her aura depends on the President, or the idea of the President; or whether, in fact, her aura increases when he's *absent*. It is possible that Jackie watchers may thrive on his disappearance. Jackie looks richer and realer with Jack gone.

Now that she is dead, and buried beside him, Jackie's constituency—we are millions—may feel that she has been completed, as if Jack and Jackie were two halves of a single soul. And yet her career as a photographic star depended on Jack vanishing; in all the post-Dallas photos of Jackie, he is of course absent, dead, but he remains the widow's implication, a ghostly emanation whose absence gives Jackie's face its glow, its look of startled sufficiency.

JACKIE'S SUNGLASSES

AND SCARF

JACKIE WORE SUNGLASSES: they disguised her but were also her trademark, announcing identity. What did we guess about Jackie from her sunglasses? We may have imagined grief-swollen eyes—or even bruised eyes. Shades implied problems: Had she been beaten? Was she drunk? Mourners wear sunglasses to hide tears; alcoholics, to disguise the effects of a bender, or to shield hungover eyes; gangsters, to be incognito when on the lam. Carlo Ponti wore sunglasses because he was a mogul; James Dean, because he was disaffected; John Lennon, because he was countercultural; Anouk Aimée, because she was Continental. Jackie's black wraparounds advertised a mode of self-evolution: they announced that she would remain blind to impediments, that she would keep her own counsel. But the lunettes were so dark, so huge, two protective bubbles, that she seemed a baby in a Skinner box; or a patient with dilated eyes; or a woman going blind. Like her hairdos, the sunglasses demonstrated audacity: few could get away with sunglasses so grand, and to wear such an attention-getting accessory under the guise of wishing to deflect notice seemed disingenuous, or foxily paradoxical.

Jackie Onassis wore sunglasses more frequently than Jackie Kennedy: Mrs. Kennedy had civic responsibilities, while Jackie O had none. The shades reminded us that

Scarf and sunglasses: disguise, purdah,
self-evolution.

she was no longer First Lady, that she had no votes to
win. Sunglasses reinforced her silence: no way to read
meanings in her irises. Jackie O's gaze is too precious to
waste: when she moves through a crowd, why should she
bother to lock eyes with strangers? Jackie's immense
round lenses imply that she is, like Catwoman, a cartoon
vigilante with an illicit goal, requiring tunnel vision and
anonymity. Blinders, the glasses are also panoptic: they
shut off distraction and detour (lest Jackie suddenly veer),
but they also give her leave to scrutinize, to enjoy pe-
ripheral vision sans detection.

Sunglasses made Jackie seem chilly but also needy. "I

am too busy, too important, for you," they said; but also, "I am endangered, I need protection from assault and mockery." "Poor Jackie," we thought, "living in sunglass purdah"; or we thought, "Why doesn't she take off the shades and look us straight in the eye, like a good American?"

Symbolically she wore sunglasses because she'd been wounded by JFK's assassination: she'd seen the sun implode, and, blinded, traumatized, could never again face light. Maybe she had no eyes! Maybe if she were to unpeel the shades, there'd be just blankness.

Jackie donned scarves, with the sunglasses, to conceal her primary armament, the hairdo. Often the hairdo must have required protection. Often she must have wished to save the coif for a finer occasion. With scarf and sunglasses combined, she could cover most of her head, revealing little. In a scarf, she's the epitome of the incommoded, belligerently private star: she becomes momentarily unexceptional, even dowdy.

The scarf may have implied ordinariness (did curlers, straighteners, or appliances fill out the scarf?), but the scarf, perfectly tied beneath the chin, extended her fastidiousness. One never saw it fall off or slide. Was it stapled in place? In photographs, it never shifted. Winds of change and revolution blew around Jackie's head, but the hairdo stayed intact because the scarf's silken epoxy held it fast.

The scarf, like a sari, covered. Less of Jackie was exposed; mantled, she could move—drawl—through public spaces, businesslike but also sultry.

To give scarf: to put on a scarf and thereby avoid the world; to imply "I am who I am, get out of my face"; to brook no dissidence. Warhol called it *wrapping*; he knew the Bouvier women were adept at it. Jackie in scarf was like a landmark wrapped by Christo: *wrapped Jackie*. In one of her last photographed appearances, aboard the *Relemar*, Maurice Tempelsman's yacht, with the Clintons as guests, Jackie wore what *The New York Times* called a "concealing scarf." In the photograph almost none of Jackie's face is visible. Not obeying the head's or hairdo's curve, the scarf juts out with independent, starched stiffness, a shelf. At this nearly final sighting, wrapped Jackie seemed almost to have vanished beneath the scarf, as if it were soaking up her identity's dregs.

Anyone can mimic her signature style. Anyone who thinks he or she deserves Jackie's eminence may start the trek by donning a concealing scarf and sunglasses. The unlikeliest Jackie imitator was Marguerite Oswald, mother of Lee Harvey. Wishing to exculpate her son, she'd embark on research junkets, wearing what she called, with unintended irony, her "Jackie Kennedy disguise": scarf and sunglasses. She didn't want to be pestered, and she knew how to put people off the scent.

One makes metaphor of Jackie's scarf and sunglasses: scarf reminds me of X, sunglasses of Y . . . and then retreats from the enterprise of mythmaking, wondering, "Is it fair, is it moral?" and then remembers that celebrities, in photographs, harden into truism and object. The metamorphosis of Jackie, in a photo, is like Daphne's: she turns into a tree (scarf and sunglasses are bark) because she does not want to be seen, does not want to be pursued.

JACKIE VERSUS LIZ

JACKIE FUNCTIONED as a movie star in American culture. She originated as a political figure, a President's wife, but even during the Kennedy administration, she was treated, in the popular press, like a film star. Was Jackie the first White House resident or semipotentate to appear in fan magazines like *Photoplay*, *Movie Mirror*, *Movie Life*, *Screen Stories*, *Motion Picture*, and *Modern Screen*? And does her unprecedented migration from her proper sphere (First Lady) to an improper sphere (profligate actress, Queen of Wish) explain her unique appeal?

Jackie appeared on the cover of *Photoplay*, for example, regularly from 1961 to 1973. Only Elizabeth Taylor clocked more time there. But because Jackie acted in no movies, her presence in *Photoplay* was, from the start, incongruous. A movie star needs publicity, but Jackie didn't; at least she feigned not to, and during the Kennedy administration it was considered indecent for the First Lady to be written about as if she were a second Liz. Editorials denounced movie magazines for their indiscreet treatment of Mrs. Kennedy. And since she appeared in no films, there were no ready-made narratives in which to fit her. Liz had *Cleopatra*, *Butterfield* 8; if the magazines covered Liz's life as if they were reporting the life of Cleopatra or of Gloria Wandrous, there was the justification that Liz had impersonated the Queen of the Nile and the self-proclaimed "slut of all time" (so Liz-as-Gloria tearfully describes herself in *Butterfield 8*). But because Jackie never impersonated anyone, the movie magazines were forced to fit Jackie's life onto the template of the divorce-prone love-mad star; "movie star" became Jackie's role.

Jackie materialized in movie magazines alongside a motley assortment of stars and has-beens. As weird stars like Liberace or Wayne Newton have cult followings in Las Vegas but never break into America's recognized big time, so the popular stars in the movie magazines weren't necessarily nationwide box-office draws. Cruising twenty years of *Photoplay*, I'm shocked to discover Jackie juxtaposed not only with magnitudes like Liz and Elvis but with minor figures. For example, according to *TV-Radio Mirror*, in 1963, the hottest stars were Jackie, Liz, and the Lennon Sisters. What traits does Jackie share with the Lennon Sisters? Relation to a family? Sanctity? Were the Lennon Sisters truly on Jackie's level? It's shocking to see Jackie cohabit the magazines with forgotten immoralists like Gary Lewis, Annette Funicello, Dolores Hart, Michael Cole, Jim Nabors, Vince Edwards, Glen Campbell, Jimmy Darren, Paul Anka, Phyllis Diller, Dorothy Malone, and Paula Prentiss. Why was Jackie accompanied by such lusterless stars? Why was JACKIE: THIS IS MY SUMMER FOR LOVE juxtaposed on the cover of *Movie Life* with SCOOP! DAVID MCCALLUM'S 60 SWINGING SECRETS!? Does David McCallum occupy the same orbit as Jackie? Perhaps Jackie's allure included her dangerous proximity to the nobody: in the midst of her enormousness and power, she quite lacked attributes. Like the star on the verge of invisibility (returning from the unseen, or headed toward it), Jackie was a woman without qualities.

Jackie's adjacency to fly-by-nights proves that stardom

has no absolute ground, and that even Jackie was subject to laws of fade-out and fall. She might last no longer than Dolores Hart. That Jackie lingered, in the twilight of *Photoplay*, does not mean that she acquired substance or wholeness. Rather, she lasted *as* ephemera; she lasted as someone we could not pin down or understand. Jackie seemed oxymoronically *eternal ephemera*: our interest remained, though it never deepened. The passion for Jackie never ceased to be shallow. She persisted, season after season, in the magazines, without any songs or films or TV shows to back her up, without granting interviews, without doing anything (beyond remarriage) to provoke commentary, but her persistence was not like Liz's, grounded in film work and divorce and perfume. Jackie's longevity was a consequence of how little could be proved about her.

The star with whom icon Jackie had most in common was Liz. The magazines explicitly linked the two through compare-and-contrast headlines, such as JACKIE WILL MARRY! LIZ WILL DIVORCE!, or JACKIE'S HOPES FOR CAROLINE, LIZ'S FEAR FOR LIZA, or LOVE . . . THE JINX THAT HAUNTS LIZ! TRAGEDY . . . THE JINX THAT THREATENS JACKIE! Sometimes they were bound even closer: JACKIE AND LIZ FIGHT TO KEEP THE SAME MAN. Or JACKIE & LIZ: SOUL SISTERS. Or THE SHOCKING PHOTOS! JACKIE DISGRACED AS ARI BOOZES IT UP WITH LIZ IN PUBLIC BAR! Jackie and Liz were most explicitly juxtaposed on June 1962 *Photoplay*'s cover. Its headline read: AMERICA'S 2 QUEENS!

At least during the Kennedy administration, however, the two Queens represented contradictory moral principles. Liz was the swinging vixen, greedy for love and

THE NIGHT LIZ & BURTON DESTROYED EDDIE FISHER!

PHOTOPLAY

25¢
June

Jacqueline Kennedy vs Elizabeth Taylor

AMERICA'S 2 QUEENS!

A comparison of their days and nights!
How they raise their children! How they treat their men!

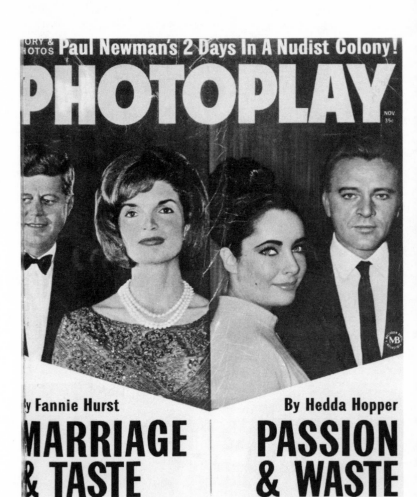

ORY &
HOTOS **Paul Newman's 2 Days In A Nudist Colony!**

PHOTOPLAY

NOV.
35c

By Fannie Hurst

MARRIAGE
& TASTE

By Hedda Hopper

PASSION
& WASTE

Why One Love Grows Despite Fame... The Other, Despite Shame

jewels; Jackie was the princess, tasteful and decorous. Liz was trash; Jackie was royalty. *Photoplay*'s November 1963 cover (issued *before* JFK's assassination) immortalized the contrast in the twin captions: MARRIAGE & TASTE, PASSION & WASTE. Jackie and JFK stood for marriage and taste, Liz and Burton for passion and waste. Jackie loved her man and treated him right; Liz did not. But Jackie soon migrated from taste to waste, and joined Liz, who became her partner in crime. Increasingly Jackie was portrayed as a big spender, a pleasure seeker. If an early 1960s *Movie Mirror* could say about Liz, BURTON TELLS WHY LIZ WANTS LOVE MORNING, NOON AND NIGHT!, by the end of the decade Jackie too (according to *Motion Picture*) would be CAUGHT IN THE ACT: JACKIE'S LOVE EXERCISES. HOW SHE STAYS ALL WOMAN ALL THE TIME. My favorite: SCOOP! FLESH PHOTOS OF JACKIE & ONASSIS: BIKINI LOVERS IN BROAD DAYLIGHT! She'd traveled far from JACKIE'S FIRST MOTHER'S DAY ALONE . . . THE LOVE THAT KEEPS HER GOING. And yet even during the White House years, her time of "taste," the magazines were glad to report that Jackie was caught dancing the Twist.

Though inevitably the stories themselves are saccharine, and reveal at the end only that Jackie is a good-hearted ordinary woman who wants marriage and children, the headlines imply that Jackie has suddenly acquired salacious freedom. Via the gossip scoop, Jackie explodes out of her image's claustrophobic box and finds a venue for extravagance—*extra vagance*, wandering (vagrancy) beyond law. The movie magazines offer soft soft porn: LIZ & BURTON ATTACKED FOR THROWING NUDE BEACH PARTY! or

JACKIE BUYS SEE-THROUGH BLOUSES TO PLEASE HUSBAND. The gossip scoop performs a punitive function—clamping down on the desires of readers, presenting a spectacle of impermissible conduct only to tame the sin and scapegoat the star. Alternately, Jackie's "Liz" immorality, in the movie magazines, was a welcome chance for icon and reader to be hedonistic. We turn to gossip scoops about Jackie & Onassis as Bikini Lovers because we want, against every dull precept, to see desire affirmed.

What did Jackie and Liz have in common? Their shared salvation was a soupçon of vulgarity, and hair the intensity of black-velvet paintings. Jackie was pseudo-French; Liz was pseudo-British. Each had insubstantial voices on the verge of disappearing. (Think of how frequently Liz swallows her lines.) As Jackie O emerged from the chrysalis of Mrs. JFK, America's Saint, so Liz spent most of her career breaking free from the original pristineness of *National Velvet* and *Father of the Bride*. In movies and tabloids, Liz could never swear, drink, or smooch enough. In film after film in the 1960s, Liz conspicuously desired; though she'd be pilloried in the press for weight gain, in movies she eats with abandon. "Eat, Velvet," says the austere Anne Revere to Liz in *National Velvet*, but in later parts, Liz would need no encouragement: in *Butterfield 8*, she says, "Waitress, could I have some more french fries?"; in the first scene of *Who's Afraid of Virginia Woolf?* she eats cold meat straight out of the fridge; "I'm a wolf," she confesses in *A Little Night Music*.

The most important point of convergence between Liz and Jackie was the role of Cleopatra, which they each played to distraction. On the cusp of Second Wave Feminism, Liz's Cleopatra, for which 20th Century–Fox paid her an unprecedented $1 million, may have seemed a misogynist fantasy of what happens when a woman rules: disaster. The history of the film's making, like the history of Cleopatra's reign, seemed meant to prove that women should not govern, that it is catastrophic if a Queen like Liz is granted centrality. The film was the costliest and longest made to date (originally twenty-six hours, it was eventually pruned to four); Liz wore sixty-five different costumes, designed by Irene Sharaff. Liz has always been the aesthetic and fiscal scapegoat for *Cleopatra*'s failure: supposedly it fails as art because Liz couldn't convey a "real" Cleopatra, but only resembled herself. Dismissal of her "superficial" performance seems, in fact, criticism for behaving like a plump, audacious version of Jackie Kennedy. *Time*'s critic complained, "When she plays Cleopatra as a political animal she screeches like a ward heeler's wife at a block party"; wasn't Jackie a refined version of a ward heeler's wife? Judith Crist lamented, "She is an entirely physical creature, no depth of emotion apparent in her kohl-laden eyes, no modulation in her voice that too often rises to fishwife levels. Out of royal regalia, *en négligée* or *au naturel*, she gives the impression that she is really carrying on in one of Miami Beach's more exotic resorts." Didn't Jackie's glazed eyes, too, reveal no "deep" emotion? And Stanley Kauffmann in *The New Republic* tartly observed, "Miss Taylor is a plump, young American matron in a number of Egyptian costumes and makeups. She needs do no more than walk around the throne room to turn Alexandria into Beverly Hills." Elizabeth Taylor is accused of flattening history and turning it into spectacle; of transforming a throne room (the White House?) into an exotic resort. Jackie, too, was a fake queen, expensive and well dressed. She didn't attend political functions; instead, she consulted with Oleg Cassini and rode horses and sailed on Onassis's yacht (as early as August 1963 he took her for a cruise). A journalist called her the "Cleopatra of the Potomac." Would a woman of Jackie's extravagance and beauty— a woman so gifted at turning herself into *spectacle*—ruin empire?

Liz's principal crimes were not lack of verisimilitude, but adultery (her affair with Richard Burton began on the Rome set of *Cleopatra*, and caused her to be denounced by the Vatican as home wrecker and erotic vagrant) and costliness. Not only was her salary $1 million, but the film was shot in Todd-AO, a process on which she profited (it was the property of her late husband Mike Todd). She was notoriously extravagant; the epic scale of *Cleopatra*'s production was seen as a reflection of Liz's personal grandiosity. (At "Casa Taylor," the house that Fox rented to serve as Liz's dressing room, she had a separate room for her wigs alone, and another room in which to put on her makeup.) If Liz seemed a fake, expensive, squandering queen, her performance as Cleopatra confirmed this persona. Like Cleopatra, Liz ruined men's empires. As Cleopatra mythically caused Caesar and Mark Antony, and their empires, to fall, so Liz seemed to cause 20th Century–Fox's decline, or, more generally, the collapse of the star system. How did Liz acquire this destructive power? Liz could topple masculine structures (Rome, 20th Century–Fox) because she had a knowledge of men's secret weakness. In *Cleopatra*, Liz spies on Rex Harrison (Caesar) falling down in epileptic convulsions; through her effeminate brother, Ptolemy, she gives Caesar the severed head of his beloved

Liz as Cleopatra: flattening history?

Pompey; she divines Caesar's assassination. Liz understands male vulnerability, just as Jackie did. Recall the picture of Jackie riding beside ailing Jack in an ambulance, early in their marriage; recall the lore of Jackie nursing him back to health. Once she described him as a boy who was sick all the time and who sat around reading about heroes. We give her credit for understanding his frailty.

Scars underscore stardom: Liz's and Jackie's intimacy with collapse (their own or their men's) increased their star power. Liz nearly died several times: her first Oscar, for *Butterfield* 8, was supposedly a sympathy Oscar, in honor of her recent tracheotomy and pneumonia. Liz became an icon because she'd survived her own death (in an autobiography she reports several near-death/out-of-body experiences); the death (by plane crash) of Mike Todd; the death of *Giant* co-star James Dean; and the disfiguring car crash of co-star Montgomery Clift. Similarly, Jackie was canonized because of her proximity to JFK's assassination. Jackie is symbolically scarred by Dallas, while in *Cleopatra* one can clearly see the tracheotomy scar on Liz's throat: I think of it as her O/scar, her (Jackie) "O" scar, announcing her wounded stardom, the connection of *star* to *wound* or *disfigurement*. When Liz says, in *Cleopatra*, "I *am* Isis—I am worshipped by millions who believe it," I proleptically or perversely intuit the presence of "Onassis" in the word "Isis." What Isis does: reunite the dispersed limbs of Osiris. Isis/Liz/Jackie Onassis is the star who surveys and controls dismemberment, sometimes putting the body's pieces together, sometimes leaving it attractively broken.

In the United States during the era of *Cleopatra* and Jackie Kennedy, African Americans were dramatically initiating a struggle for civil rights; the Cold War had reached its apex. Representations of Jackie and Liz as Cleopatra figures reflect the imagined decline of traditional white male power structures, proposing, as alternative, a fictional realm where women were disastrous Queens, fickle and prescient, changing costume every scene, wearing elaborate wigs, and squandering budgets. (Imagine Eartha Kitt starring in another version of 1963's *Cleopatra*: what if Hollywood had dared to portray Cleopatra as an African Queen?) We're accustomed to denigrating fakeness in art or in politics. However, obsession with fake Queens might have been a useful force: it might have been salutary to realize that we wanted not an Emperor (Caesar, JFK) who ruled the world and vanquished Communists, but a mysterious Queen (Cleopatra, Jackie) who represented another order of power. What kind of strength did Jackie and Liz propose? The power of fakeness, when it knows itself as fake; the power of wish, when it has the audacity to unveil itself. Liz was criticized for failing to portray Cleopatra realistically; for flattening the film's historical ambitions, and seeming to care only about her costumes. Similarly, Jackie did not communicate overt politics. She supported the arts; she looked good in clothes. She whispered, and restored the White House. But one step toward revising politics is self-consciously dwelling upon its glazed, seductive surface. Caring more about Jackie than about JFK, a populace might have been obliquely saying: (1) we prefer women to men; (2) we prefer surfaces to depths; (3) we disregard, altogether, the fallacy that Jackie's appearance can be dissociated from issues of nation, body, and border. Would Elizabeth Taylor have made a worse President than Ronald Reagan? Liz as Cleopatra, or Jackie as

Queen of America, are no less probable, and infinitely more desirable, than Reagan. Liz is certainly a better actor than Ronald. If American politics has long represented the triumph of style over substance, why not have some style worth dying for?

The strong Liz/Jackie symbolic connection, narrated in the fan magazines and enacted in *Cleopatra*, represents an American fantasy about leadership: a desire for incommensurate, unearned, and artificial largeness; a longing to be led by a woman; an acknowledgment that politics, as presently practiced in the United States, is nothing but a costume drama, and that politics may be revised and revived *on the level of costume*, Liz and Jackie's sphere of mastery. Jackie once asked, in response to the hysterical media coverage of her clothes and her hairstyles during JFK's campaign, "What does my hairstyle have to do with my husband's ability to be President?" *Cleopatra* implies that the realms of "presidency" and "hairstyle" are not easily separated. (Think of JFK's constant haircuts, or Reagan's shiny, shoeblack cowlick.) Jayne Mansfield summarized this line of argument—this gesture of leveling the distinction between *bombshell* and *President*—when she angrily said to JFK: "Look, you'll only be President for eight years at the most. I'll be a movie star forever!"

Jackie's and Liz's heads loomed out of proportion to their frames. In Richard Avedon's extraordinary 1964 photo of Liz, she's at last been authorized to be huge in temperament and self-presentation. She's taken the role of Cleopatra to heart, as a new model for how she might behave. (How many women, inspired by *Cleopatra* or by *Vogue*'s article "The New Cleopatra Complex," modeled their own maquillage and coiffure on Liz-as-

Queen?) Her cleavage—how can one discuss it? She's impossibly bosomy; she's flat Jackie's opposite. And yet one learns from Jackie, as one learns from Liz, lessons of space. What Jackie taught with her piled hairdos, Liz taught with artful display of her cleavage—how to split open the world.

Another variety of star who bears comparison to Jackie is the Hitchcock frosty blonde—Doris Day in *The Man Who Knew Too Much*, Kim Novak in *Vertigo*, Julie Andrews in *Torn Curtain*, Tippi Hedren in *Marnie* and *The Birds*. Jackie, like Doris Day, was the paradoxical Cold War woman, alternately frosty and hot. A cover headline from *Life* magazine (October 10, 1960) summarizes the paradox: BOX OFFICE BONANZA SUNNY DORIS DAY IN A SHIVERY ROLE. A goody-goody? Or a cheerful woman in arctic circumstances? In *The Man Who Knew Too Much*, Doris Day reveals her gunmetal core: no innocent, she has a wonderful screaming fit, sings "Que Sera Sera" as subversion, and manages to look radiantly and menacingly sexual while maintaining overtones of sanctity she'd exploit in *Teacher's Pet*. In *The Man Who Knew Too Much*, or *Vertigo*, or even Liz's *Suddenly, Last Summer*, the woman must survive a man's trauma. By surviving JFK's death, with her temperament of frost, Jackie earns a place in the *Vertigo* Hall of Fame: as icon, she's a sunny woman caught in a shivery role. Cold War gales inundate her. Odd, how Doris Day and Jackie could look at once highly sexed and radically frozen. The necessary pretense of hygienic frigidity—a self-protective coolness—magnified their allure. *Some Like It Hot*, *The Seven Year Itch*: Marilyn's heat, whose connection to JFK we know, was the itchy opposite of Jackie's Kim Novak/*Vertigo* waxiness—the waxiness of a double agent, of a live woman impersonating a painting. We're accustomed to thinking of Marilyn Monroe as summarizing paradoxes of 1950s American white womanhood; Jackie, however, seems an equally representative and poignant figure—Marilyn's thin, dark doppelgänger. If Marilyn represented white womanhood as bruised fruit, palpitating and tragic and "natural" (as critic Richard Dyer explains in *Heavenly Bodies*), Jackie typified a condition of deadness, coldness, the otherworldliness of Tippi Hedren fleeing the attack of *The Birds*, the self-sufficiency of Doris Day in *Lover Come Back*, Doris manufacturing an eroticism of penury and the nunnery.

Grace Kelly, Jackie's Monaco equivalent (tabloid headlines asked IS GRACE JEALOUS OF JACKIE?), served as Hitchcock's cool blonde in *Rear Window, Dial M for Murder,* and *To Catch a Thief.* Who can forget, in *Thief,* Grace semi-sadistically and suavely accelerating her car around dangerous curves, while Cary Grant sweats? Forever one would associate Grace (like Jackie) with fast, faster vehicles, and a royal urge to race away. And in *Rear Window,* Grace must pretend, as Jackie pretended, to be the demure fashion-crazed nursemaid to the man-of-war, the Jimmy Stewart, the Jack; yet Jimmy is immobilized in his leg cast and his voyeurism, and Grace possesses latent friskiness, climbing, with her Edith Head-designed skirt, into a murderer's window, while Jimmy gapes—just as Jackie, in pink suit, would climb out of the Dallas car. (Edith Head would later call Jackie, in terms of fashion, "the greatest single influence in history.") Grace, like Jackie, must pretend that being a fashion plate is a condition of paralysis; yet, in fact, the man, the photographer, is the paralyzed one, and Grace/Jackie, reading *Harper's Bazaar* in the film's final shot, has the power to look, to flee, and to desire. Incidentally, Grace Kelly visited JFK in the hospital in the 1950s: Jackie oversaw the visit. She knew how to watch, elegantly, over a man's sickbed.

The other royal-seeming star parallel to Jackie was Audrey Hepburn—with her slenderness, her carriage, her queer accent, her ballerina background, and her perennial role as naïve girl who becomes a princess but whose relation to splendor and royalty is tenuous, sham. Most Jackie-like about Audrey Hepburn was her long retirement: her evident satisfaction in *not* appearing, for swaths of dry years, in movies. And isn't Audrey Hepburn in *Wait Until Dark* a blind sister to Jackie O in sightless sunglasses? Audrey Hepburn photographed in mini-dress outside the Rome church where she'd just married Andrea Dotti, a psychiatrist (I think: "At least Audrey will be in good, safe, shrink hands"), is a fetching document of a 1960s "impulse" marriage, like Jackie and Ari, or Sinatra and Farrow, or Garland and (Mickey) Deans—unions that once symbolized redoubtable flair, but then quickly fizzled, just as a hairstyle, once as upbeat as a nuptial, eventually reveals its latent evanescence. (Always look at the hairstyle when studying evanescence: a new hairdo can make a star look either ravaged or redeemed.)

In this survey of stars whose allure echoes Jackie's, I must not forget two queens of New Wave cinema, Monica Vitti and Jean Seberg. Jackie screened *Breathless* in the White House, as well as such other *nouvelle vague* films as *Last Year at Marienbad* and *Jules and Jim*. (Jackie even had Jean Seberg to dinner at the White House!) Monica Vitti, in *L'Avventura*, coined new modes of ennui connected to lost identity and artiness—the artiness of no plot, of a girlfriend disappeared on a nameless island, of bourgeois society's rottenness. Didn't Jackie, too, seem to know—and savor—the rot? Jackie had artiness and spaciness to match Monica Vitti's. And in *Breathless*, Jean Seberg has *le style Jackie* because she has vague affiliations with diplomats and because after she rats on Jean-Paul Belmondo to the police, she sees him die. This is like the Jackie we'd come to know: a Jackie who's intimate with dying men, a Jackie whose style seemed an affected American's in Paris (think of Jean Seberg saying, in English, against the film's French, "New York *Herald Tribune*, New York *Herald Tribune*"). What do we learn about Jackie from Jean Seberg in *Breathless*? We learn that consciousness might resemble a French *nouveau roman*—a story without point of view. We learn how to be seductively alienated. We learn to move through foreign locales with minimal gestures, blunted speech. We don't fall in love. We assume that the world will blow up in a few years. We condone adultery. We realize that best friends are easily kidnapped. We take long train rides nowhere, and drive a convertible toward seedy apartment houses. Our life resembles film noir, but our attitude is sunnily democratic, and we pretend that our stilted and sullen gestures, our resemblance to a pert mannequin, is a terminal, exotic variety of American optimism.

JACKIE AND ORIGINS

JACKIE GILDS HISTORY by providing it with a photogenic and unverbal instant of origin: the Inauguration, the moment she emerged into First Lady status, the moment her identity became public property, and the moment she made her indelible fashion statement (the pillbox hat). Just as JFK did *not* wear a top hat during his Inaugural Address, so Jackie (who professed indifference to millinery) chose a hat whose sheer dumb roundness, whose resemblance to a unisphere or cinnamon bun, became her logo. I want to reimagine Inauguration pictures now, to figure out Jackie's role as *she who inaugurates fantasy*, as *mute instance of commencement*.

In some collective, mystified heart, Jackie set up reverberations of a beginning. I was two at the time—hardly myself—but when I look at these pictures in retrospect they seem images of *my* origins. The notion of young beautiful Jackie open to states of wonder and awe (her face registers *appreciation of the new*) invokes fantasies of initiation. Why? Because we demand that every story recapitulate the dreary arc of our own life?

The famous image, from *Life* magazine, of Jackie stepping out from her house to go to the pre-Inaugural gala (always *pre-*, never *post-*): now the punishing specificities of 1960 have vanished, and in the frozen realm of photos, Jackie is simply leaving one house to enter another, quitting private life to enter public life. The outfit of this princess of the *pre-* seems a wedding dress. If she's the bride, is Jack the husband or father? Jack stands in the background, his face blurred. The photographer has chosen, wisely, to focus on Jackie. As always, a man—chauffeur?—offers an umbrella. Jackie lifts her long skirt so it won't trail in snow. Easy to look clumsy lifting one's skirt, but Jackie never looks awkward. She stares straight ahead, certain of destination. Everything in the photo is dark except Jackie's dress, and the falling and fallen snow. It's imperative that Jackie not sully her silk crepe dress. Hence she keeps herself aloof from snow. And yet the snow matches her dress and her own frosty nature, and seems the intended element for her passage from ordinary life into her new, bleak immortality. A journalist said of Jackie in 1961 that she had a "woman's instinct for entrances." She has the ability to effect, in the viewer, an initiating reverberation, a shudder that announces origins. She was, at this moment, losing her identity: she said, "It is terrifying to lose your identity," and also "It's really frightening to lose your anonymity at thirty-one." The Inauguration was a ritual purgation; Jackie was shedding common identity and taking on a *nouvelle*, blank self, matte and unmarked as the snow she stepped through, transparent as her Bergdorf Goodman sheer chiffon overblouse revealing underground silver filigree.

In another photo, Jack and Jackie make their entrance at an Inaugural Ball: they look like bride and groom. This was a *romantic* occasion; the country was marrying Jackie. Jackie seemed fatigued: shockingly, the announcer on the air actually mentions Mrs. Kennedy's recent caesarian. As the newscaster tells us: "The other Kennedy ladies all got together and agreed they would

84

Origins: Jackie steps into her new,
bleak immortality.

eschew white as a color and leave that for the belle of the ball." Is Jackie a belle? Does the Inaugural Ball represent Jackie's romantic conquest of the audience? Is she vanquishing the hearts of men only, or of women, too? Are women swooning in identification? Is the Inauguration a moment for a belle to shine—a woman's event, like a woman's picture? (Not that Jackie was grateful for the hoopla. She described the Inaugural Ball as a bunch of people milling around like "mesmerized cattle.")

Though Jackie leaves early, and Jack stays out late, the evening represents Jackie's inauguration as Queen of America. She wears no glitter, no showgirl frills. The evening advertises her austerity. We see the new presidency from her point of view: we imagine her pride, savor her triumph. We don't consider all of JFK's new duties and responsibilities. Instead, we focus on Jackie's new opportunities as symbol, her new ability to be the camera's obsessive center.

Image: Jackie rides in the Inaugural Parade. It looks like Dallas: after November 22, 1963, we can't look at photos of Jackie and Jack riding placid in an open car without thinking of possible disaster. She must have wanted sunglasses, but she's not wearing them. JFK squints so much that his eyes are almost entirely obscured, but even Jackie's squint is photogenic and endearing, and does not preclude a good view of her eyes.

Image: Jackie sits beside Pat Nixon, Mamie Eisenhower, and Lady Bird Johnson, listening to Jack's Inaugural Address. Against dingy minks, Jackie's fawn-colored coat with huge round buttons and matching pillbox stands out. At least she's not wearing the pelt of a murdered animal! Even her outfit seems pacifist, nonviolent. When Robert Frost's pages blow around in the

Jackie, dispenser of magic pills from her divine pillbox hat: a secret, ulterior Inauguration.

wind, and he can't read his Inaugural poem, Jackie looks worried. In the photo, an expression of sympathetic distress crosses her face. This proves Jackie's sensitivity, her understanding of Frost.

Until the Inauguration Jackie had not yet "come out." Yes, she'd been a deb, a bride, and a campaign wife. But the Inauguration represented the moment of Jackie's national—international—initiation into a new, consecrated identity. She was reborn into her snowy nothingness, her public-servant large-buttoned "peau d'ange" sacrificed status. She was now prey to fantasy, prey to being looked at.

A common, "normal" romantic fantasy of Prom supremacy took flight: Jackie was triumphant, Jackie began her career as goddess, and if we called her hat a "pillbox"

we wouldn't look too deeply into its medicinal under-
tones; we wouldn't remember Benzedrine or Valium or
Thorazine, we wouldn't consider Jackie—not yet—a
denizen of the valley of the dolls. Her pillbox, creamy
and uncollapsible, would seem, instead, her regal tiara,
easily copied, poignantly dented. At least two different
designers would take credit for having designed it. But
we designed it. Or at least we *designated* it—as the hat
of origins. Putting it on, Jackie started all over again, and
we started all over again, this time as Jackie. She has a
phantasmal ability to *generate* us. Put into motion by
Jackie-at-the-Inauguration, we may fumble through our
lives without direction. The country may veer off track.
But a fantasy remains in place: that a woman in pillbox
hat and large-buttoned coat cut a ribbon, blessed an endeavor, christened a weapon.

When did Jackie subordinate at the Inauguration? Jack gave
the speech, but Jackie radiated her subversively nonverbal
charm; cat looking as if she had eaten the canary, she
smiled, said nothing, looked gratified over a conquest
without a name.

When did JFK learn the atomic codes—before or after
the Inauguration? When did the power to blow up the
world shift to him? Wasn't the Inauguration the moment
that he took on apocalyptic agency? Against the *fact* that
JFK was now responsible for our possible fiery termina-
tion, note the *fantasy* of Jackie as the belle of the ball.
The buttons on her coat are big as sweet *galettes*. Do
the buttons, promising edibility and succor, perversely
echo the nuclear button (wasn't it always called a button?)
that JFK might push, setting off atomic war? Were her
buttons neutral, or were they part of a national defensive/
aggressive machinery?

Just now I reread JFK's Inaugural Address. Does it shed light on the meanings of Jackie at the Inauguration? No. She was not merely JFK's illustration. She demonstrated other values and principles: the call of sleep, the pull of stillness. A secret, ulterior Inauguration overshadowed JFK's. Jackie was crowned the princess of stasis and silence, the dispenser of magic pills from her divine pillbox hat. Fairy godmother of America, she looks stunned and dreamy; the glitter she sprinkles on our eyelids ensures our stupor, and prevents us from asking impertinent questions.

JACKIE AND
ORDINARY OBJECTS

JACKIE TURNS the ordinary object into something extraordinary—simply because she notices it, points to it, names it. We're consoled, imagining Jackie's simple side. Jackie may have had fabulous wealth and recherché tastes but she was also a figure of what Jane Bowles has called "plain pleasures." Jackie performed her alchemy mostly in our heads—when we read about her banal actions; when we heard, for example, that she once liked to dance the rhumba.

Press accounts, particularly during her time as First Lady, emphasized her association with commonplace actions and objects—on the one hand, to strengthen her tenuous connection to "the people," and, on the other hand, because icon Jackie was herself objectified, a commonplace *petite chose* in mass consciousness. Everything ordinary that Jackie did, owned, or discovered becomes evidence that (1) Jackie is really just one of us, despite her elite veneer; (2) we, despite our relentlessly ordinary lives, are secretly magnificent, because we share plain objects and practices with Jackie; (3) icon Jackie is an unpretentious object in the American home, and that's why she is fond of ordinary things—she identifies with them. Whatnots are her peer group.

Jackie plays Scrabble. Scrabble! We, too, have played it. Scrabble becomes our link to Jackie—as well as her symbol (Scrabble cubes jumbled in a pile, enigmatic letter-buttons combining to form full-size words). Jackie memorizes the poem "John Brown's Body." "John Brown's Body": ordinary poem, ordinary name! Jackie's not a Euro-snob, she's linked to American particulars like "John Brown's Body." When Jackie searches through the White House for treasures, her nylon stockings tear. Laddered hose! Jackie, just like the ordinary woman, has laddered hose. Laddered hose becomes a symbol of a common plight, a common dignity. Jackie says, in an interview, that she wants Caroline to be able to do "all the normal things she'd do normally." Jackie understands the value of normality! Jackie wants Caroline to do normal things! The message: *Jackie is normal.* Who's really normal? No one. But against all evidence of the senses, all proof that Jackie was supernaturally beautiful and eerie, there remained these stubborn particulars in the Jackie legend, mooring her to earth and to us.

Someone quotes Jackie using the word "delish." "Delish"! What an ordinary, slangy word. Jackie said "delish." Maybe Jackie and I have something in common: we share *delish*. We share era-specific conversational banalities.

Such Jackie gossip demonstrates Jackie's endearingly trivial traits—those which link her fate to ours. And we can use these minutiae, in turn, to help us navigate our own lives, armored by Jackie identification.

In 1961, *Life* magazine covered the First Lady's White House restoration project. In a photo, Jackie bends down to lift a carton, doubtless filled with antiques. But it is a used box. On it is printed, in bold letters: "SPECIAL CORNISH HEN FROZEN CHICKEN KEEP AWAY FROM HEAT." If only by the logic of juxtaposition, Jackie—the princess—is linked to the world of frozen chicken. Why does Jackie's tendency to bump against ordinary objects and practices transform her?

Simply this: nothing in her carriage or her deportment ever capitulates to the rude force of the ordinary object she encounters. Even in the photo of Jackie bending down to pick up a box labeled "SPECIAL CORNISH HEN FROZEN CHICKEN KEEP AWAY FROM HEAT," her arms are superbly and leanly biceped, her carriage impeccable. Frozen chicken can't reduce Jackie's mystique, because her aura surrounds the particle of banality (the "FROZEN CHICKEN") but doesn't change shape from having encountered material impediment. Tangibles like "FROZEN CHICKEN" offer a route into her imagined consciousness, and also create a sense that *it could be me, lifting the heavy carton, enduring laddered hose.*

Frozen-chicken-style particulars also serve as symbol of Jackie's resistance to interpretation and understanding. We will get no farther into her mind than these blunt dull facts. We discover, for instance, that Jackie served Kool-Aid to women reporters visiting the White House. Kool-Aid! The least distinguished drink. It became the punch of suicide in Jonestown; but until then, no beverage was more banally typical of early 1960s America. And Jackie served it! We may harbor a secret belief that Jackie would never drink Kool-Aid; that, instead, she drank Puligny-Montrachet. But she served Kool-Aid to women reporters, a set whom she notoriously disliked. Does Kool-Aid prove Jackie's meanness, stinginess? Certainly we can glean, from Kool-Aid, that the surface of Jackie Kennedy, in the media, will be littered with powdery, sweet commonplaces.

Jackie lived among whatnots, vegetables, beverages. A

painting Jackie liked was William Chase's "Lettuce and Tomatoes." How American, how plain: lettuce and tomatoes. One imagines Caesar dressing, or Thousand Island. One hears that Jackie said, while on her restoring mission, "Look at that Lincoln cake plate." What is a cake plate? I didn't know there was a special variety of plate called "cake plate." But Jackie knew, and she pointed to it. "Cake plate" becomes another molecule in the Jackie pointillism—another detail, mysterious, unsymbolic, that helps to compose icon Jackie.

For lunch in the White House, Jackie would often have a grilled cheese sandwich sent up on a tray to her bedroom, before her nap. Grilled cheese! No sandwich more customary, more homespun. It is easy to identify with Jackie if she is the kind of person who eats grilled cheese for lunch. Or Jackie's beverages: the icy pitcher of daiquiris for cocktail hour. Here is her White House recipe: "2 parts rum, 3 parts frozen limeade, and 1 part fresh lime juice. Add a few drops of Falernum as sweetener." You may think of Jackie as a reader of Colette and an intimate of Margot Fonteyn—and yet, look, the evidence proves that Jackie knew frozen limeade and Falernum. I can't quite picture Jackie holding an upended can of frozen limeade (certainly a servant prepared the daiquiris), and yet the existence of this recipe helps me locate Jackie amid mundane murk.

Juxtapose *icy daiquiri* and *cake plate* with glamorous photographs of Jackie, and thereby double her allure. We hear that she danced the cha-cha to "Never on Sunday." We know that song. "Never on Sunday" becomes a bridge to Jackie. We may see a photo of Jackie in galoshes. Or we may read, in one of the biographies, that she bleached her arm hair, used Phisohex, and ordered powder puffs from Julius Garfinckel's for $1.13. Phisohex roots Jackie in a brand-name world, our world. Icon Jackie equals Phisohex plus Inauguration, or cake plate plus Dallas, or "Never on Sunday" plus pillbox hat. It's the incongruity that snags my attention—that moves me. It's not just Jackie's brocade cocktail suit—it's the juxtaposition of brocade cocktail suit with unsymbolic whatnots like Falernum.

Jackie's enthusiasm about plain objects and pleasures made it seem that she was pulling the public's leg, or else that she was "dippy," or else that she was endearing. It wasn't just the plainness of the objects, it was the pleasure Jackie evinced—gleam on face, rapturous openness of gaze. It was our ability to imagine, based on photos of Jackie looking astonished (astonished by the Taj Mahal, by Pablo Casals, by flashbulbs, by crowds), that Jackie was equally astonished by pink opaline cigarette boxes.

We hear that Jackie, after her nap, every day at the White House, would put on slacks and a turtleneck pullover for her afternoon's work. *Turtleneck pullover* becomes a link to Jackie. We can imagine that she enjoys these unsentimental items of apparel; that she would rather slouch around the private quarters of the White House in a turtleneck pullover than appear at a state dinner. Probably Jackie delighted in turtleneck pullovers and looked wonderful in them even when not in the presence of photographers. The most regal element of Jackie's attire or milieu has an underground link to the realm of the petty particular, the whatnot: elbow-length gloves, though fancy and elite, can be traced, down the juxtaposition chain, to turtleneck pullovers and daiquiris. How wearied she must have been of elect and prestigious goings-on. We imagine that the turtleneck pullover and the privacy in which she eats grilled cheese are blessed balm; we imagine that Jackie needs plain pleasures to recover from the rigors of being an icon.

Because she was silent, we'd have to rest content with news of her whatnots. Because we were unspeakably drawn to her, the whatnots surrounding Jackie took on a supernal glow. Because, eventually, we recognized that our own lives were tapestries of trivialities, we allowed ourselves, at moments, to feel Jackie-esque, as we ate grilled cheese, played Scrabble, and bleached our arm hair.

IT MAY CONTRADICT intuition to consider Jackie "exotic." Wasn't she white-bread Americana? And yet an essay in *Paris-Match* (1961) described Jackie's appearance as follows: "Her full lips, high cheekbones, widely spaced, heavily lashed eyes, and black hair all give her an exoticism which emphasizes her strangely toneless and beautiful voice." She seemed to have originated far from here. *Here?*

Jackie seemed exotic, inward, and venereal, from a parochial Anglo-American point of view, because of her glamorous yet suspect ties to France. Think of the French cuisine Julia Child introduced to American middle-class households: icon Jackie was exotic as quiche lorraine, croque-monsieur, La Vache Qui Rit cheese, and Leslie Caron as TV's Lili. Press accounts of Mrs. Kennedy emphasized her Bouvier genealogy: the Bouviers, albeit French, were not of aristocratic "stock," though a Bouvier-penned account, *Our Forebears*, tried to prove the clan's pedigree. Articles appeared in movie magazines about French branches of Jackie's family. And much was made of Jackie's time abroad, studying at the Sorbonne, and of her "perfect" or "fluent" French (others claimed it was merely "schoolbook" French). Jackie chatting with Charles de Gaulle, with André Malraux—these encounters define Jackie's cosmopolitanism. Despite her ineffably French nature, she was trapped in an American incarnation; a changeling, lost in America, misunderstood, in exile, she only found her true self when, in 1961, she traveled to Paris with JFK, where at last she achieved symbolic supremacy over the man to whom she was supposedly mere accessory. Before, she had seemed passive, shy; in Paris, as crowds shouted "Vive Jacquiii!" or "La belle Jackie!" she seemed vigorously pleased at the attention. She rose to her iconicity, relished it; Paris was the honeymoon period of her fame.

Apparently Jackie was caught reading Proust at a campaign stop. In her last interview, she mentions Proust: "Proust? I'd read that long ago." In early coverage of Mrs. Kennedy, much was made of her recherché tastes in reading (everything from "Colette to Kerouac"). Jackie's "beat" or "bohemian" side (Kerouac) balanced her allegiance to French sensualists and hedonists (Colette, Proust)—intellectual heavyweights that the American public would take as evidence of Jackie being quite "other," and untranslatable.

Legendary are Jackie's trilingual abilities: Spanish, French, Italian. She spoke Spanish in Spanish neighborhoods, Italian in Italian neighborhoods, a few words of Polish in a Polish neighborhood. Newsreel footage of Jackie on a South American trip (1961) shows her speaking Spanish in Bogotá and Caracas; compared to JFK, who mispronounces Venezuela as "Ven-zue-la," Jackie seems awake to difference, interested in the foreign cultures she visits. Venezuelans held up signs as the Kennedys drove past: "Kennedy, No. Jackie, Sí." Unlike the President, whose office is xenophobia, Jackie radiates a charming xenophilia. That's why she was welcome where her husband was not. Newsreels document Jackie visiting a Caracas kindergarten, where she leaves a record player as gift. A Caracas kindergarten was not Jackie's usual Mecca. "This tour was a Jackie Kennedy triumph," said the newscaster. "Wherever she passed, the word was 'how lovely.' " By speaking a few words of Spanish, Jackie gave the impression not only that she was an adept diplomat, or open to otherness, but that she contained a tablespoon of understated, unpermitted alterity.

In search of Jackie's foreignness, I watch a televised 1961 interview with Jackie—held in French—on the White House lawn. She seems more at ease in French than she does in any extant American interview. She laughs, smiles; a secret drollness emerges, and her voice, for once, is not breathless Ophelia's, but the "low" and "cultured" voice that Jackie's intimates describe. On this show, her French is rudimentary, much of it Franglais. She mentions "un petit peu de punch"; she describes a "garden party" but pronounces the words "garden party" as if they were French; talking about the White House, she says, "Voici le diplomatic reception room." Of Jack, she says "il ne relaxe pas." After Jackie's segment of the interview is over, the French host braves the White House to interview Jack, who can only muster one sentence of execrable French. It would be unseemly—un-masculine—for JFK to speak French as comfortably and seductively as Jackie. *Time* describes her speaking "low, slow French to De Gaulle," and *Life* captions a picture of Jackie and the French President, "The wooing of Charles de Gaulle," as if her diplomatic victories were also sexual triumphs. Indeed, Jackie's Frenchness matches her femininity, her artistic tastes, her aristocracy, and her appearance of being in exile from husband, country, and her own body—didn't she give the impression of wanting to escape? Frenchness also afforded sexual leverage against philandering Jack: with her "fluent" French, she could "woo" Charles de Gaulle and upstage JFK in the French heart. As *Paris-Match* said, referring to Jackie's trip to France: "*A Paris, l'Elégance de la First Lady Subjugue le Général.*" Jackie's elegance *subjugates* the General. If Jackie was subordinated by JFK in America, then in France through elegance she achieves erotic dominance. "I'm enjoying this trip terribly," said Jackie. *Terribly?* The word "terribly" is an American-aristocratic affectation, pseudo-British, like other words Jackie is often quoted as using ("dreary," "rather"); *terribly* sums up her ability to overpower through style, through a "terrible beauty."

The photos of Jackie in Paris show a hyperlegible elegance, whose effect on the viewer might have been terror: terror that her beauty and chic might be getting out of Jack's (or the United States') control; terror that her beauty constituted a covert declaration of war. The preparations for Jackie's costumes on the Paris trip received much press: would she wear a Givenchy gown in honor of the French? Was a lock of her hair really sent, a week in advance, to noted coiffeur Alexandre of Paris, so he could conceive a proper wiglet for her? And was the wiglet called a "curled torsade"? Was her lipstick, "Tender Red," really designed by Nathalie? (Who was Nathalie? One account calls her "Europe's leading makeup expert." But what was the significance of "Tender Red"? The difficulty of assigning meaning to Jackie lore does not diminish its resonance. If anything, such resistance to meaning highlights her lore's exoticism.) Even today, looking at photos of Jackie in Paris, I'm struck by the over-the-top gorgeousness of the Oleg

Cassini "Greek-style" gown she wore to the official reception at the Elysée Palace. Do I call the gown "pink-and-white straw lace," the gloves "above-the-elbow"? The gown—its line simple, its lace detailing complex—renders De Gaulle speechless, advances America's cachet, and reveals Jackie's veiled Frenchness. No one wears dresses like this anymore. The retrospective eye, then, knows the ephemeral nature of Jackie's triumph (JFK would soon be dead, Jackie would never again have official opportunities to dress this opulently, Jackie would never again be so tolerant of photographers). Why does Jackie look exotic, in the straw-lace gown, standing next to De Gaulle? Because she is a young woman, dressed in a decadence that declares originality, and he is an old fat man, dressed in a uniform that declares conformity. That her youth and beauty and heightened elegance are here finding *political* or *diplomatic* use makes the beauty seem "exotic" because it is pretending to be natural and sympathetic (as if it took no effort to coif her hair into this bizarre shape) while secretly serving a coercive and aggressive function (she is "working" her labor-intensive loveliness overtime). Americans, looking at these pictures in 1961, might have felt linked to (proud of?) Jackie but also estranged: is this truly our Jackie or has she sprouted a new, foreign identity, behind our back?

She pretends not to notice her dress. She *can't* notice it in public; that's the etiquette of being a superbly dressed woman. And yet *I* notice her dress. Photographed talking to André Malraux, Jackie's not obsessed with her pink frock, but certainly André is aware of its effect; Jackie's "terrible" poise comes from her ability to look beautiful and then *ignore it*. She walks through the Versailles Hall of Mirrors but she can't be photographed staring at her

*Labor-intensive loveliness: she pretends
not to notice her dress.*

own sublime reflection; she must avoid any appearance of narcissism, even though gowns this exorbitant and gemmed must have given her a rise as she looked in a mirror before embarking for Versailles—Versailles, where America's anachronistic queen belongs, Marie Antoinette returned to the century (eighteenth) about which she professed to know and care the most.

Jackie in India achieves exoticism by seeming merely to point at it. She poses as Western tour guide to Eastern strangeness, but the tables turn, and India uncovers Jackie's exoticism instead. Of her visit, the U.S. Information Agency made a film, "Jacqueline Kennedy's Asian Journey," shown in 106 countries. In the documentary, Jackie against the splendors of India seems quintessentially a Westerner abroad, and yet she also seems a woman in search of her ideal context. On the one hand, she is cruising for wonders, seeking stimulation and exoticism. On the other hand, *she* is the sought-after stimulus; *she* is the seventh wonder of the world. And so, in a *Life* photograph of Jackie at the Taj Mahal, she seems not only an American wife contemplating her dream house or the woman on *Let's Make a Deal* pointing to a prize washing machine, but the Taj Mahal's eerie twin, its friend and reflection. Like Versailles, or the White House, the Taj Mahal is a monument that mirrors Mrs. Kennedy's scale and sublimity. Photographed in front of it, she seems tiny—but it's also as if the Taj Mahal has become her extension, proxy, and possession, and so she can absorb and claim its size. The Taj Mahal is closed to the Western eye; the Westerner can't size up its significance, can't know its history or context. Similarly, Jackie, though an American property, can't be evaluated. She stands, opaque, in front of a treasured palace whose enigmas echo her own. That's why she's smiling: not just because she's found a beautiful building, but because she's found a partner in deception and avoidance.

This documentary of Jackie's trip to India seems like a version of *Gidget in India*. Jackie is the ingenue who visits a far-flung locale and makes friends there, proving that her normalcy can subdue even a subcontinent of strangers. Also, however, the film seems a documentary of Jackie's raptness, her ability to express unfeigned wonder. A similar "documentary" of the period comes to mind: *The Wild, Wild World of Jayne Mansfield*—in which Jayne tours Europe's capitals, interviewing transvestites, discovering kinkiness abroad. Jackie, like Jayne, functions as the tabula rasa against which the otherness of sinful Europe or inscrutable India can reveal itself. Jackie and Jayne, tour guides in the manner of Lowell Thomas, seem to be showcasing the wild wonderful world but really are just showcasing their wild wonderful selves.

Jackie's dream house.

Jackie went to India without JFK; therefore the trip was her first independent venture as cruiser and traveler, as talent scout for marvels.

Jackie liked the Taj Mahal so much that she returned at night to see it marked by moonlight; this seemed to prove Jackie's seriousness, her deep regard for wonders. But it also proposed the Taj Mahal as the lost key to Jackie's sphinxlike character. If she wanted to see the Taj Mahal twice, maybe the Taj Mahal can tell us something new about Jackie! Thus icon Jackie drained the places she visited of their history, and rendered them fragments of the Jackie travelogue. The Taj Mahal, no longer simply itself, became Jackie's acquisition, and a clue to her heart.

When, no longer official, Jackie Kennedy visited Cambodia in 1967 (evidently there was a secret diplomatic reason for her trip, but it was not made public at the time), she seemed once again on the lookout for world-class treasures. Touring Angkor Wat fit her agenda as connoisseur of historic sites. It also replayed her visits to Paris and India. Now, in 1967, in Cambodia and in Thailand, she looked even more like America's Queen, with her off-the-shoulder green gown and her upswept high-flown hair, while Prince Sihanouk kissed her hand, the wife of a police official fanned her, and extras strewed jasmine petals in her path—but she was no longer the real Queen. She symbolized no official American function, but she came, still, in her capacity as overseer of the marvelous, visiting Angkor Wat like a second Taj Mahal. Now, however, in certain pictures, she assumed modness, foretelling Jackie O. Wearing what Catherine Bowman in the poem "Jackie in Cambodia" calls her "heavenly wardrobe / from iceberg to tangelo," she was an agent of surrealism: it defied logic for the widow of JFK to be visiting Cambodia in a tangelo dress, showering Courrèges-style glory upon ancient civilizations. In Bangkok she stood next to the Emerald Buddha, illuminated at night so Jackie could see it better, as if the Emerald Buddha and Jackie were unchanging quiescences. Jackie had Emerald Buddha characteristics; she glowed, she uplifted, she said nothing, she was illuminated at night for superior viewing. For icon Jackie, wars and insurrections vanished; the world was a disconnected sequence of holidays and grandeurs. Simulacral herself, she rendered simulacral any monument she posed beside.

Jackie at Angkor Wat, Jackie at the Taj Mahal, Jackie at Versailles (and, finally, Jackie on Skorpios): Jackie visiting foreign civilizations enacted her own distance from self—how faraway she seemed! But wasn't Jackie always in exile from herself, a bemused visitor to her own body and outfits? Every occasion she graced seemed an Angkor Wat, a ruined staircase she numbly descended. We pitied Jackie for her numbness. Poor Jackie, standing beside the Taj Mahal: why couldn't she seem more "real"? Her unreality was touching, poignant; because we felt sorry for simulacral Jackie, isolated from experience and sensation, her unreality became the badge of her pathetic authenticity.

JACKIE AS HOUSEWIFE

WAS JACKIE KENNEDY a housewife? Her most famous political intervention was the restoration of the White House, her lengthiest public appearance the televised tour of its rooms. Though a woman identified with housecraft, naturally she delegated house*work*. Jackie Kennedy lore includes detailed accounts of her helpers —Providencia Parades, her maid; Pamela Turnure, her assistant; Mary Barelli Gallagher, her unofficial personal minion, whose resentment-laced account of servitude, *My Life with Jacqueline Kennedy* (edited by Frances Spatz Leighton, who also co-wrote *Bum Voyage* and *I Prayed Myself Slim*), is indispensable reading; Maud Shaw (whose unauthorized *White House Nanny* infuriated Jackie); and Mrs. Mini Rhea, who wrote *I Was Jacqueline Kennedy's Dressmaker*. Everyone who worked for Jackie seems to have written a memoir: the usher (J. B. West's *Upstairs at the White House: My Life with the First Ladies*) and even the kennel keeper (Traphes Bryant's *Dog Days at the White House*). And never forget Nancy Tuckerman, buffer extraordinaire, whose memoirs I eagerly—if unrealistically—await. Like the loyal servant in *The Remains of the Day*, Jackie helpers sometimes portray their labor as a morally superior endeavor, as if Jackie's good taste and eminence redeemed the act of serving her, despite the rigors of her fastidiousness. When

Pamela Turnure interviewed Irvin Williams, the White House gardener, for the JFK archives, she queried him about Jackie's taste. Turnure said, "I know that Mrs. Kennedy liked very simple flowers." Williams responded, "That's right, she did. One of her favorites was the dianthus, called bravo, a little, eye-catching, red flower." Turnure asked, "She had really very good taste, didn't she, in flowers?" and Williams answered, "She sure did." Turnure persisted, "Just the way she did in art and in other areas." Williams, docile, answered, "Yes, ma'am." Mrs. Kennedy dignified the house of which she was chatelaine, but it would be a misnomer to call her a "housewife." In her Miss Porter's School yearbook, she listed her ambition as "Not to be a housewife."

Jackie lore centers on her extravagant abhorrence of visual flaw. She might have learned fussiness from her mother, who had twenty-five servants at Hammersmith Farm, including one whose full-time job was emptying wastebaskets. In the White House, Jackie wanted her sheets changed before she took naps. When she moved into the White House, she quipped, "Throw out all the crap," and "Let's have lots of chintz and gay up this old dump." Did she mean to sound like Bette Davis? Or did Kitty Kelley, who quotes these lines in *Jackie Oh!*, invent them in order to portray Jackie Kennedy as a snobby wit? Another bon mot: "Why the hell should I traipse around to hospitals playing Lady Bountiful when I have so much to do here to make this house livable?" Although she professed to "hate to make changes," she brought back highballs and ashtrays, hired a French chef, altered the seating arrangements at state dinners (numerous round tables rather than one large ceremonial banquet table), expanded the guest lists to include artists, and favored

"Flemish" floral arrangements. Jackie's changes incited emulation: *House and Garden* advised how one could reproduce her decor at a lower cost. Propaganda: the White House was a representative domicile; Jackie Kennedy, the paradigmatic housewife, was rewriting the style of the American home. Jackie gave lip service to this doctrinal mission: about the White House she observed, "Every boy who comes here should see things that develop his sense of history. For the girls, the house should look beautiful and lived in. They should see what a fire in the fireplace and pretty flowers can do for a house." She also said, "I'll always do anything my husband asks me to."

But there are alternative interpretations of Jackie's housekeeping and her wifely subordination. Think of Emily Dickinson's poem "I'm 'wife' . . ." Dickinson, unmarried, nonetheless dubbed herself "Wife," as if the "Wife" identity served as a screen beneath which she could carry on unconventional business:

> *I'm "wife" — I've finished that —*
> *That other state —*
> *I'm Czar — I'm "Woman" now —*
> *It's safer so —*
>
> *. . .*
> *I'm "Wife"! Stop there!*

So Jackie might have said, "I'm Wife, I'm Czar. Stop there! Now that I'm Wife, I'm safe from your questions and your commands." Jackie's "Wife" identity gave her immunity; we may enjoy imagining her as "Wife" not because we wish to deify the role of American "Wife" but because the "Wife" disguise gave Jackie room for unregimented expenditure. Imagine the White House as site where she had unlimited power over local matters— a domestic caricature of Cold War JFK, Leader of the Free World, without rival Kremlin. As White House Wife, who could stop her?

Jackie may have sounded as breathless as Marilyn, but backstage, if we can trust the gossips, Jackie could command like a drill sergeant. Or so I want to believe. Tales of willfulness nicely balance out the public shyness, and make Jackie seem attractively powerful, incendiary, as if the White House were a good location for a surreally magnified personality to disport. Usher Mr. West generously quotes from Jackie Kennedy's memos, which substantiate her coldly exacting eye. My favorite Jackie memo concerns lawns:

Mr. West.

The White House lawns are a disgrace. . . .

1. It is a sea of brown as one looks across the South Lawn.

2. Clover, weeds and crab grass are mixed in.

3. On the hillsides there is a completely different kind of stringy, long green grass. —It is driving the President crazy—and I agree with him. In Glen Ora we have one man who cuts the lawn every two weeks, it looks like green velvet—and this place does not look as well as cowfields in Virginia.

. . . I have never bothered much about lawns—but every place I have lived—with a part time gardener—the lawn has been beautiful—so surely with twelve gardeners that is possible at the White House—

By the East Wing—the hill and gardens are truly atrocious . . .

AND—*the big problem now is LAWNS—am sure you will solve it—*

Thanks JBK

My second-favorite memo concerns curtain braids: "Also in the Blue Room make sure the braid on curtains is turned in as if the braid faces out it gets sun-burned." Who but dream Jackie would have noticed the braid's sunburn? Who but dream Jackie would have noticed the difference between a braid turned in and a braid turned out?

One unexpected effect of Jackie's "Wife" persona was *defamiliarization*. Rather than seeing, on the televised White House Tour, a picture of a woman comfortable in her home, with "pretty flowers" and a fire, we saw a stiff, attractive, but oddly inanimate woman who didn't seem to belong to her role, or to the house she was leading viewers through. Norman Mailer criticized her aloof falseness. But wasn't it more subversive and estranging that this quintessential woman of appearances and of housecraft should reveal, via TV, how unhomelike—*unheimlich*, uncanny—her home truly was? Jackie on the White House Tour may have lent herself to parody because she was already subtly engaged in self-parody: with convincing unsuccess she mimicked a role whose hollowness and constriction she could not deny.

Jackie was "Wife," but also her image resisted certainties of wifely identity. Men don't stick to Jackie; or Jackie doesn't stick to men. She moves independently of JFK, travels to India with Lee, cruises on the *Christina* with Onassis, doesn't accompany JFK on campaign trips; then Jack dies, and she has a succession of escorts (Mike Nichols, Lord Harlech, Pete Hamill, Roswell Gilpatric) but

I'm "Wife"! Stop there!

none of them adhere; rumors of romance are never clarified, and Jackie, as media image, remains on the prowl but unattached. Then she marries Onassis, but public speculation on their conjugal life takes the form of disbelief. False rumors circulate of a marriage contract stipulating how many nights a year she has to sleep with him; she spends most of her time in New York; when he dies, she is not by his side. In a movie fable of her life, *The Greek Tycoon*, Jacqueline Bisset plays Jackie O (called, tellingly, "Liz") as frigid. Moody, withdrawn, she's too upset and delicate to have much sex. Jackie's escorts often seemed, to use the gay phrase, her "beards"—her covers, her alibis. One didn't imagine that Jackie was really having a romance with them; they served as decoys, to deflect press attention from some truly weird hypothetical erotic life we were free to imagine and never substantiate.

Jackie gave no clear sexual messages. Her sexuality was subordinate to her identity as an extravagance, a slim fastidiousness; as she undercut the sacredness of housewife on the TV White House Tour, by pointing without affect at objects, so she complicated the role of male-affiliated woman. Yes, she was wife of JFK, wife of Ari, companion of Tempelsman; always, she'd appear with a man on her arm. But their auras paled before hers, and the sole concern of the camera, facing Jackie, was not companionship but aura. The camera didn't care about the man she was photographed beside. The camera only absorbed Jackie's solitary frequencies, her wavelengths as a privacy. If we asked her how she felt about her house, how she felt about men, she might have said, with Emily, "I'm 'Wife'! Stop there!" Sometimes a strict role— "Wife"—makes a hiding place, a way to tell the world to lay off.

The nomenclature of wife: Mrs. Kennedy, Mrs. Onassis. "Mrs. Kennedy" sounded ironic because Jack was dead, or, even while he was alive, ironic because there were so many other Mrs. Kennedys afoot, the identity invalidated by sheer multiplicity and repetition. "Mrs. Onassis" sounded ironic, too, either because she wasn't living with Ari, or because Ari was dead and she was living with Tempelsman; or because "Mrs. Onassis" seemed a coy euphemism, a way of avoiding rudely having to say "Jackie." (Posthumous sycophants, to this day, call Jackie "Mrs. Onassis.") At 1040 Fifth Avenue, her apartment was listed, long after Ari's death, under the deceptive name "Mrs. Aristotle Onassis." "Mrs." seemed, in Jackie's case, always to be a concealing half-truth.

MOST OF THE PRESS around Jacqueline Kennedy, as First Lady, centered on her clothing, interpreted as an allegory of her soul. Being well dressed was her professional obligation, choosing a designer a political act: prudently she opted for an American, Oleg Cassini, although rumor has it that she surreptitiously wore French designers. She complained about the undue and inaccurate coverage given her clothing purchases; famously, she once said that she couldn't spend $30,000 a year on clothes "unless I wore sable underwear." JFK feared her clothing could be a political liability, and Jackie claimed, "I don't want to be a fashion symbol. I just want to be appropriately dressed. Clothes are a nuisance to me." Hairdresser Kenneth said of Mrs. Kennedy, "She cares less about her appearance than many other women, but puts beauty care automatically into her routine." And yet, throughout her career as icon, she'd be identified as a clotheshorse; a Ron Galella candid of Jackie shopping at Bonwit Teller makes her seem dizzy with desire for the clothes she is cruising.

Was Jackie in charge of her clothing? Were they uniforms? Or is it accurate to read her outfits as acts of will and volition, as expressions of personality? Were Jackie's costumes a theatrical effort—a work of performance art? She didn't "express" herself in her outfits; rather, she reduced the number of clues by which we could "read" her. Through fashion, she flaunted ("Look at me") and she concealed herself ("You're not supposed to look at me," says Liz-as-Cleopatra to Burton, during her ritual initiation into Queen identity).

"She's a mess," said a queeny gay man at a showing of Liz Taylor's *Cleopatra* at New York's Regency Theater in the mid-1980s, a long-overdue revival of a maligned classic. He said "She's a mess" with a lisp, so it sounded like "She'th a meth," as in "methadone." He meant it as praise. He said it loudly whenever Liz appeared on-screen in a new, garish, transcendent costume. "She's a mess" means: she's too much. Or: her degree of preparation for role-playing excites amused commentary and admiration. Each outfit implied calculation, but pretended to be off-the-cuff. Like Liz, Jackie was a mess because her outfits, despite their vaunted simplicity, were *too much*. They demanded response but it wasn't polite to comment on them. Think of the gown she wore when she met the Shah of Iran: starburst jewel in her brioche hairdo spoke a wish to be royal, to be a show. (In retrospect how sordid the occasion seems: the Shah!) Any of Jackie's exquisite off-the-shoulder gowns or sari dresses proclaimed, "I, Jackie, am treating this drab event like a fancy occasion. I defy the rest of the dressed-down world." Jackie seemed an ad campaign for Fanciness— the "fancy" as an antidote to dreariness and desuetude. And in response to photographs of Jackie as First Lady in fancy dress, I find myself giggling: why? Because the uncanny has entered the room in the form of "mess"— Jackie's superbness as inverse "mess," Jackie's unornamented unfatty gown as a symptom of the "mess" it claims to be the obverse of. In real life the effect might not have been *de trop*. But in photographs, Jackie's outfits prove her idol-worshipping Old Testament attachment to color, shape, design, and gewgaw. All her innovations and preferences call attention to themselves, and seem "too much," even though they pretend to be ascetically simplified, all ego burnt away. Her unusual color combinations (hot pink and orange); her Somali leopard coat; her lace mantillas, worn to church, and worn in mourning; her occasional polka dots; her red-ruffled organza early-1970s Valentino dress: if only there were one thing wrong or "off," then the look would fall down to earth, from its "too much" aerie.

Jackie's look is "too much" because it's recognizable: in retrospect the outfits are so indelibly and irrefutably Jackie that they seem, in their own historical moment, excessive by virtue of self-consciousness. Surely the dress she wore to the Mount Vernon party knew it would typify an era! Surely Jackie's slubby Dallas suit knew it would be immortalized! Surely the pillbox hat and the braid edging and the above-the-elbow gloves knew they contained a surplus of aura, a surplus of Jackie essence that allowed the outfit, even in its own moment, even in 1961 or 1963, to preen!

It's paradoxical that Jackie should be a "mess," given that her look was streamlined and minimalist. Her keynote was simplicity, modesty. Note her famous pumps ("stacked heels"); her modified Chanel suits; her lack of jewelry. Jackie's own sketches (as seen in the volume she co-authored with Lee, *One Special Summer*, a scrapbook of their European Grand Tour) were exaggeratedly linear, like Lord & Taylor's ads: skeletal pick-up-sticks. Jackie's look reduced flesh and bauble, and emphasized outline —a Givenchy-Mainbocher silhouette. She liked a "Balenciaga covered-up look." She favored "French con-struction" in her dresses, at least in the 1950s—support (bra and petticoat) "built right into the dress." Conspic-uous darts made the dress know itself as architectural. The effect of a Jackie dress, writes Mrs. Mini Rhea, was as if "a whole piece of cloth [were] held up on her," and she became the cloth. Her trademark bateau necklines, supplemented by pearls, emphasized her collarbone, and made her seem radically underdecorated. But even in her plainest outfits, a small detail would rise to the sur-face, proclaiming secret "too-muchness," proclaiming that beneath the veneer, Jackie was still "a mess." Among the most arresting pictures from the last year of her life is the photograph of Jackie sitting between John Jr. and Bill Clinton at the rededication of the JFK Memorial Library. John and Bill are wearing dark suits. They have no choice. Jackie, too, is wearing a dark dress; but one sees, around her neck, a gathered necklace, knotty and obstreperous, which works against minimalism. And she is wearing gloves—in this day and age! The properness —gloves and necklace, accoutrements of the well-mannered lady—undoes the wished-for unobtrusiveness, and turns into a sign of incipient and desirable vulgarity, as if minimalist Jackie held within her a maximalist per-sona, like Zsa Zsa Gabor (who remembers meeting Jacqueline Bouvier on a plane, and recalls her "kinky hair and bad skin").

The slubs on the suit that Jackie wore to Dallas typify the "too-muchness" of Jackie, as does its "Schiaparelli pink" hue. Slubs and pinkness draw attention to Jackie's surface, and serve, in the morality tale of Jackie's ap-pearance, as individualism's indices.

Two absences in Jackie's look: absence of fingernail

polish, absence of conspicuous makeup. Sometimes the lipstick's color seems bold, interestingly dissonant. An observer reports that Jackie Kennedy had twenty-five different lipsticks on her dresser; among her favored shades were Nearly Peach and Strawberry White Pale. Other than lipstick we never see her makeup. Nor do the eyebrows look effortfully plucked, though they might secretly have been. According to Mrs. Mini Rhea, Jackie avoided sleazy and clinging materials, and "had a perfect horror of overdressing." Jackie's tasteful disdain for excess shows her classiness; she skipped such questionable fads as "slave bracelets."

Another allegorical Jackie look was her horsewoman apparel: jodhpurs. Camille Paglia has noted that Jackie's body language reflected horse-riding expertise, including the art of "dressage." Certainly Jackie has moved through public occasions as if she were foxhunting—radiating prim gamble and dare. Many quintessential Jackie outfits implied athleticism; maybe she required simple clothes so she could run away from crowds and cameras. Think of Capri pants (slacks had their own minor radicalism, if only because Jackie Kennedy's predilection for them outraged a Republican dowager): Capri pants urge us to get lost. Think of sandals for Mediterranean shopping; pants for walking around Manhattan; sweater tied around her neck, as she hails a cab after work. These outfits are signs of her everydayness, her love of sport, and the lurking, lean presence of a trained body, a body that wants to move and to act, rather than be photographed or emblematic. And even in Jackie's state outfits, we can often see her entire muscled arm, for she favored sleeveless dresses; even in the realm of the "fancy," a long, slim, elastic body was waiting to break free of the occasion of her own iconicity.

Talking about her clothes was a way of talking about her body without seeming to. Indecorous to speak about the First Lady's body. But not out of line to speak about her clothes, which were the body's map, speaking unseen hills and dales. What one knew of Jackie's body: she had a difficult time bearing children. Her slimness became proof of these travails: we could think, "Poor Jackie, she desperately wants to have more children, and can't, because she's *too skinny*." What one knew of Jackie's body: flat-chestedness, collarbone, long neck, muscled arms, big feet (size 10A), large hands, broad shoulders. Did Jackie eat enough? How could she stay so thin? Only in the post-Dallas months did she look slightly bloated. Was she thin because she was morally superior? Was she thin because she was rich? Thinness seemed an allegory of the well-functioning Jackie economy: no waste, no waist. (One reads gossip about Jackie's exercise regimes—including Yoga?—and her spare, low-fat lunches.) Muscles meant she could take care of herself. But large feet, large shoulders, and flat-chestedness raise the specter of androgyny. (Catty Cecil Beaton reported the "suspicion of a mustache," and described her "huge baseball player's shoulders and haunches, big boyish hands and feet.") Jackie's slenderness places her in the category of the "boyish," like Vanessa Redgrave's impersonation of transsexual Renée Richards, or Audrey Hepburn's tomboy gamine roles. Note Jackie's look-alike, the spookily androgynous Lee: aligned with sister not husband, Jackie inhabits a dynasty of Bobbsey Twins, adolescent and not yet boy-crazy or "stacked." And note Jackie's collarbone in her wedding pictures. The collarbone, a genderless feature, speaks: always revealed, it substitutes for cleavage as the primary marker of her upper body, and in Jackie's case it symbolizes bone structure, breeding, athleticism, stick-to-itiveness. The collarbone is always perpendicular to the line of her arms, of her down-tending dress; the collarbone gives her body, in its long gowns, the look of a crucifix. Notice in photos how tightly she holds her hands to her sides—or how she keeps them folded in front of her. Icon Jackie does not wish to interfere with the symbolic work that her body is performing.

Jackie's face: eyes wide apart. Her gaze was 180 degrees—like theater in the round, available to all spectators. If the photo is taken frontally, she looks walleyed (split personality, eyes going in opposite directions). If the photo is a three-quarters view (the customary angle for a Jackie photo), the eyes appear closer together, and relate more naturally to each other. The eyes radiate a bonny Bouvier glow: their wide span always seems to recall photos of baby Jacqueline, pet of Black Jack. Because, looking at grownup Jackie's wide face, we can divine the presence of baby Jackie, the face's adult squareness reminds us of Jackie's wounded daughterly desire; beneath the political wife and mysterious Jackie O lay an identifiable and sympathetic hunger. Thus it was always possible to use Jackie's wide-set eyes as a path toward identification with wounded baby Bouvier, whose stare meant want.

Was Jackie "beautiful," and is it necessary to decide? Instead of beautiful, let's say that Jackie was utterly *legible*. Her face's size, and the space between the always open eyes, left room for visual rapture. A front-runner's appealing "cameo-faced" wife, said *Life* magazine in 1959. Why cameo-faced? Because she made cameo appearances? Because she seemed an inanimate ring or locket? Two stars with wide cameo faces like Jackie's are Raquel Welch and Sophia Loren: Cinerama face signifies

Beauty; boyishness; collarbone; note Jackie's noninterference with the symbolic work her body performs.

exoticism as well as sexiness. So Jackie's wide face increased her spiciness and uncanniness: it was too square a face to fit into cramped, conventional canons of taste.

Axiom: the relation of Jackie's head to her body resembles the relation of a baby's head to its body. Thus Jackie's head is a *needy* and *center-of-attention* head.

Axiom: Jackie's beauty—or her legibility—invokes jealousy. I envy Jackie's beauty. Or I may obliquely claim it, by staring at it.

What Jackie's body language taught: how to inhabit our bodies, and how to divorce ourselves from our bodies. Her head floated above her body like a worthy globe. Is it possible to imagine that our own heads are as central, as spherical, as Jackie's? Can we take the evidence of her androgynous collarbone and use our own as a navigational tool—as if the collarbone were prow of a Viking ship? Or her feet: can we, with or without pumps, step through adversity with the forthright, bowlegged, perfectly timed steps of Jackie walking behind JFK's casket, of bereft Jackie approaching JFK's catafalque? She positioned her pump-shod feet demurely in campaign appearances. That seemed a trying aspect of being a polite wife—making sure that you walked in the appropriate, finishing-school fashion. Note how, when she is seated, Jackie's knees are neatly pressed together. She knew how to arrange her body decently for photographs; she knew how to walk, how to hold herself erect. She never slumped. She seemed unimpeded by her body, unembarrassed by it. The bare collarbone, in particular, signifies Jackie's refusal of mediation toward her body: she didn't need a wrap, she was unafraid to let her shoulders, naked and Samothracian, ride the photographed air.

JACKIE'S MADNESS

IS ICON JACKIE a freak or a madwoman? JFK, when asked to characterize his wife, called her "fey." Jackie allegedly said of herself, when, in the late 1960s, fame threatened to overwhelm her, "I suppose I shall always be a freak." She stood apart, in the intensity of her celebrity, from other stars. Next to Jackie, even other luminaries seemed normal. (Only the likes of Liz or Michael Jackson—called "Jacko" in the tabloids, as if acknowledging his affiliation with Jackie O, who edited and wrote the introduction to his *Moonwalk*—occupy her level.) Therefore, like Diane Arbus's photographs of freaks, photos of Jackie seem evidence of human weirdness: a sighted UFO.

Mad Jackie troubles the received wisdom that she is normality's paragon—ideal wife, mother, fashion symbol. Look again at photos of icon Jackie; reconsider them as glimpses not of a woman after whom we should model our conduct, but as portraits of an exception, an abnormality. See Jackie as part of a long tradition of *photographed oddities*: although Jackie, in her unsigned *New Yorker* "Talk of the Town" piece, quoted Lewis W. Hine on the connections of photography to delectation (through photography he "wanted to show the things that had to be appreciated"), it's equally true that photographs appreciate their objects by representing them not as beau-

123

tiful but as "other." Looking at Jackie in a photo, she's vested with an alterity that refuses pat summary. We may envy her wealth and her beauty, but we also understand that the photo represents a supernatural being—a species of the undead. Didn't she survive JFK's murder? What explains her poise and stillness, unless she's an immortal automaton, superior because remote from flesh and blood?

Aspects of the Jackie legend establish her iconic madness. She had no memory of climbing on the trunk of the car in Dallas. She'd blanked out: amnesia. JFK's assassination functioned as shock treatment, wiping out parts of her memory. She received tranquilizer shots, but they couldn't cut through her arrested wakefulness. Reading William Manchester's *The Death of a President*, or other accounts of Jackie in the aftermath of the assassination, I see Jackie as a character like Olivia de Havilland in *The Snake Pit* or Elizabeth Taylor in *Suddenly, Last Summer*—movies in which women suffer traumas that cause them to dissociate, repress, go dead. Kitty Kelley reports Jackie receiving shock treatments for depression at a private clinic. These have been refuted; but "shock treatment," and the shoddy realm of "shock," redolent of Sylvia Plath's *The Bell Jar* and Samuel Fuller's *Shock Corridor*, fit the iconography of Jackie as contained madwoman, whose fidelity to proper conduct straitjackets her. An article in *The Village Voice* after her death compared docile Jackie Kennedy to defiant Sylvia Plath as two extremes of 1950s/1960s elite white feminine identity. But strong strange icon Jackie's shocked stillness exists in a continuum with images of Sylvia Plath, genius madwoman suicide. If we never worried that Jackie would commit suicide, she nonetheless had the leonine, abstracted, tormented look of Anne Sexton holding a cigarette on the back cover of *The Death Notebooks*, her face schizophrenically split, like the daughter of Dr. Jekyll. Jackie's intense composure implied shock or trauma, which increased public sympathy. Admiration of Jackie's cool maturity was a tacit acknowledgment that she might easily have gone crazy, and that her public manner held madness at bay.

For Jackie appears, in photographs, as if she's in shock—as if the act of paparazzi transgression traumatizes her. A friend confided to *Newsweek* (1962): "That smile on her face is just *there*. I've leaned over and spoken to her in public and she just keeps on smiling. She gets sort of dazed when the flashbulbs go off." Photographers immobilize Jackie, or surround her in an amniotic bath of welcome yet dread flashbulbs. It's possible to interpret Jackie's avoidance of cameras and publicity as a form of phobia: she seemed to have a paranoid relation to her own persona and myth, as if any public attention were inevitably a murderous repetition of Dallas.

Did Jackie misbehave? It seemed not. Always she held her head high, sat up straight. She seemed the antithesis of Rosemary Kennedy, the lobotomized sister-in-law; even the antithesis of alcoholic Joan. Except for the assassination moment, when she climbed backward, Jackie never lost it. (Nor was climbing backward necessarily a lapse; indeed, it may have been instinctive valor.) Part of the fascination of Jackie watching was the spectacle of her self-control. Would she keep her sanity? We watched to see if she'd crack up in public. A famous Jackie anecdote: when Stephen Spender asked her of what accomplishment she was most proud, she responded that it was keeping her sanity under difficult circumstances.

Madness was displaced, in the Jackie legend, onto her aunt and cousin, Edith Bouvier Beale and Little Edie. A debutante with aesthetic inclinations like Jackie, Little Edie never achieved independence; after trying to live alone in New York, she moved back to take care of her mother, at their East Hampton estate, Grey Gardens, and, until her mother's death a quarter of a century later, never left. A *folie à deux*, they lived in squalor, bickering, retelling and reinventing the past in a house infested, said Little Edie, by "sloats, otters, badgers, possums, raccoons," and condemned by the Health Department. Their oddly glamorous delusions—virtuoso canticles of incrimination and self-justification—were immortalized in the Maysles brothers' vérité documentary, *Grey Gardens*. Jackie's image never appears in it—except in a montage of newspaper clippings about the scandal (the Edies were threatened with eviction, and Jackie was photographed helping to houseclean: it was considered unseemly that her cousin and aunt should rot in poverty while Jackie partied); and yet it seems reasonable to view this portrait of Little Edie as a skewed, uncanny case study of the Jackie who might have been.

Little Edie sheds light on icon Jackie: in Jackie's image there lies latent madness, a rakish instability linked to the Bouvier heritage. In *Grey Gardens*, Little Edie dresses with colorful, disconnected eccentricity, wearing a sweater as substitute skirt, a makeshift snood concealing her shaved head. (She called her bizarre getups her "revolutionary costume.") I interpret Little Edie's endearing, loony nonconformity as a sinister shadow of icon Jackie—a portrait of Jackie gone bad, Jackie if she'd not married Jack but remained a Bouvier, losing money, indulging obsession, becoming paranoid. (Little Edie

Jackie's starstruck shadow?

says, "They can get you in East Hampton for wearing red shoes on a Thursday . . . they can get you for almost anything.") Little Edie uncannily speaks with Jackie's accent—the Bouvier dialect, including "litra-choor" for "literature." Little Edie didn't have to face the paparazzi, but she had to face her mother, the Maysleses' camera, and East Hampton's scorn. Like solitary Thoreau in *Walden*, Little Edie—and Jackie?—are privileged eastern seaboard nonconformists. "Staunch," Little Edie calls herself, and spells it for us: "S-T-A-U-N-C-H." Says Little Edie, "In dealing with me the relatives didn't know that they were dealing with a staunch character, and I tell you, if there's anything worse than a staunch woman . . ." Jackie, like Little Edie, was a staunch woman the world feared and loved. Little Edie, in one scene from *Grey Gardens*, reads—with a magnifying glass!—an astrology paperback called *It's All In the Stars*; Warhol reports that when he visited the Edies, their beds were strewn with fan magazines, including stories about Jackie and Caroline, stories which Big Edie took at face value. One headline was CAROLINE LEAVES HOME! Big Edie reportedly said, "Why is Caroline doing that to her mother? She's such a nice woman." For evidence about the icon, *we* need to turn to fan magazines. But does Edie? Can't Edie call Jackie directly? Certainly Ari liked the Grey Gardens gals: he gave them a blanket, which they dubbed "the Onassis blanket." (Assignment: name a blanket in your house "the Onassis blanket.") Despite the comforting presence of the Onassis blanket, Little Edie remains far from the Jackie O glow, and therefore inhabits our distant position—the outsider, the Jackie watcher. Although her cousin is Jackie O, Little Edie lives light-years away from celestial machinations, and needs to rely on horoscopes and fanzines to plot a safe course.

Because Jackie never appeared in a real movie, it's ironic that her balmy cousin should become a sort of movie star, achieving underground notoriety in *Grey Gardens* (discovered by Andy Warhol, she even had a brief nightclub career, like Sukhreet Gabel, "bad seed" daughter of the judge who gave illegal preferment to Bess Myerson's companion), and that "Sister Woman" Lee Radziwill should attempt an acting career, appearing in a production of *The Philadelphia Story* and in a TV-movie remake, scripted by Truman Capote, of *Laura*—the story of a woman who disappears and then reappears; the story of a woman who survives her own death and becomes (as in *Vertigo*) her own stand-in. Lee was, by some reports, a poor actress; certainly Jackie disapproved of her sister's bid for notoriety and fame. Lee and Little Edie are starstruck doubles of our Jackie, who never starred in *Laura*, but whose life seemed more baroque and noirish than anything Otto Preminger could have concocted, and whose ostensible normality cast our own misbehaviors as forms of madness, even as her normality seemed claustrophobic, or proof that poise and etiquette were self-contaminating practices. If Jackie seemed "fey" or freakish or mad, it was not because she indulged in demented monologues on film but because she'd been stunned, zapped—corrected out of the kinds of labile behavior that Little Edie theatrically displayed.

JACKIE RECURS: her specialty is repetition. Mass media's adoption of Jackie as slogan and image ensures that no sighting of her can ever claim to have been the first: it will always rest upon a prior occasion. Thus Jackie, as image, is necessarily cliché and revenant.

Events recur in Jackie's life: her narrative depends on erotic and morbid déjà vu. Black Jack returns as Jack Kennedy, and then again as swarthy Ari; Lee is Jackie's double. After Jackie almost dies in childbirth, and baby Patrick dies (the second of her children to die), then her husband is shot, a death itself echoed in 1968 with Bobby's assassination. A 1973 *Photoplay* headline summarizes Jackie's connection to repetition: DEATH IN JACKIE'S LIFE AGAIN: GOD, NO MORE!

The Jackie look repeats itself. Every mock Jackie echoes the original, as homage or unintended parody; every new photograph of Jackie repeats the foundation we've already seen, the progenitive Jackie, whose good taste mandates a fawning series of imitators.

Andy Warhol, in such silk screens as "Gold Jackie," "Round Jackie," "Red Jackie," "Jackie (The Week That Was)," "Three Jackies," "Nine Jackies," and "Sixteen Jackies," was the first intellectual or artist to reflect on Jackie's status as repeated icon. These Jackie portraits, some pre-assassination, some post-assassination, bor-

Warhol's "Sixteen Jackies."

rowed the format of his electric chair, car crash, Liz and Marilyn series. All of these subjects are spectacles associated with disaster and shock: Liz, Marilyn, and Jackie faced disasters (illness, suicide, assassination); witnessed electrocutions turn death into spectacle, just as a car wreck attracts voyeurs and photographers. Furthermore, as critic Richard Meyer has observed, Warhol conflated celebrities and criminals; John Waters would do the same with Divine, who achieves apotheosis, in such films as *Multiple Maniacs*, when she goes on killing sprees. Fabulousness lies in Divine's imagined likeness to Liz Taylor, as well as in her theatrical, overplayed monstrousness. Jackie, Marilyn, electrocuted convict: the silk-screened figure, in the Warhol oeuvre, is (like Divine) interchangeably a glamorous female star, a criminal, or a victim.

Warhol rendered Jackie—celebrity/victim—in his standard grid, repeating images as if they were mug shots, frames of documentary film footage, or a fan's clippings. Repetition implies mourning: the Dallas scene is a trauma, and mourning takes the form of recycling and recall, a process that unsettles chronology (images of Jackie before and after JFK's death get jumbled). Repetition implies commodification: Jackie no longer has control over her own image, nor do we, as consumers, for it is dispersed in culture with a rapidity and vehemence that do not obey the laws of individual desire. And repetition implies obsession: the Jackie photos are cropped —narrowing the focus onto Jackie alone, myopically isolating her from context. In Warhol's "Sixteen Jackies," she's alone in a hall of mirrors, like Rita Hayworth in the final scene of *The Lady from Shanghai*; lonely Jackie is trapped among reflections of herself, without companion. Though the Warhol silk screen announces no individual or psychological point of view—it seems to erase individuality, its technique underscoring the "inhuman" processes of mass media reproduction—it betrays the emotions of a saintmaker. To repeat Jackie sixteen times requires energy, momentum, and love: Andy evidently cared enough about Jackie to multiply her. Or else her aura was tenuous, and it needed bolstering through multiplication. One would never get deeper into her experience; one could only repeat the faint glow, and hope to acquire a vivid Jackie through stolid accretion.

Camille Paglia, arguing that Warhol's "Jackie" silk screens emerge from his lapsed Catholicism, considers them images of a *mater dolorosa*. True: but they were also a gay fan's cutouts, images from a "pervert" scrapbook. What's remarkable about Warhol's "Sixteen Jackies" isn't any specific emotion that accrues to the images. We don't know what the spectator feels, the spectator who repeated and tinted Jackie. All we know about Jackie worship from "Sixteen Jackies" is that the procedure has sixteen stations; that this fan desires sixteen copies; that her value increases with each repetition.

Warhol not only silk-screened celebrities: he also befriended them. He knew Jacqueline Onassis; they even went to the Brooklyn Museum together. He describes the visit: "Being with her is like walking with a saint. . . . It was like she was in a trance." Jackie told him about a Haitian artist who charged according to how many figures or objects a painting contained. Warhol remembers: "The first three are included—cows, dogs, and chickens. Sheep and goats are extra, and if you throw in some people and houses it gets really expensive. Jackie thought that was an interesting concept of art." It's odd to think of the real Jackie having a conversation about aesthetics and value with the artist who, in his silk screens, commented on (and perpetuated?) her commodification. She also asked him, "What's Elizabeth Taylor really like?" Onassis gave Warhol credit for knowledge of the "real" Liz, even though he was famous instead for repetitions of a "false," silk-screened Liz. This scene—Onassis discussing iconicity with Warhol—suggests that Jacqueline Onassis, living in a world saturated with images of Jackie and Liz, may have looked toward "Jackie" or "Liz" as the type of alluring stranger about whom ordinary people might ask, "What's Jackie really like?"

The images in "Sixteen Jackies," however, are *not* identical copies of each other. For example, the four smiling Jackies in the top row are the same photo, but the third from the left is not level with the others (like a TV with a vertical-hold problem). Although the image of Jackie doesn't change, our angle of vision might; the picture may fade, or be artificially brightened; it may fall off-center, or drop below the line of visibility. Each time Jackie gets repeated she alters. A narrative emerges, and it is not the story of Jackie's life or the growth of Jackie's soul—but the narrative of the image and of our relation to the image.

PASSÉ JACKIE

ICON JACKIE'S ALLURE rests on pastness; since November 1963, she has been a dated image. For most of her career as symbol, she'd be the *former* First Lady. The look she popularized while in the White House: this, too, would become profoundly retro, even as Jacqueline Kennedy Onassis herself survived. Jackie watchers would savor the ambiguous pleasure of juxtaposing, in their minds, the "former" Jackie with the "current" Jackie (pillbox hat at the White House versus slacks at Doubleday). When, on the cover of *Spy* magazine, just a half year before Jackie's death, a Daryl Hannah look-alike was photographed wearing a copy of Jackie's famous Schiaparelli pink suit, the morbid parody depended on the viewer's certainty that Jackie Kennedy's look was, though immortal, also firmly in the past tense. Always Jackie would seem to evoke *temps passé*—whether fallen Camelot, lost elegance, or shattered innocence.

The realm of the lost, the former, and the passé may inspire sentimental nostalgia. Or it may strike the viewer as kitschy. When Coco Chanel accused Jackie, at the time of her marriage to Onassis, of having "a touch of vulgarity," she meant, I think, not exclusively that Jackie Kennedy herself was vulgar but that the *image* of Jackie was passé (redolent of the early 1960s) and therefore touched by vulgarity, as former fashions, until they're resurrected, are doomed to be. Because Jackie was associated with the early 1960s—the Kennedy administration—but consistently remained in the public eye *after* that moment of star emergence, she'd always seem a leftover from a discontinued feast. Time moved on; Jackie remained. A piece of history or popular iconography that stays in circulation past the time of its acclaim becomes either monumental and mythic, or it becomes tawdry and démodé. Women's magazines and the popular press always gave Jacqueline Kennedy Onassis credit for being a fashion trendsetter long after she was First Lady; the real Jackie may have retained impeccable chic, but as icon she functioned as a figure poignantly *behind the times*. The underside of "Jackie survived!" was always a jaded "She's still here?"

One can see the tawdriness of icon Jackie in the commemorative magazines that emerged in profusion after the death of JFK (similar magazines came out after Jackie's own death), or in the cheapness of the tabloids and fan magazines which were icon Jackie's element. One found her image at the supermarket beside Pall Malls, Lady Gilettes, and Tums. One didn't see her in sacrosanct or elect public sites; rather, the appearance of a Jackie story meant that the magazine was "garbage," or that the coverage was unreliable and ephemeral, soon to be outdated. No Jackie scoop could last for long: it would soon be contradicted or superseded by new evidence, new speculation. And Jackie herself began to resemble the tabloids in which she appeared. Best-dressed as Mrs. Kennedy, as Mrs. Onassis she'd be voted worst-dressed. Like Liz, she didn't remain for long in the safe realm of taste; quickly she repatriated to waste. Partly because photos of Jackie are obsessively recirculated and recycled, the images of survivor or widow Jackie in late 1960s bell-bottoms or mid-1970s natural fibers, next to images of Jackie in classy pumps and bateau-neckline dresses from the early 1960s, remind us that in each of her fashion incarnations Jackie seemed at once up-to-the-minute and passé—not because the real Jackie's taste was flawed, but because the images are recycled, and therefore we see pictures of Jackie after the fact, when the fashions have dated.

Jackie's dated side didn't diminish her appeal; I find succor in images of Jackie precisely because they no longer serve a current function in culture. Because Jackie no longer had any concrete acts to perform in American life (all her duties were now symbolic), she had the leisure, as icon, to serve as memory aide and as reliquary; if one was concerned with Jackie, if one eagerly read magazine articles about her, it was a spiritual exercise at odds with practical or political necessities.

One miracle of icon Jackie is that although the images of her always seemed passé, a new, living Jackie was here to correct and update the old Jackie. Real, current Jackie would serve as rebuke to the static, outmoded images of past Jackie; and yet so haunting were the old images that "real" Jackie often seemed the anachronism or the error, not measuring up to the truth standard of the fawn-colored pillbox hat.

Since 1963, Jackie had no legislated public or political function. She was an entirely private citizen. And yet because her image continued to extract fealty from us, she seemed dethroned or exiled; like Russian royalty living away from the Soviet Union after the Revolution, Jackie seemed an escapee from an earlier, aristocratic regime, trying to live incognito, but still possessing a latent legitimacy—waiting for the proper moment, so she

137

could be restored to her sovereign seat. The fact that Jacqueline Onassis edited a book on imperial Russia—*In the Russian Style*—seemed to substantiate icon Jackie's status as an unjustly deposed monarch. The book's respectful attitude toward pre-Soviet Russia seems obliquely to comment on Jackie's own position as passé princess, or princess of the passé. Although Jackie published the book as "Jacqueline Onassis" (dropping the name "Kennedy" for the moment), the book's reverence for outsized and opulent monarchs commemorates Camelot. Photos of headless mannequins dressed in imperial Russian fashions, posed in original locations, remind the reader of Dallas (JFK's lost head), of Jackie's own "mannequin" aspects, and of our relation to Jackie as if she were royalty, defunct, sapped of volition, haunting an obsolete castle. Looking at these images of displaced monarchy, do we wonder if Jacqueline Onassis pines for the pomp of her White House years? Additionally, in her introduction to *The Firebird and Other Russian Fairy Tales*, Jacqueline Onassis sounded the note of melancholy exile, evoking a culture of artists and monarchs wrenched from their former center: writes Onassis, "At some point in the 1920s, years after the Russia he knew had disappeared, Boris Zvorykin, in exile with many of his former colleagues, tried to recapture the richness of that distant culture he held in his heart. Against a background of gray Paris skies and mansard roofs, he painstakingly wrote out in French the Russian phrases long familiar to him, and brushed his brilliant colors into the pictures of onion domes and flowing rivers, gray wolves and exotic princes and princesses that you will see in the pages that follow." Earlier in the introduction, she alludes to "blind men" who "used to apply for positions as tellers of tales in rich houses." Uncanny, that Jacqueline Onassis, in print, mentioned rich houses and princesses. And blind men: in dream Jackie's household, who are the blind storytellers, and what tales do they tell?

Another aspect of Jackie's dated nature was her fondness for the antique and the departed. The few opinions she publicly proffered concerned her passion for history and for the preservation of old monuments (whether furniture and wallpaper in the White House, or Washington's Lafayette Square, or Grand Central Station). A journalist once described her as a "Beaux Arts type of girl." Visiting the Parthenon as First Lady, she said that she wanted the Elgin Marbles returned to Greece; she helped save ancient Egyptian temples from ruin; she said, "I adored Latin"; when she assembled an exhibition of JFK's mementos after his death, she chose a tiny figure of "Herakles and the Skin of a Lion," about which she said, "It is very early (around 500 B.C.) and not as beautiful as some of the other pieces, but he loved it because it was older than any of the others." Even her famous Paris hairdo—terribly à la mode—was based on a Carlo Crivelli painting, and was called "Gothic Madonna."

Devoted to the safely, monumentally antique, Jackie also was associated with the shock of the New—or at least the New refracted and domesticated by a nostalgia-inducing historical distance. On her 1961 Paris trip, she visited the Jeu de Paume museum, and when asked to name her favorite painting, chose Manet's "Olympia"— an image of a nude prostitute posed as an odalisque, with a black serving girl behind her. In it, the odalisque's gaze is unashamed, direct, confrontational. It is a painting intended to *épater le bourgeois*. It seems risqué for Jackie as First Lady to have selected this scandalous nude as her favorite. Whatever Jackie meant by citing "Olympia," it's clear that Jackie herself functioned as an odalisque, a figure of exotic come-hither allure; that she, like Manet's painting, was an expensive and mystified commodity; and that Manet's trick of having a modern-day prostitute pose as an art-historical odalisque was a stratagem with which Jackie had reason to be familiar, given that she, too, was a vulnerable and contemporary woman inhabiting an age-old, compromised, exposed, and hieratic symbolic position.

Can the passion for Jackie endure? In five years, how passé will my worship of Jackie seem? Does it already seem dated, trivial? Or will Jackie's aura deepen? Will her capacity as symbol of the tragically outmoded and deposed enable her, in future time, as gyres turn, and styles dissipate and fail to replenish themselves, to seem more monumental and lasting—precisely because of her evanescence—than when she was alive? In twenty years, in fifty years, what resonances will Jackie still possess?

Shocking, that we remain interested in Jackie. Isn't she the past? Our continuing fascination with Jackie represents one of the few available instances of *collective* retrospection. In a country where events of a year ago are forgotten, it's unusual to care still about a figure whose legitimacy as Empress ended over thirty years ago.

WAS ICON JACKIE a saint or a sinner? Was she an image of the perverse or the pristine? She oscillated between the two—now sacred, now profane. Some Jackie lovers would be shocked to hear me suggest that icon Jackie was a pleasure principle, a libidinal wild card, symbolizing jackpots and orgasms and autoeroticism. Others would think it ridiculous to claim that Jackie O could be taken seriously as a saint, even if she did, once, meet with the Pope, and even if Cardinal Cushing said to the world, "Stop criticizing the poor woman."

Jackie's sanctity was former (it ended when she married Onassis) and it goes, more or less, without saying. Rarer are explorations of her perversity.

"Jackie O": one of the nickname's origins must have been *Women's Wear Daily*'s use of the phrase "Daddy O and Jackie O." From that jingle we know that the former First Lady has chosen a sugar daddy; that she is sleeping with a man old enough to be her father; that she has prostituted herself. That's probably why "Jackie O" is considered a disrespectful sobriquet for a saint.

"Jackie O": the nickname implies orgasm, and summarizes the public's prurient fantasies about what attracted Jackie to a man as seemingly irregular as Ari. Ari gave Jackie her "O." Just as Ari satisfied Maria Callas after her unromantic marriage to dour Meneghini, so Ari could teach Jackie the secrets of love, after her widowhood and after inattentive Jack.

"Jackie O": priapic, Dionysian Jack departed, and Jackie symbolically inherited his priapism, his "jack" nature. J.O.: Jackie's initials are slang for "jacking off." *Onassis* even shares a prefix with *onanism. Jackie Onanism*: an unstated aspect of the allure of J.O. has always been her onanistic subtext, the sense of orgasmic release that her very name and lifestyle (big spender) implies. Autoeroticism: is it perverse to look in solitude at Jackie? Jackie herself is usually pictured as a loner: in photos she's cropped away from companions, and the image of her face works best as a religio-erotic incitement to empathy when it is isolated from context. The "J.O." aspect of "Jackie O" rests in her identity as a financial escalation (more and more wealth) and in the alternately pathetic and privileged solitude in which she is usually depicted as dwelling. "Jackie O" is Jackie Kennedy finally having a good time: what gives her the right at last to tap her "O" potential is solitude, a mirror of the Jackie watcher's onanistic isolation. Studying Jackie, empathizing with her, dreaming about her, you and I are alone with an unspeaking image; we use Jackie to bring us toward a state I'd call pleasure if it were not also morbid and neurasthenic.

How many nightclubs are named after Jackie O? I know of one in Rome ("Jackie O") and one in New York ("Jackie 60"). Is the connection between "nightclub" and "Jackie O" based on her identity as jet-set international partygoer and her connection to the splurge? What might happen at a nightclub named "Jackie O"? The name strives to point out her passé nature; "How dated!" says a nightclub named "Jackie O." And yet calling a night-club "Jackie O" announces rarefied and ritzy pleasures. Jackie O is a "party girl." Regardless of how infrequently she was actually sighted at clubs, in her "O" incarnation she typifies a kind of 1970s pleasure allied to Studio 54, the Warhol "Factory," and to a sophisticated, fatigued understanding of celebrity's commodified nature, of the dictum that all celebrities (Jackie O, Halston, Roy Cohn, Marlon Brando, Liza Minnelli, Liz Taylor, Leonard Bernstein, and Rudolf Nureyev) are created equal. Andy Warhol photographed Jackie backstage with Bianca Jagger in Liza Minnelli's dressing room: Jackie, Bianca, and Liza, three paradigmatic 1970s celebrities, were famous as much for themselves as for the dead or absent figures they conjured—Judy, Mick, Jack. Liza and Bianca and Jackie deserve to have fun now because they're wounded; they deserve to get high, or need to, after a bruised life up close to colossal, demanding figures.

The public may have imagined that Jackie Kennedy was "frigid" (aristocratic women don't feel sexual pleasure, according to one Victorian myth that associated female sexuality with the working class and with prostitutes), and that only a vulgar, dark, and exotic man like Ari could give her pleasure and liberate her "O" nature. Certainly "Jackie O," as nickname, intersects with Pauline Réage's *Story of O*—a sadomasochistic and pornographic novel of the sexual odyssey of a woman named, simply, "O." "Jackie O," as salacious nickname, implies that Jackie, by marrying Onassis, had deliberately soiled her image—a masochistic plunge in reputation.

Via stories and speculations about the sex life of Jackie and Ari, we could imagine a Jackie no longer erotically deprived, a woman at last allowed, on her outlaw island in the Aegean, to sate herself. "Jackie O" helped us dream of pleasures and sufficiencies beyond our own humble ken. "Jackie O" justified pleasure, even if she seemed scapegoated for her imagined transgressions against Camelot and Catholicism.

Though the public imagined that Jackie did not find Ari sexually attractive, in photographs from the early 1960s—the time when Jackie met him, and when (according to C. David Heymann) Lee and Ari had a "sometime romance" (which makes Jackie's own liaison with him wonderfully incestuous)—he had craggy good looks. It was intolerable, though, for some Jackie worshippers to imagine that she could desire a short dark Greek. (Irish-Catholic Jack and French-Catholic Jackie were equally ethnic, but this understanding goes against the grain of American racial thinking, which insists that certain people are unmarked, "white," while others are stained by race and ethnicity.) I have no difficulty discerning Ari's sexual magnetism when he's photographed beside Liz, in 1964, at the Lido nightclub in Paris. He seems a good match for Liz: strongly limned features, as if outlined with charcoal or eyebrow pencil; a fondness for holding cigarettes and wineglasses; a penchant for swearing; an affinity for jewels. We must also remember that before the 1970s, when gay standards of male beauty began to enter mainstream media through such vehicles as Calvin Klein ads, the paramours of conventionally lovely women need not have been attractive. Rather, these homely men seduced by virtue of their power or their money. Compare Burton's pockmarks to Liz's perfect skin. Vivien Leigh and Laurence Olivier, among starry couples, are one exception to this double standard, which demands that the woman be beautiful but forgives the man his physical flaws.

"Jackie O" was an object of prurient voyeurism, even if in all but one set of photos she was clothed. But scopophilia is so universal, even Jackie succumbed. Stories exist of Jackie peering down from her Fifth Avenue apartment through a telescope; and there are famous pictures of Jackie holding a camera, as Inquiring Camera Girl, or the unusual candid photo of Jackie, in India, flashing her miniature camera at the photographer, in mock retaliation, as if proving that she, too, likes to look and to snap.

If the perversity and prurience of the Jackie watcher was summed up in the figure of paparazzo Ron Galella, who, Jackie claimed in court (if we trust the *Photoplay* account of the trial), made "grunting noises" as he took pictures of her (the noises of a sex maniac), and allegedly said, "Hi, baby," to Jackie, as if she were his "babe," then the dominatrix aspect of Jackie was summed up in her vigorous response to Galella and other paparazzi. In a famous set of pictures, Jackie is shown exiting the arty porn movie *I Am Curious (Yellow)*; she's wearing a black leather miniskirt. Here, definitively, is pleasure-seeking Jackie O, keeping up to date on sexy trends, the Jackie who "went see-through" to please Ari. If "curiosity" is pornographic, then Jackie, by seeing *I Am Curious (Yellow)*, proves herself as curious as the rest of us. (And yet, supposedly, she left the film before it ended. Because it bored her? Because she wanted to avoid photographers? Why did Ari stay behind in the theater?) The frisson of this photo is the presence on the pavement of prone, humiliated paparazzo Mel Finkelstein, whom Jackie allegedly judo-flipped in self-defense. Jackie's secretary averred that it was "silly to think Mrs. Onassis could flip a 168-pound man. . . ." Who knows if she really flipped him? The *Life* magazine photo is captioned: "The real thing: did she or didn't she?" Several kinds of curiosity, and several kinds of "real thing," overlap here: Did Jackie really flip the paparazzo? Are Ari and Jackie really in love? Is this really Jackie (her back is turned to us) or is it a fake Jackie, a Jackie impostor? Is the sex pictured in *I Am Curious (Yellow)* the real thing, or is it simulated? Is pornography, whether actual or simulated, ever "the real thing"? How "real" is Jackie, how "real" can Jackie ever be to the Jackie watcher? Can photos of Jackie ever be "the real thing"? And is our curiosity about the "reality" of Jackie equivalent to the prurient curiosity that drives us—that drove Jackie—to see a porn movie? If "pornography" was originally defined as art about prostitutes, are not all photos of Jackie in her role as "trophy wife" a form of pornography, in the root sense? And is not all curiosity indirectly pornographic? These ambiguous photographs attempt to capture Jackie in a moment of sexual willfulness (seeing porn) and aggressiveness (flipping a man); but it's also possible to read Jackie's exiting the theater and Jackie's flipping of the photographer as acts of moral protest against the regime of prurient looking, a regime in which these photos of Jackie-as-dominatrix in leather miniskirt also participate.

"Smash his camera," she once told her bodyguard, in reference to intrusive Galella. The Jackie who flipped Finkelstein (a Jew) and who wished to smash the camera of Galella (an Italian) was portrayed as an aristocratic Francophilic sadist: a woman whose refusal to grant the public a glimpse amounted to a Mrs. Grundyish disdain for the popular media and for the "low-class" or "ethnic" types who produce such stories and consume them. A headline about Jackie's suit against William Manchester for *The Death of a President*: JACKIE'S CRACK-DOWN ON THE JFK BOOKS. Jackie's sadism—the woman in black leather, cracking down, flipping photographers—was part of her mythic snobbishness and wish for privacy. Ron Galella, in his picture book *Jacqueline*, uses class envy as justification for his quest to photograph Jackie; he often refers to her money and privilege, and to himself as a working man (in fact, he sued her for "malicious prosecution," claiming that by thwarting his attempts to take her picture, she was interfering with his livelihood). A working stiff, he'd have no place on Capri or on Fifth Avenue if he didn't have the pretext of following Jackie to these exclusive sites. Jackie O, unwilling object of public delectation, metamorphoses into a dominatrix, a woman whose spending and whose aggression against photographers establish her as a figure of private will and pleasure; Jackie's "O," her private zone, is the cipher that every photograph tries unsuccessfully to capture.

Icon Jackie's willfulness and caprice allowed her to play the role of sadist against our role of masochist: the public became an unwanted suitor whom Jackie, once she married Onassis, had the power to "bump," just as she bumped all passengers off the Olympic Airlines flight she took to Skorpios for her wedding. Jackie could bump the unwanted, the ancillary. All that was not central, she could ignore. In photographs, she can't see us, the viewers. She stares right through us, erasing us. That's symbolically an aggressive act: she unwrites our existence by not seeing us, refusing to know us. Similarly, Jackie was mythically a "no show"—she'd decline to appear at most social events, even Kennedy-sponsored shindigs. A famous instance of Jackie snubbing company occurred when she was staying at the Kennedy home in Florida, and Rose had important guests; though Rose insisted that Jackie join them for lunch, Jackie refused, staying in her bedroom. Similarly, we hear of Jackie keeping Jack waiting—before the Inauguration, and even on the morning of November 22, 1963. This image of Jackie as imperious, as a "no show," as a woman who refused to allow the public to gaze at her, confirmed that her libidinal specialty was refusal, disappearance. In our imaginary relation with Jackie, she's flipped us. First, we've "flipped" for her: we are head over heels, infatuated. Second, there's a literal sense in which Jackie *flipped us*: as the camera's eye reverses the up-down axis, so Jackie "flips" (or inverts) our position. In an act of imaginary sadism or aggression, she turns us upside down, making north our south, undoing our orientation.

I'm still haunted by one of the questions Jackie asked when she was Inquiring Camera Girl for the *Washington Times-Herald*: "Do you consider yourself normal?" I wonder: Did Jackie consider herself normal? Do we consider her normal? And are we, looking at pictures of Jackie, normal? Is it normal to perceive the tendrils of relation that bind together a public figure and her legion of followers?

If you are searching for Saint Jackie, recall that she was voted, in 1963, the Catholic Welfare Council's "Woman of the Year," and that Cardinal Cushing suggested that the public should imitate Mrs. Kennedy instead of movie stars; consider the pictures of Jackie entering or exiting mass, or conversing with the Pope. When she married Onassis, however, she was declared

"Do you consider yourself normal?"

a "public sinner" and was barred from the sacraments (because Onassis was a divorced man). The "O" was her scarlet letter. Henceforth she'd be identified, like Hester Prynne, by a mysterious and allegorical "O," as if she were the fallen woman in a morality play.

JACKIE AS A
FICTIONAL CHARACTER

MOST OF US didn't meet Jackie; to us she remains an abstract collection of irreconcilable images and qualities. We know her only as we know a character from literature or film: a figure in narrative, who may quicken our pulse, wring tears—but who has no tangible reality beyond words or pictures, or beyond the figment's circulation in our bodies and psyches. Each of us might suggest a different gallery of fictional characters whom Jackie resembles; mine reflects my own idiosyncrasies and prejudices.

Emma Bovary. Jacqueline *Bouvier* may have wished, with the other Bouviers, that her ancestors were French aristocrats, but in fact they were shopkeepers. The original meaning of "bouvier" is "oxherd"; "bovine" shares a root with both "Bovary" and "Bouvier." The sentimental plots that Emma swallows, and that inspire her to derange her life, as if in imitation of the novels she's read, are like the plots constructed around Jackie's life (as rendered in miniseries, fan magazines, newspapers). The ruination of a modern-day Emma Bovary would not be romance novels but adulation of stars like Jackie: for example, Michelle Pfeiffer, in *Love Field*, idealizes Jackie Kennedy (because the Michelle character, like Jackie, lost a baby), and makes decisions based upon this mistaken identification. Ultimately, the quest to emulate Jackie leads Michelle out of a settled bourgeois world of material comfort and complacency, into an interracial relationship and an expanded moral vision.

The Princess Casamassima. In Henry James's novel *The Princess Casamassima*, Hyacinth Robinson, an impoverished young bookbinder with delusions of grandeur, befriends anarchists who want to use him as linchpin in their plot to change the world (he's to assassinate a public figure); but meanwhile he falls under the enchanting sway of the Princess Casamassima. He must choose between the revolution and the Princess, who represents civilization's splendor, however contaminated by inequities and suffering. Here, James describes Hyacinth's vision of worldly delights the Princess embodies: "He saw the immeasurable misery of the people, and yet he saw all that had been, as it were, rescued and redeemed from it: the treasures, the felicities, the splendours, the successes, of the world. All this took the form, sometimes, to his imagination, of a vast, vague, dazzling presence, an irradiation of light from objects undefined, mixed with the atmosphere of Paris and of Venice." Shall Hyacinth choose the Princess's dazzling world, or sacrifice his life, instead, to the anarchist cause? Jackie, like the Princess Casamassima, represents society's ambiguous splendor. Diana Vreeland, who appreciated society and splendor, said (as recounted by Jacqueline Onassis in her 1977 essay "A Visit to the High Priestess of Vanity Fair"): " 'Society has *splendeur*. It is something the world envies, to be a member of society. What is the point of money without being in society? . . . It used to be birth and wealth. Today it's SCOOP and anything of talent.' " Dreaming of Jackie, we envision *splendeur*: we dispense with the mundane, and dip our feet in perfumed ichor. Jackie and the Princess *Casamassima* (does the name mean "maximal *casa*," "big house," as in Jackie's White House?) represent an aristocratic world where female beauty and aesthetic cultivation garnish wealth.

Is Jackie Marxism's decadent antithesis? For Jackie's charm and beauty, wouldn't we give up the revolution? She leads us from small towns into the velvet metropolis; she beguiles us away from socialism, back into monarchy. Jackie is capitalism's finest flower: when she visited Vienna with JFK, and posed next to grandmotherly Nina Khrushchev, Jackie seemed evidence that, if choosing between capitalism and communism were a choice between Jackie and Nina, one would be smart to pick capitalism. American news coverage of the Vienna summit emphasized how Jackie "charmed" Nikita Khrushchev —as if her personal, seductive diplomacy could convert a hard-line Red. Looking at Jackie's face, *exalté* during the overture to Mozart's *Marriage of Figaro* (at a TV broadcast concert of the Vienna Philharmonic, attended by the Kennedys and Khrushchevs), one imagines that siding with America in the Cold War was an aesthetic imperative.

In her Princess Casamassima guise, Jackie poses an old moral dilemma: is she a progressive or a regressive cultural current? Is preoccupation with Jackie, in mass culture, a retrograde nosedive toward the past, a nostalgia trip? Or is it a way to reconstruct origins that never existed, and thus to hurtle toward a future we haven't begun to imagine? I would answer that icon Jackie is neither progressive nor regressive; she confounds the urge to judge cultural forms and representations as either positive or negative. One doesn't have a choice as simple as Hyacinth's—to follow Jackie or to embrace, instead, the anarchist revolution. Jackie might represent her own variety of anarchy; associated with numbness but also with autoeroticism (J.O.) and the night, Jackie is uncategorizable ingot in the blood veins and imaginations of millions.

Lily Bart, in Edith Wharton's *The House of Mirth*, depends on the kindness of strangers, and therefore it is fatal for Lily not to please. Lily ends up overdosing in a rented room. We sympathize with Jackie if we consider her a modern Lily Bart, if we sense that Jackie isn't as rich or secure as she wishes, and that her movement toward prominence is suicidal, for it involves moral compromise.

Jackie O, Lily Bart, Emma Bovary: the story of a woman who attempts to rise into a higher class, or who is victimized by her own class instability. Gore Vidal said that Jackie and Lee were raised to be "adventuresses." If Jackie was an adventuress, she was cast in a classic melodrama of a woman fighting destiny, the double standard, male duplicity, and her own sentimentality. If we loved Jackie's story, and identified with it, that was because we could grasp its contours from afar, and flesh in the particulars from novels and movies.

As I've described, two basic plots determine my appreciation of Jackie. In one, the Lily Bart/Emma Bovary story, the woman tragically tries to social-climb, or loves the wrong man, or seeks to live by an outdated etiquette. In another—the story of *my* infatuation—Jackie plays the Princess Casamassima, and I play Hyacinth Robinson. Proust's *Remembrance of Things Past* recapitulates the Hyacinth plot: this time, the Jackie character is the Duchesse de Guermantes, who represents to Marcel the splendor of society, the antiquity of an illustrious house, the disastrousness of modern marriage, and the erotized unattainability of the art object. Another Duchesse de Guermantes figure is Garance, played by the alluring Arletty, in Marcel Carné's film *Children of Paradise*. When pale Baptiste, shouting, "Garance! Garance!," runs through the Paris carnival crowd at the movie's end, and loses her to a mob that signifies the extinction of illusion, I think of Jackie, because she is always lost to us; because, like Arletty, she is French, vaguely collab-orationist, and therefore disgraced (wasn't marrying Ari considered her defection from Kennedy-style democracy into the arms of an unscrupulous empire builder?); be-cause she moves, within the space of a single epic movie, from an identity as thief to an identity as aggrieved prin-cess; and because Baptiste sees Garance as Hyacinth sees the Princess or as Marcel sees the Duchesse—from the point of view of an aesthete whose keenest pleasures are conceptual and impossible.

Either I see Jackie as the heroine of a novel. Or I consider myself, as Jackie lover, to be the protagonist of a novel in which Jackie represents the elusive object of desire, whose evanescence blesses (and disintegrates) the speaker's melancholy, fragile identity.

Jackie Kennedy herself summoned the King Arthur plot to explain her life to the public. By allying her husband's administration to Camelot, she cast herself— a mixed blessing—as Guinevere. For in Camelot, the Queen, not the King, commits adultery. Thus Jackie, by evoking Camelot, graciously took on the adulterous role, displacing JFK's infidelities onto herself.

The nickname "Jackie O" recalls Anna O., the famous hysteric whose case study Sigmund Freud and Josef Breuer included in *Studies on Hysteria*. On the basis of the name, I'm tempted to conjecture a place for Jackie

O in the history of psychoanalysis. If Anna O. is its obscure and garrulous origin, might not Jackie O represent one of its veiled continuations, if not its expensive, invisible end point? Was Jackie O America's premier hysteric? Is our interest in Jackie O a symptom of collective hysteria? Or does Jackie O demonstrate the social (rather than individual) nature of psychic forces?

The letter O is an exclamation: Oh! Kitty Kelley titled her exposé *Jackie Oh!*, suggesting that we're shocked at Jackie's conduct, and that she regularly provokes open-mouthed awe. American astronauts in space, upon hearing of Jackie's marriage to Ari, said "Oh my!" That is the classic response to a Jackie sighting, or to Jackie's aura: "Oh my!" Or, to reverse the outburst: *My O*. Saying "Oh my!" in response to Jackie's presence, I claim her; I say, "Her O is mine." O is the peephole through which I see her. O is the circularity of this collective dream of Jackie. O is the nothing I can see and know of her famous nature. O is an unspecified orifice. Her O is *not* mine, and therefore I have "O envy," and need to give myself an "O" by saying "Oh my!" in response to Jackie; I must say "Oh my!" ("I'm astonished!") in front of a photo of Jackie O, to confirm and attain an aura as open and vast as hers, and as pop.

When I think of the exclamation "O!" I think of lofty, dramatic utterances. It is not a letter that I take lightly. Jackie's "O" does not tarnish her but lends her a tragic raiment. Here are some instances of "O" in *King Lear*: ". . . now thou art an O without a figure"; "O most small fault"; "O, are you free?"; "O, reason not the need!"; "O fool, I shall go mad!"; "O! O! 't is foul!"; "Sick, O, sick!"; "O, our lives' sweetness!"; "O ruined piece of nature!" Entire books have been written on the Shakespearean

I have "O envy."

significances of the O. Suffice it to say that the O in Jackie O establishes her as naught and naughty and also introduces the "I" into the equation, if we flip "Jackie O" to form the "I"-implying invocation "O Jackie."

The O puts Jackie in places she doesn't belong, in places that the real Jacqueline Onassis would hate to be. The O shames Jackie; the O turns her into currency, a gold piece. If money is shit, as Freud speculated, and Jackie, marrying Ari, becomes filthy rich, then the O puts the onus of dirt on Jackie, branding her with an O that signifies lucre gained through the gold wedding band (also an "O"). The O puts her in the shoes of Ingrid Bergman in chilly *Gaslight*, a woman stuck in the house of a man who's trying to prove she's mad. Like the Ingrid Bergman character, Jackie is an innocent. How can Jackie O, in our serialized comic-strip novel, *The Story of Jackie O*, escape from Charles Boyer? Our role, as Jackie watcher, is to understand her inner dignity, beneath the ratty vestment of myth. She has, for us, the reality of all heroines—we imagine that her reminiscences and sorrows have a depth lacking in mundane, real life—or else we use icon Jackie to articulate our own ambiguities, those that don't easily surface into speech, and that only stammer into audibility when we see them mirrored in art.

JACKIE VERSUS

MARIA CALLAS

JACKIE ONASSIS made no recordings. Now that she is dead, all we have are the books she edited, and photographs, and rumor's distillate—the sentences of biographies and of news accounts. When Maria Callas, Jackie's rival, died, she left numberless LPs and tapes; after life, she still sings to us, still wins acolytes. After Jackie died, I listened to Callas's recordings to imagine that Maria had softened toward her enemy, and that she was now singing posthumous requiems for Jackie's soul.

Consider Jackie from Maria's wounded point of view; imagine what Maria thought of Jackie; use Callas's recordings as oblique documentation of her heartbreak (even if the original LPs *predate* the marriage of Ari and Jackie). Recall that Maria Callas's sister was named Jackie, and that Maria, as a child, was dumpy and awkward, while her sister was attractive and well liked (or so Maria believed). With what horror Maria must have greeted the news that her rival for Ari's love was also named Jackie!

Jackie O is mythic without Maria's aid. But Callas provides musical commentary to Jackie's story. Thinking of Maria's woe adds texture to Jackie; allows us to see Jackie as victorious, rather than victimized; allows us to see Jackie from a myopic rival's jealous point of view. Why did Jackie choose Maria's man? It makes Jackie seem less vulnerable to know that she "stole" another woman's guy.

Fan magazines frequently reported on the rivals: would the two meet? Allegedly the ex-diva sought reconcilement with the ex-First Lady, but, said Maria, "it is not wanted by the other side." The phrase "the other side," bringing to mind the title (now lost to me) of a reincarnation/ESP tome about life after death, seems to describe not *the other side* of a romantic triangle, but *the other side* of the life/death divide: Jackie was often portrayed as denizen of *the other side*, a ghoulish beauty wandering the Elysian fields. Jackie was *the other side* to Rose Kennedy; Jackie was *the other side* to Marilyn Monroe. To all of us, Jackie is *the other side*—demon or angel beyond our ken. It may comfort us, reading fan magazines, to know that even someone of Maria's stature felt divided from Jackie. One provocative headline enticed readers with the fantasy of Jackie, Ari, and Maria forming a hedonistic ménage in the style of *Bob & Carol & Ted & Alice*:

MARIA
CALLAS
ASKS
JACKIE:
*"Let's make it
a threesome"*
JACKIE'S
STRANGE
ANSWER

(In a photo accompanying the article, Jackie is smoking, as if to demonstrate her wickedness.) If they formed a threesome, would Maria and Jackie desultorily caress? This was the era when Elizabeth Taylor performed two lesbian scenes—with Mia Farrow in *Secret Ceremony* and with Susannah York in *X, Y and Zee*. The Gumby-like flexibility of icon Jackie! It is our prerogative to hypothesize about Jackie and Maria and Ari, even if our conjectures never match up with decent biographical truth.

Compared to glacial Jackie, Maria seems rather clumsy and human. Maria was a star for actual, not mythic, reasons. Fearless of the media, she used gossip reporters as allies in demolishing Ari's and Jackie's reputations. Maria commented to the press that Ari was "beautiful as Croesus," and that Jackie was smart to give a grandfather to her children. She called Jackie "America's sweetheart," and said, to an interviewer, "I am like you. I am sitting back and watching the scene. All I know about Mrs. Onassis is what I have read about her in the newspapers." Odd, that Maria should pretend to depend on the media for Jackie knowledge. Of course Maria had reliable insider sources. But note that Jackie had the power to make *even Maria Callas* seem like an ordinary person, remote from the throne room of Jackie presence.

Jackie went backstage after Maria's return performance as Tosca, at the Met, in 1965. According to Heymann's biography, Jackie said to Maria, "You were magnificent," and Maria responded, "You are magnificent, too." What does this anecdote teach us? That Maria and Jackie, parallel deities, once intersected in actual space; that they traded pat praise; that Maria acknowledged Jackie's stature as a performance artist (her star turns included JFK's funeral). It must have been customary, in polite discourse, for people to compliment Jackie on her "magnificence," whether they were referring to her heroism, her style, or just her air of seeming to be giving a performance.

At her hardest, whether pre- or post-Ari, Jackie in

sunglasses and scarf looks like Maria Callas. But in general, the rivals represented opposite physical types. With Maria as dramatic foil, one could notice, anew, Jackie's gauntness. One had no problem imagining Maria comfortable in a muumuu. Jackie, however, though often casually dressed (her jeans phase, her ribbed turtleneck phase), seemed anorexically suspicious, primed—vigilant against fat or interference.

In the famous picture of triumphant smiling newlyweds Jackie and Ari aboard the *Christina*, Jackie looks like the coldhearted absence of Maria; Jackie seems, simply, *not Maria*. Jackie smiles, perhaps because she's proud of having ousted the diva. Ari's toplessness—naked dugs—proves him daredevil, sexual; we know that he will make "demands" on Jackie. Maria's absence from the picture—her obsolescence—helps us see that Jackie disturbs and reshuffles environments, and that, as one gossip piece reported, "when Jackie wants to go out she borrows other women's husbands as freely as the woman next door borrows a cup of sugar." Even the *Christina* is not without its shadows: Maria's vanishing makes Jackie's arrival as "Mrs. Onassis" seem tragic, or proves that her newfound security came at the other star's cost. Not that we blame Jackie. Rather, Maria's sudden absence seems a warning that Jackie should have heeded—proof of Ari's cavalier and impulsive mode of picking up and discarding a trinket. And so we may imagine Jackie's and Maria's solidarity. What Maria could have told Jackie!

The contrasting example of Maria reminds us of Jackie's untheatricality, her American silence. Not only doesn't Jackie sing, she doesn't even speak—at least not in public. Compared to Clytemnestran or Medean

Jackie is not *Maria.*

Maria, Jackie is undemonstrative, nonexhibitionistic. To understand icon Jackie we need the clarity that opposition—Jackie versus X—offers. "Oh, so Jackie is *not* Maria," we think, and thereby imagine that we comprehend Jackie.

JACKIE AND WATER,
JACKIE AND WIND

AMONG THE FIRST widely seen photographs of Jackie was the cover of *Life* magazine, July 20, 1953—image of Jackie and Jack sailing, with the caption: "Senator Kennedy Goes A-Courting." Jackie, unidentified girl beaming so widely her face must hurt, is merely the lucky object of JFK's courting. She is casually dressed—blouse, shorts. Bare legs. No sunglasses. And yet already she dominates the photo; her pleasure exceeds Jack's, though she's less toothy. The wind seems more interested in Jackie than in Jack. She leans into the spray as if she were the fo'c'sle. She's not buffeted by waves; she masters them. This photo establishes Jackie's blustery complicity with water and wind.

Aquatic Jackie was married near the water, in Newport; from her bedroom at Hammersmith Farm she could see the bay. At Jackie's funeral, Caroline read an Edna St. Vincent Millay poem about the beach at Truro; a childhood poem written by Jacqueline Bouvier, signed "Me —1939," called "Sea Joy," confesses, "Oh—to live by the sea is my only wish," and as illustration, Jacqueline drew a picture of herself stoically facing scud and sea swirl, her body a sheer uninterrupted line. The JFK Memorial Library at Columbia Point, Boston, reigns in splendid isolation, a hermit staring out to sea. On its lawn is Jack's sloop, the *Victura*. After Ari died and the

Skorpios years were over, Jackie built a Martha's Vineyard seaside house, hundreds of acres, private beach—the climax of her life as ocean maven. The Kennedys used Cape Cod and Hyannis Port as propaganda: the "Compound" proved that they were rich, but also that they were beachcombers, given to meditative walks along the sea. (The water image backfired when Mary Jo Kopechne drowned at Chappaquiddick: the Kennedys became associated not only with ocean but with drinking and drowning.) Jackie took the Kennedy predilection for ocean and turned it into a wuthering, introspective tendency. In a photo of Jackie wading in the sea and tossing Caroline into the air, Jackie's pants are wet up to the knee. Another often-reprinted photo shows Jackie walking by the beach after JFK's election has been announced: here, ocean offers protection from the publicity she'll have to face. Ocean, for Jackie, means respite from iconicity. The sea is just as much an icon as she; they can compare notes. Or else Jackie can be comforted by the sound of waves drowning out her celebrity. Also, there's a photo—on the back of Mary Van Rensselaer Thayer's authorized *Jacqueline Bouvier Kennedy* (which, allegedly, Jackie herself ghostwrote!)—of young Jackie Kennedy walking by the C&O Canal, holding her jacket. The day must have been terribly humid. Visionary Jackie, surrounded by the canal's lush foliage, stares out over the water, away from the camera. Water is as mythic and uncommunicative as she; it has a personality, but we don't know much beyond that. As in photos of Jackie beside the Taj Mahal, she's not dwarfed by canal or ocean. No more can Angkor Wat diminish Jackie than can the Atlantic; she needs large, silent buildings and natural wonders to serve as counterpoint to her own sinewy muteness.

Jackie on the *Honey Fitz*, the Kennedy yacht: no one from the madding land can interrupt her. The Kennedy boats foreshadow the *Christina*. And Skorpios: the direst retreat. Water mirrors the Jackie consciousness we can never enter (we wonder what Jackie is really thinking, but she is inarticulate as the sea); water, a moat, isolates her from us. But we, too, know shores. Poking toes in beach sand, we can pretend we're Jackie, photographed in a candid with Lee by the sea. When we can see Jackie's bare feet actually touch the sand, then we know her need to be rooted, ordinary, and pebbly. No mediation rises between Jackie and the waves.

Jackie and Jack, before his presidency, swim at Hyannis Port, frolicking around a tiny, modest boat, in shallow water: Jackie wears a foolish fringed bathing cap, the sort anyone can wear. Gaily holding flippers, she's kin to starlets in a teen film like *Beach Blanket Bingo* or *Where the Boys Are*. That she should be deprived of beach pleasures constitutes one of her life's tragedies.

Water and tragedy: *The Greek Tycoon* represents the President's assassination taking place while the Jackie and Jack characters are taking a quiet stroll on the beach. If we consider the Liz Taylor character in *A Place in the Sun* to be a Jacqueline Bouvier type—rich girl enjoying water sports—then the Monty Clift character's complicity in drowning dreary Shelley Winters reminds us that for every Liz or Jackie, finding tranquillity by the sea, there is a Shelley Winters, a jilted, plump, and drowned Cassandra. A *Photoplay* headline proclaimed in August 1967, JACKIE NEARLY DROWNS! WHY NO ONE ANSWERED HER CALL FOR HELP. Writes Fred O'Brien in the accompanying story: "The photographers clicked away as she backed out into the ocean. . . . She could have been doomed, yet she courageously refused to come in out of the water. She just kept on pleading and crying for help."

In photos of Jackie sailing or Jackie by the beach, her hair is windblown. Pregnant, smoking Jackie photographed in pink maternity shift aboard the *Honey Fitz* (in 1963): breeze, our friend, ruffles her hair, and she can't bother to keep it orderly. She's reading a book—trying to ignore the camera? Since she'll lose the child, Patrick, and since JFK himself will soon be dead, when we look at this photo in retrospect Jackie seems sweetly vulnerable, and her position, windswept and pregnant, on the open deck of a boat, proves her risky exposure to destiny's whims. Even when she christens the Polaris submarine in Groton, Connecticut, wind disturbs her tresses, renders them human, captive to mutability. In the November 1963 newsreel footage of Jackie before the assassination, she pushes back a stray lock that falls onto her forehead. Delicately and automatically adjusting her hair, Jackie confesses (if we view the gesture retrospectively) that she is vulnerable to the upcoming bullet. If Jackie's helmet hair represents her static and monumental qualities, her likeness to sculpture, then her vulnerability to wind (and her secret sympathy with its gusts) shows her pixie and pathetic aspects. As a public figure who cares about propriety, she can't afford to have messy, breeze-blown hair. But sometimes she forgoes scarf or hair spray, or else the wind, too strong, disturbs her, and someone photographs the disturbance, and we have thereby a memento of Jackie's willingness to abandon pride and brave the elements. So many photos of breeze arresting or tantalizing Jackie! A Ron Galella candid of Jackie shows her crossing the street in Manhattan—wearing tie-dyed or faded jeans and a ribbed jersey. The

Breeze.

clothes cling to her exceptionally trim form and she moves limberly, athletically: who wouldn't wish to be Jackie, at large in Manhattan with an extraordinary body and no packages to hold, just her own slim sublime person? But the most remarkable feature of the photo is Jackie's windblown hair—it covers most of her face, like an impromptu veil. Wind-tossed hair proves that the photo happened in real time, real air; and it suggests that Jackie, like the wind engaging her, cannot be seen, touched, or verified, but is an immaterial current.

Thinking of Jackie disturbed by breeze, I remember Iphigenia sacrificed by Agamemnon: Iphigenia at the edge of the water. I think, "Jackie doesn't seem to mind the fierce encroachment of the elements—wind, water. She thinks the breeze is just playing around, toying with her. Doesn't she know how dangerous husbands and nature can be when unleashed?"

Of course, I am reading too much significance into Jackie's friendship with wind and ocean. But because icon Jackie rises into life only out of photographs, the pictures ask for interpretation. Every fillip of nature or culture adjacent to Jackie seems oblique commentary on her enigma. Even such universals as "wind" and "ocean" seem her property, seem uniquely expressive of her character and her plight.

DOES JACKIE SYMBOLIZE "family values"—that loathsome reactionary phrase? The press has always defined her as wife, mother, daughter, sibling—as someone who functions not independently but in relation to an extended and a nuclear family. Icon Jackie is a primer, guiding us through every kinship position. Contemplating her, I'm overwhelmed by a maelstrom of nosy hypotheses.

Glam mom: Jackie avoids realities of diapers, colic. She endures tragedies of miscarriage, stillbirth. She plays with her children. They pose beside her. Obsequies remember her as ideal mother. Utility of icon Jackie: imagine her as your mother, imagine yourself as a Jackie-style mother. Imagine the leisure: nanny Maud Shaw takes care of dirty details. You're at liberty to enjoy your children. Jackie made mothering seem like an elegant hobby. In a photo, infant Caroline grabs Jackie's beads, mouths them. Coiffed Jackie holding baby Caroline always looks cool yet tender. On the Hyannis Port porch, solitary Jackie in yellow-and-white-checked print dress seems perfectly single, without impediment or duty, but in another photo from that same session, Jackie holds a dog in one hand, Caroline in the other. The same imperturbable, abstract, and solitary Jackie now touches dog, touches Caroline. "She's a mother," I think. "She takes care of her pets," I think. A dim, dull knowledge dawns: the reality of Jackie's affection for Caroline and John. Photos of Jackie pregnant intrude the same, persistent knowledge: the reality of Jackie's pregnancies. The knowledge of Jackie as mother enters the mind *after* the knowledge of Jackie as glamorous wife has already found habitation. Wishes flutter to the mind's surface: to mother Jackie; to be mothered by Jackie; to free Jackie from motherhood's burdens; to give Jackie peace, so she can be a mother without surveillance. The "mom" aspect nudges icon Jackie in an unaccustomed direction. No Joan Crawford, Jackie was headlined in movie magazines as a paragon: WHAT HOLLYWOOD MOTHERS CAN LEARN FROM JACKIE KENNEDY ABOUT BRINGING UP CHILDREN; THE THREE DAYS JACKIE HID FROM THE WORLD— HER BIGGEST CRISIS AS A WIFE AND MOTHER. Propaganda of Jackie-as-mom photos proclaims that she was a good mother, and that you, reader, should imitate her, and that if you, reader, fail, you fall beneath Jackie's sublime standard.

Jackie as daughter: think of Janet Auchincloss's pride, having a beautiful daughter whose husband became President; recall alleged strictness and severity, and hope that Janet was "nice" to Jackie; observe well-adjusted Jackie and think, "Janet Auchincloss did a good job"; remember that Mrs. Auchincloss released a formal announcement of Ari and Jackie's marriage (manners still applied, Jackie was staggeringly famous but she was still a daughter, and Mother must do what's proper). Or turn to Black Jack, in the dark night, and imagine Jackie's love for him, and wonder if he pushed that love too far; imagine Jackie visiting Black Jack's apartment, after the divorce, and Black Jack giving Jackie the money to house her horse

Danseuse, and later visiting Jackie at Farmington (Miss Porter's School). Idealize the relationship of Black Jack and his Jackie; mourn his untimely death, gone before he could see Jackie in the White House. (A maudlin biography, Kathleen Bouvier's *To Jack, with Love: Black Jack Bouvier, A Remembrance*, gives him credit for raising a daughter destined to be First Lady, and speculates that if Black Jack had lived, he'd have been as famous as Jackie. The author describes Jackie's evening in Versailles from the point of view of a father who obtains posthumous vindication through his daughter's triumph: "Yet that night of palaces and nobility, of opulence and fine wines, powerful and handsome men and women of global importance, was a salute to Jack as clearly as it was to his daughter. It might have been the greatest night in Jack's entire life. He never made it to see Jackie at Versailles. For that I nearly wept.") Picture Jackie accompanying Janet to the Lazy-A-Bar Ranch in Reno, where Mother divorced Black Jack. Imagine Jackie's grief that Black Jack was too drunk to lead her down the aisle; imagine her tears, savor the melodrama. Or else take on Black Jack's point of view, and imagine what a sensational daughter Jackie must have been, so sly and artistic. The possibilities of Jackie cogitation are manifold, intoxicating. Did I neglect to say that you may imagine Jackie as Baby Bouvier, beautiful and weeping, gurgling "goo-goo"? Note that star mouths are infantile and only vaguely gendered: note Liz's "bleb," her shiny underlip, and note Jackie's upper lip, which often aristocratically subdivides, a lip crinkle caused by a swiveled eyetooth, a lip crinkle I think of as a classic Bouvier signature of infantile yet high-class need.

Then turn to Jackie as daughter-in-law: a fruitful path.

Imagine Rose's point of view: imagine her envy, upstaged by Jackie. Watch a 1958 campaign TV spot called "At Home with the Kennedys," in which Rose and Jackie sit together, awkward, on a couch; Rose has an obstruction in her throat, and she coughs, reaches offscreen for a glass of water. Be happy that Rose is fumbling her performance, looking foolish on the air, next to composed Jackie, or that Jackie cattily says to Rose, "Jack has been ungallant enough to say in speeches that you've been campaigning for sixty-five years." In every picture of Rose and Jackie together, stories simmer: facing a photo of Jackie, Rose, and Ari in a limo, you may wonder, "Did Rose forgive Jackie for marrying Ari? Did Rose and Ari get along?" Looking at a photo of Rose at the Inauguration, in sunglasses that make her seem Ma Barker, head of a criminal clan, wonder if Rose at last realizes Jackie's supremacy. Wonder, when considering the assassination, whether Rose was more unhappy than Jackie, or differently unhappy, and wonder how Rose and Jackie comforted each other. Imagine Jackie charming Joe Sr.; imagine Jackie wiping drool, later, from paralyzed Joe's mouth; imagine (a rumor) Joe offering Jackie $1 million if she stays with Jack. And imagine Rose Kennedy and Janet Auchincloss in Newport confabbing about the upcoming Jackie/Jack wedding—moment lost in a later whirlwind! Imagine antagonisms; imagine wounds magically healed.

Consider the possible jealousy of the other Kennedy wives and sisters—Jackie the only one among them to become a true icon. Or did they feel sorry for Jackie? Is it true that Jackie was the only member of the clan who understood Joan Kennedy? Remember Ethel mocking Jackie's pronunciation of "Jack-leen": "she says it rhymes with 'queen.' " Assume Jackie's point of view, and think with disdain of Ethel, whom, according to Kitty Kelley, Jackie described as "the type who would put a slipcover on a Louis Quinze sofa and then spell it Luie Cans." Look at the famous photo of Jackie on the porch at Hyannis Port with Ethel, Joan, Eunice, and Jean, and note that Jackie alone among them seems coolly porcelain. Think: "Poor Jackie, I hope the other Kennedy women were nice to her." In photos of Eunice and Pat and Ethel and Joan campaigning with Jackie, notice how "rah-rah" the other girls look, how bored and distracted Jackie seems. Then turn to the brothers. Think of Jackie's fondness for Bobby, and of Bobby's for Jackie; speculate about romance. Did Jackie consider Bobby a kid brother, or did she consider him morally superior to Jack? Think of Ted serving as Kennedy patriarch by talking marriage contract details with Ari and, later, escorting Jackie to Ari's funeral, where Christina snubbed her.

Then consider Lee: imagine complicities, jokes. The trip to India, the European Grand Tour: think of the confidences exchanged. Imagine Lee's probably ferocious jealousy of Jackie (imagine your sister turning into an icon) but also imagine Lee's sense of being the lucky one, spared tragedy. Imagine Jackie's jealousy of Lee: reportedly Jackie insisted to a clothing scout in Europe, during the early 1960s, that she send news of "treasures" to Jackie *before* sending them to Lee. A treasure war between Jackie and Lee! Imagine the sisters roasting Ari together; imagine Lee supporting Jackie's marriage to Ari, or envying it. Use Lee as launching pad into Jackie's consciousness: "Lee is *almost* Jackie, and Lee is a much more accessible person. I could imagine being Lee, and then, by a quick switch-over, could turn into Jackie." Look at a photo, in

175

One Special Summer, of the sisters dining in what Jackie (or Lee?) described as "a latticed restaurant where you talk all afternoon," and imagine the languor of Lee, whose sister is not yet an icon but is on the verge of becoming one. Andy Warhol called Jackie and Lee the best "sister act" in town. Give incidental thought to "Yusha" Auchincloss, Jackie's stepbrother, who allegedly had a crush on Jackie. Yusha's room, in Hammersmith, was down the hall from Jackie's. Imagine Yusha in his room, in the 1940s, a few steps down the hall from young Jackie, and wonder. Imagine Jackie as a stepsister; imagine suddenly discovering yourself in demi-relation to Jackie.

Think about Jackie from the point of view of John and Caroline: imagine seeing Jackie stumble around the apartment in a bathrobe, her wet hair wrapped in a towel. Think of John and Caroline from Jackie's point of view. Wonder whether Jackie approved of John Jr.'s romantic life, or whether she was fond of Edwin Schlossberg, Caroline's husband. Imagine the son-in-law's point of view. Imagine what it would be like to have Jackie as mother-in-law: surreal bounty! Or imagine whether Jackie approved of Caroline's fine arts major, whether Jackie advised Caroline on dress and decorum. In pictures, notice how Caroline's poise has increased over the years, and wonder whether she consciously styles herself after her mother, and wonder what it would be like to think "Mother" and "Jackie" and for the two incontrovertibly to be one. Surreal! Then imagine Jackie's closets from the point of view of Maurice, or John, or Caroline, or Ari. Imagine their attitudes toward the rows of shoes. Imagine how they conceptualize "Jackie's closet," or whether they conceptualize "Jackie" at all.

Then turn to Jackie as wife. Think of Jackie from Jack's

point of view, from Ari's. Or from the point of view of John Husted, her first fiancé. (Did he regret that the engagement foundered?) Wonder whether Jack felt guilty about his philandering, or whether Jackie hit him, yelled at him, gave him ultimatums ("If you don't stop sleeping around, I'm leaving you!"). Wonder whether Jackie wept over news of the affairs leaking to the world's press in the years since JFK's death. Think about JFK's infidelities and their effect on Jackie. Wonder whether Jackie truly loved Jack, or vice versa; whether they were cold to each other; whether, in 1970, Jackie still considered Jack to be the only love of her life, or whether love for Ari had begun to cast its own worthy shadow. Wonder whether Jackie felt sorry for Jack because of his ill health, his grueling ambition. Consider Maurice Tempelsman and imagine happy Jackie, love found at last, respect, equality, and other words from magazines.

The position of Jackie's stepdaughter is rife with possibility. One *Movie Mirror* headline, before the fact, revealed: THE HIPPIE WHO MAY BECOME JACKIE'S STEPDAUGHTER TELLS ALL!!! Instead of a hippie, Jackie got Christina: think, briefly, of Christina—how she, riven by envy, must have hated Jackie. Did Jackie really call Christina (so reports Kitty Kelley) a "spoiled monster with fat legs and chunky ankles"? Someone must feel sorry for Christina, dead so young, at thirty-seven, and forgive her for calling Jackie an "Angel of Death" with a "hyena-like smile." Then think of Alexander Onassis, and imagine Jackie comforting Ari when his son died in a crash, and imagine the sibling relations (awkward?) between John, Caroline, Alexander, and Christina.

I imagine Jackie in relation to other members of a

mythic family: she is an occasion for thinking deeply and obsessively about the roles of mother, father, wife, husband, daughter, son, sister, brother, sister-in-law, brother-in-law, mother-in-law, father-in-law, stepsister, stepbrother, stepson, stepdaughter. Her family history is an international reference point—a theme park; all the different kinship roles, so close, so claustrophobic! The magazines loved to classify Jackie according to her position in a family: MY SISTER JACKIE, AUNT JACKIE . . . How could Jackie keep track of all her different emotions? Life in a clan, life with husbands, life with children, life with Christina and Rose and Teddy and John-John and Lee and Black Jack and Ethel—was it fun or exhausting, does it resemble your life, were Jackie's filial, maternal, and sororal emotions a rarefied distillation of yours? Every family is a ruined family. Jackie, embedded in an idealized family, kept silent about the ruin.

JACKIE AS DANDY

JACKIE MIGHT HAVE archly manipulated her own iconicity; or if she couldn't control the ways she was portrayed in the media, at least she knew herself as "show," as "appearance," and her sensibility and her aesthetic philosophy dictated the show's plot.

Considering Jackie as the artificer—the architect—of the Jackie Show portrays her as an entrepreneur of appearances. Unlike Madonna, however, Jackie did not directly profit from her production; not an entertainer, Jackie lacked syndication or copyright over her image, which could be used against her will. A more fruitful comparison is between Jackie and the nineteenth-century dandy. Imagine that Jackie considered herself in the dandy tradition, and that the tenets of dandy philosophy influenced her self-presentation and her peculiar, shy exhibitionism.

Jacqueline Bouvier invoked dandyism in the essay she wrote for the *Vogue* 1951 Prix de Paris contest (which she won, and, on her mother's urging, turned down); in this essay, she chose Charles Baudelaire, Oscar Wilde, and Sergei Diaghilev as the three dead figures she'd most like to meet. The first two—if not all three—were dandies. Baudelaire theorized the dandy, a type of city dweller, antibourgeois, aristocratic, bohemian, whose "being" or whose process of self-realization and self-exhibition is conceived as a performance and as a deliberate subversion of the work ethic and the emphasis on useful production. The dandy produces nothing but himself, his airs, his effects, his bons mots, his costumes. (The dandy was usually a "he.") Oscar Wilde's dandyism—his subversion of the work or production standard, and his act of replacing it with "useless" words (art for art's sake) and with flamboyant and avant-garde self-promotion and self-commodification—had the important distinction of being antimasculine, or was interpreted as such: following Wilde, the dandy's modes were branded as effeminate or even "sodomitical," and thereafter the inheritors of the dandy mode would primarily be either self-conscious homosexuals, artists, or impresarios (for example, Sergei Diaghilev, Carl Van Vechten, Lincoln Kirstein, Andy Warhol). But mostly the inheritors of the dandy mantle would be rich (or rich-seeming) women. Of Jackie's circle, Diana Vreeland most perfectly embodies the dandy type. Wildean wit, Baudelairean synesthesia, and aristocratic hedonism migrated into this *Vogue* editor and fashion-for-fashion's-sake sage, whom Jacqueline Onassis profiled in "A Visit to the High Priestess of Vanity Fair," an essay for an exhibition at the Costume Institute of the Metropolitan Museum of Art. Onassis also edited Diana Vreeland's *Allure*, which, although no photos of Jackie appear in it, obliquely comments on the Jackie myth. Vreeland praises, for example, the glamour of widows: "It's this realization that they're *alone*—that wherever they put their hands, there's no one to help them in anything." The publication of *Allure* assures us that Jacqueline Onassis appreciated female allure enough to edit a book celebrating it. The clearest indication of Jackie's "dandy" strain, however, remains the V*ogue* essay, in which she describes Baudelaire and Wilde as "dandies," and in which she praises Wilde for being able, "with the flash of an epigram, [to] bring about what serious reformers had for years been trying to accomplish." Here, she invokes two kinds of politics: the politics of "serious reformers" and the politics of the dandy, achieved through wit and style. The importance of "serious" reform notwithstanding, we can credit Jacqueline Bouvier with knowing, at the beginning of her ascent to stardom, the limits of seriousness, and the usefulness of "flash" and wit and superficiality—even the *political* usefulness of "flash." This is the politics of the dandy, and, in Jackie's case, it depended on the "flash" of the paparazzo's camera.

Praising Diaghilev, Jacqueline Bouvier indicates her respect for transitory performance, and for entrepreneurs who create ephemeral atmospheres. Dance, the most bodily of the arts, remained her favorite (among her first guests at the White House was Balanchine); but in the following passage, she describes not only the art of dance, valuable *because* impermanent, but a dandyesque conception of life in which the fleeting impression, the evanescent (unserious?) tableau, is valued more than the monumental and the willed: "Though not an artist himself, [Diaghilev] possessed what is rarer than artistic genius in any one field, the sensitivity to take the best of each man and incorporate it into a masterpiece all the more precious because it lives only in the minds of those who have seen it and disintegrates as soon as he is gone." She seems, proleptically, to be describing the effect of "Jackie" as masterpiece—momentary odalisque that disintegrates as soon as she turns her back. Jackie, though not an artist in the conventional sense, produced a public persona that had attributes of an artwork. Jackie, in other words, was the *auteur* of "Jackie": as a director (in so-called *auteur* theory) is imagined to be the author of the film, so Jackie was the *auteur* of her own persona and show. In her essay, Jacqueline Bouvier imagined herself as "a sort of Over-all Art Director of the Twentieth Century, watching everything from a chair hanging in space," and said that "it is their theories of art that I would apply to my period." She did apply their theories to her period; she did become an Over-all Art Director of the Twentieth Century. Reigning from an unseen chair hanging in space, she seemed to "direct," like an *auteur,* a fantastic show, which, like the production of the ideal dandy, was gratifying for flouting the moralistic bourgeois division between *waste* and *use.* Part of the show that Jackie directed, of course, was our desire, our attentiveness, our spectatorship.

Jackie-as-dandy did nothing, but her inactivity was glamorous. What were aspects of Jackie's "uselessness"? She never defended political causes—even in the White House, her only interest seemed to be the White House itself. Although Frances Spatz Leighton recalls that Jackie "seemed much more interested in charitable work, such as helping retarded children, than she was in the social whirl," this is hardly the general impression that Jackie gave in any of her public phases. Openly affiliated with no charity except historical preservation, supporting no amendments, no movements, Jackie stood aside, for her entire career, from active politics, as if with distaste for its boorishness; politics seemed a Kennedy touch football game she was too delicate and refined to play. Seen in light of her dandy affiliation, Jackie's abstention from the "serious" work of politics seems not the failure of nerve or the lack of idealism that sterner critics might have suggested, but a signal of a sensibility for which American politics has had too little space: an acknowledgment of artifice's power; an acknowledgment of the reign of surfaces. In the "At Home with the Kennedys" TV spot, in which Rose and Jackie chat together on the couch, Rose notes how lucky Jack was to find a wife who loved campaigning; but when Jackie says that she feels like she's shaken every hand in Massachusetts, her singsong yet expressionless voice ("Marilyn Monroe playing Ophelia") turns the line to parody, and we realize, in retrospect, that Jackie did *not* enjoy campaigning, and that she seems uncannily to speak without affect because a deadpan manner is the only way she can acceptably broadcast her dandy sensibility while still impersonating the docile wife. Underplaying, seeming to erase herself, she's actually advertising her own brand of politics: self-parody under the guise of seeming "natural."

It's even possible to interpret, in retrospect, the questions that Jacqueline Bouvier asked for her Inquiring Camera Girl column as deliberately arch, off-center; as self-consciously parts of a dandyesque colloquy, in which, like a philosopher queen, Jackie is playing a Socratic game on the streets of Washington, querying strangers, posing koans that may mean nothing or that may, like a well-timed if nonsensical aphorism, push the auditor toward bliss and self-recognition. Some of her questions were: "Do you consider yourself normal?" "Do you often change your impression of people?" "Do you think your life story would make a good movie?" "What do you think flying saucers really are?" "Would you like to crash high society?" "Do you think Mamie Eisenhower's bangs will become a nationwide fashion?" "Would you like to see the European custom of kissing ladies' hands started here?" "If you had a date with Marilyn Monroe, what would you talk about?" "Do you think a wife should tell her husband that he's smarter than she?" "What has been your greatest Coronation thrill?" "Do you think Nathan Leopold should have been paroled?" "If you were to be electrocuted tomorrow morning, what would you order for your last meal?" The uncanny convergences between some of these questions and later coordinates in Jackie's life (Marilyn Monroe, Mamie Eisenhower, coronation, crashing high society) make her questions, looked at retrospectively, seem parts of a premeditated scheme, as if Jackie, holding her Graflex camera and asking innocuous questions, were planting clues about her personality to be parsed later by fans.

One pleasure of Jackie gossip has been the glimpses it offers of her dandy side. Although superficially the gossip indicts her as a big spender, the scoops give us a chance to enjoy the "other" Jackie. If muckraker Fred Sparks hadn't reported it, how would we know that Jackie suggested to JFK, when he was struggling with the issue of air pollution, that the Air Force spray Chanel No. 5 everywhere? How would we know, if gossips didn't report it, that Jackie would mimic diplomats after state dinners? When Billy Baldwin, decorator, came to Greece to advise Jackie on the redesign of the several Onassis domiciles, he didn't eat his dessert, and so Jackie left it on a tray outside his guest-room door with a note: "Billy: you missed your midnight sweets—and the houris have been kneading unguents all day long. . . ." She signed the note: "Mme Suleiman le Brilliant." Did Jackie enjoy considering herself a Mme Suleiman le Brilliant, an odalisque, a figure like David's version of Madame Récamier? (Jackie listed eighteenth-century saloniste Madame Récamier as one woman from history she admired.) One feels, reading accounts of Jackie's private life, that she had steady and sustaining truck not only with officials, Kennedys, and moguls but with a far more "trivial" sort: decorators, designers, hairdressers, and other practitioners of artifice.

Was Jackie a "fag hag"? Unpleasant term: but one must invoke it in order to plumb Jackie's dandy affiliation. It's important to ponder the notion that Jackie, like many great souls, might have been a "fag hag": when Jackie is accused of steering her life too avidly in the direction of *men* (JFK, Joseph Kennedy, Ari) or of being a "gold digger" or "adventuress," the assumption is that she only enjoys macho, political, financial, official men. In fact, if Jackie has been a princess of appearances, an Over-all Director of the Twentieth Century in *artifice* but not in *substance*, then the men who helped her in the business of artifice were mostly of that suspect class of designers who, whether straight or gay or neither, occupied the degraded, feminized realm of surfaces over which Jackie ruled supreme. Think of Truman Capote (although he later turned on her, calling her a "tramp"); shoe designer Mr. Mario; hairdressers Jean-Louis and Kenneth (think of how many thousands of confidential conversations Jackie has had with hairdressers); decorators Billy Baldwin and Stéphane Boudin; designers Halston and Valentino and Givenchy and Cassini (only later did she find a woman designer, Carolina Herrera). Jackie, in her role as dandy, needed the help of other dandies; it was with dandies, I imagine, that Jackie could go about the "serious" business of making a spectacle of herself.

The consumers of this spectacle, the audience of the

Jackie Show—call us Jackie lovers, Jackie watchers, Jackie fans: our contingent is, finally, partner and collaborator in Jackie's undercover dandyism. We Jackie lovers may delight in her appearance, reports of her doings; we may find glamorous or poignant the least detail about her beauty at the Inauguration, or her conduct immediately after the assassination, or her life on Skorpios. And yet this pleasure we take in Jackie lore and in Jackie beauty is useless; it does not lead to production. As object of delectation, as pleasure-inspiring personage, Jackie turns us into dandies; loving Jackie, or indulging in our curiosity about her life, we participate in an aesthetic experience without borders or design. It's like witnessing a carnival or a Passion play that disappears the moment we begin to applaud. What did we see? Where did she go? Audience to Jackie, we could make no point about her; could say nothing but, as *Motion Picture* put it: WE BACK JACKIE. All we could aver was that we stood behind her, that we advocated her. A 1968 *Photoplay* poll encouraged readers to vote on whether Jackie was trivial or serious:

I THINK JACKIE KENNEDY (check one)
_____ is wasting her life
_____ is not wasting her life
COMMENT (if you wish) _____

Readers were then encouraged to clip and mail the ballot to "Jackie Kennedy Poll, Post Office Box #1705, New York, New York 10017." What was the purpose of the poll? It gave fans an artificial sense of participation: the fan was having a say. The poll asked: is Jackie a dandy, or is she a serious, productive woman? What would it mean to accuse Jackie of "wasting" her life? (Again, note, as in the "taste vs. waste" comparison between Jackie and Liz, how important it seemed to separate Jackie from waste, and how easily she took on waste's properties.) As dandy, Jackie was wasteful; she wasted time, wasted money. She was accused of being trivial, squandering her political clout on inessentials, devoting herself to luxuries and nightlife. Loving Jackie, we, too, became trivial, particularly because there was nothing to do with the experience, nowhere to deposit or express it. At best, we could vote in *Photoplay*'s "Jackie Kennedy Poll," or comment on Jackie to a friend, or compile a Jackie scrapbook. Like the dandy, we understood that the delight taken in a glimpse of Jackie, or in the idea of Jackie as a fairy sitting on a chair hanging in space over the Twentieth Century, watching us all, must be sufficient mead. We had to turn back to the business of life—to useful *work*—and renounce useless dreams and narcotics.

JACKIE AND DRUGS

COLUMNIST Suzy Knickerbocker commented on Jackie, "If she had really wanted privacy, the way she says, she could have gotten it. But publicity is like dope and she's got to have that front-page fix." Is publicity like dope? Was icon Jackie addicted to her fame? Were we addicted to Jackie? A 1964 biography of Jackie describes her druglike effect on fashion: "models who bore a re-semblance to Jacqueline Kennedy—wide eyes, leonine haircut, square face with a full lower lip—were a drug on the market." Does Jackie function in our culture as a drug functions in the body, or do we respond to Jackie as if she were an illicit, addictive substance that changes the boundaries of experience, speeds it up, slows it down, engenders visions and delusions?

Critic Avital Ronell, in her book *Crack Wars*, has hypothesized connections between literature and addic-tion: though it's commonplace to say that a novel has the power to alter one's sense of time and corrupt one's morals, we're not accustomed to thinking of literature *as* a drug. I suggest that, loosely following Ronell's provoc-ative lead, we consider icon Jackie as a substance that induces altered states in the contemplator. Each gossip scoop about her, each photo, is a "hit," a fix. Jackie performs as a drug because she deranges our sense of scale, our hierarchies of size: imagining an event from Jackie's point of view may make one feel enormous, or it may dwarf one's own comparatively meager life, as if we, dreaming of Jackie, become Alice in Wonderland, falling down the hole, losing proportion. Thinking about Jackie alters your body image: you may feel thinner, fatter, larger, smaller. Does your head swell or shrink when you conceptualize Jackie's head?

Jackie herself may have seemed drugged. On the White House Tour, doesn't she sound as if she's on Valium? Isn't her zombie mien one version of behavior demanded from elegant Stepford Wives in the era of *Valley of the Dolls*? On the one hand, "dolls" contribute to the "partying" lifestyle. On the other hand, a woman turns to "dolls" to escape her life or to perform as expected. Jackie's attractively remote and disconnected manner had affiliations with the realm of the "doll" or the mannequin as well as with the woman who took "dolls" to become more doll-like, to have fun, to relax, to stupefy herself, to induce amnesia. We know that Jackie chain-smoked, though pictures of her in the act are rare. We know that she gave Truman Capote a porcelain jar with the word "opium" inscribed on it. Why not imagine culture as a jar labeled OPIUM, and imagine Jackie iconography as the powdery substance we ingest to make our bodies surge with false possibility, false hope?

Icon Jackie herself behaved most like an addict when she shopped. One hears that Jackie would often buy several of the item she liked. Does it clarify the nature of Jackie in our lives if we think of her as a cheap or priceless object we shop for, an object that costs everything or nothing, maharajah ruby or penny candy, that we crave again and again until repetitive ingestion or unsated restaged desire sickens us?

"Black Jack" is a card game; it is also Jackie's father. She's daughter of (to quote my dictionary) "a variety of twenty-one in which a player can become dealer." Playing "Jackie" is like playing "Black Jack": a speculation, a gamble. You may lose your fortune; you may taste a rare ether. The men in Jackie's life (Black Jack, "Hughdie" Auchincloss, Joe Sr., Jack, Ari, Maurice) were financiers, speculators, power brokers; she was evidently attracted to their games of risk. As Grace Kelly escaped to Monaco to rule as Princess over a miniature land of gamblers, so Jackie escaped to the *Christina* and Skorpios, principalities of addiction.

We OD on Jackie by considering and reconsidering her; each November 22 since 1963, she's been resummoned, like a drink we shouldn't return to. What does it teach us to interpret Jackie as a drug, to interpret Jackie as something we inject, ingest, introject? It reminds us that the pleasure she gives is short-lived; that she enters our imaginations in order to alter the perspectives and axioms on which we base our worldview; that indulging the desire for Jackie knowledge is considered wasteful, damaging to economies of work and productivity; that Jackie is a game within our volition, but that, as in all addictive games, we lose willpower as the ante is upped. We think about Jackie not because we want to remain steadily ourselves, but because we want exit.

One of my favorite memos that Jackie sent to her minions while in the White House supplies a phrase, "make-believe cocktails," for discussing the thrill of Jackie identification. I quote from Jackie's memo, concerning beverage arrangements for Joseph Kennedy, Sr., when, accompanied by his nurse, he visited the White House: "Drink tray put it on Mr. K's side—but in dining room on a suitcase stand—I don't think she drinks & he just has make-believe cocktails. Tray should have Gin &

Make-believe cocktail.

Tonic—Coke—Ginger Ale, Rum, Scotch, Ice, cocktail shaker—Lemon juice—(I think this comes in a mix already in a bottle)—Sugar syrup in a jar." Make-believe cocktails! It's an amusing phrase: Jackie is poking fun at Joe Sr. What were the ailing patriarch's make-believe cocktails? Shirley Temples? I consider Jackie a make-believe cocktail. Thinking about Jackie, I'm not ingesting an actual substance. But then why do I feel high? Why does the room around me change its shape? Why do I feel suddenly smaller, then suddenly larger? Make-believe cocktails harm no one. They don't damage the system, though they make me feel terribly adult. Thinking about Jackie, I mimic a suspect and alien state of "adultness," of maturity; even though I am now older than Jackie was in 1963, Jackie Kennedy, in photos, seems truly an adult, while I always feel rather like a child. That's the effect of make-believe cocktails, or of Jackie: she makes me *more*. More silent, more voluble. More infantile, more mature. It doesn't matter in which direction she pushes me; but be assured, she pushes. Her image draws me toward a "high" that may be followed by depression, because, like all ordinary people who become mythic, she confuses me about the difference between reality and dream, and so one second as I look at a picture of Jackie I know that she's just an ordinary woman and then the next second I realize that she's a legend and that this picture isn't really Jackie but just a religious representation, and the quick shift from the *ordinary* to the *religious* inflates and deflates me, makes me unsure of ground. Some cocktail—some goddess— has entered my chemistry. Hasn't it? I may try to purge myself, but then I take another look at historic Jackie and I'm high again.

JACKIE AND

SYNESTHESIA

ONE ANALOGUE for such highs is synesthesia—defined by my dictionary as "a sensation produced in one modality when a stimulus is applied to another modality, as when the hearing of a certain sound induces the visualization of a certain color." For example, when I smell the perfume Shalimar, I see the color blue. Or when I hear Connie Francis sing "Where the Boys Are," I taste cumin. Or when I smell fresh lavender growing on a hillside, I feel the coldness of a milk shake.

In an arresting reminiscence, published after Jackie's death, architect I. M. Pei reveals Jackie's own engagement with synesthetic experience: "We went to China together in 1982. She visited my family home and garden in Xuzhou. Old Chinese houses have carvings on the walls—calligraphy, sayings. She was particularly taken with two panels. One said 'See Fragrance.' The other said 'Read Paintings.' Of course, she thought this was fascinating, and she wrote the sayings down. After we returned, she painted a picture for me in Chinese style, with black ink. It said 'See Fragrance' and 'Read Paintings.' She was a lady of great sensitivity." *See Fragrance*: Jackie wrote down (in some private notebook?) a phrase that epitomizes synesthesia, the ability of one sense (smell) to trigger another (sight). As in: *I see the aroma of Shalimar*. I've never actually smelled Shalimar (a perfume manufactured by Guerlain, the illustrious French parfumerie), and so I can only "see" Shalimar as a concept, a word, or as a memory of the perfume's occurrence in the macabre novel *The Mephisto Waltz*, where Shalimar is connected to the transmigration of souls from a dead body to a living.

Forty years before Jackie copied down the phrase *See Fragrance*, she quoted—in her Prix de Paris essay for *Vogue*—Baudelaire's poem "Correspondances" on the magic power of colors, sounds, and perfumes to kindle each other, and, together, to suggest ineffable unities: Jackie says that Baudelaire "developed the theory of synesthesia," and that he "speaks of perfumes, 'green as prairies, sweet as the music of oboes, and others, corrupted, rich and triumphant.'" First in French, Jackie's language, and then in English, the language of her ordinary life, and of mine:

> *Il est des parfums frais comme des chairs d'enfants,*
> *Doux comme les hautbois, verts comme les prairies,*
> *—Et d'autres, corrompus, riches et triomphants . . .*

> *There are perfumes cool (or fresh?) as children's flesh,*
> *Sweet as oboes, green as prairies,*
> *—And others, corrupted, rich and triumphant . . .*

Note that in translating Baudelaire, Jackie omitted the simile about "children's flesh." In defining synesthesia, she also quotes Oscar Wilde: "the musk and gold heat that emanates from a vase of flowers in the 'Music Room.'"

Emboldened by Jackie's interest in synesthesia, I want

to speculate on how synesthesia might illuminate the flight patterns of icon Jackie.

Jackie engages, richly, our sight: we are accustomed to seeing pictures of her. Vaguely she engages our sense of hearing: we may remember what her voice sounds like, if we've seen the White House Tour, or we may have an idea of her voice, from having heard imitators, or having read descriptions of her breathlessness. But she will remain abstract until we draw in the other senses—touch, taste, smell. This is where synesthesia proves useful: it permits us to reconstruct Jackie.

For example, when I think "Jackie," or see a picture of Jackie, several objects, confections, or incidental "treasures" (as Jackie might have called them) come to mind. I think of the perfume called Jicky, by Guerlain; I think of Chiclets chewing gum; I think of petits fours; and I think of enameled clip-on earrings. Let me delve into Jicky, Chiclets, petits fours, and clip-ons to show how Jackie provokes synesthesia, and how we can't fully comprehend Jackie as icon unless we explore our own synesthetic responses.

The name "Jicky" itself seems halfway between "Jackie" and "sticky." The idea that a product called Jicky exists, waiting to be bought, excites me: icon Jackie behaves like a product but one can't buy her, she is off the market. The smell of Jicky is impossible to put into words; but I understand Jackie better by telling myself that only through the portal of a scent could I apprehend her nature. Jackie herself remains ineffable; all we have are distant approximations, like Jicky by Guerlain, to signify her. I don't insist that Jackie herself smell like Jicky or that Jackie ever have used Jicky. I don't even insist that Jackie have *heard* of Jicky, though I can't imagine that a woman of her era and her cultivation wouldn't be familiar with the names of all the Guerlain line, including L'Heure Bleue, Chant d'Arômes, Vol de Nuit, Chamade, Parure, and Jardins de Bagatelle. Men *and* women wear Jicky. Proust wore it. So did Alice B. Toklas—which makes Jicky akin to a drug, because of Alice B. Toklas hashish brownies. Alice B. Toklas had a conspicuous mustache; it pleases me to imagine that Jackie, paragon of beauty, should be held responsible to the perfume Jicky, with which even homely (yet distinguished) women scent themselves.

Chiclets: the plastic window through which one can see the gum's color (hence, too, the flavor) is like a miniature TV screen, and reminds me of the shape of Jackie's clutch purse. The hard enameled outer layer of the Chiclets pellet, sweet and resistant, gives way to chewy gum; the exterior coat reminds me of an old Cadillac, or of pills. Through "pills" I pass from "Chiclets" to "pillbox hat" and thus to Jackie. Furthermore, I find Jackie in Chiclets because Chiclets are a plain pleasure and an old-fashioned brand of gum, a kind I chew because of nostalgia, no longer because of need. I feel about Jackie much the way I feel about Chiclets: protective, sentimental. The hard coat of a Chiclet cube also reminds me of an icon (I want to spell it, this time, "ikon") and the ikon's resistance to interpretation. Finally, the shape of a Chiclet, tapered at the sides, not absolutely square, reminds me of a movie screen: thus I consider Chiclets to be the gum of stardom and exposure and exhibition.

Petits fours: petits fours are the sort of French dessert (like mille-feuille) that in the 1960s I considered fancy. Petits fours are square, with hard butter-cream frosting and soft tea cake inside, lined with jam. The inside of a petit four isn't a treat; its outside is—for the same reason (hardness, resistance, sheen) that the coat of a Chiclet pleases. I have always liked sugary glazes, and therefore appreciate petits fours, or the idea of petits fours, via the word "glacé," which enters the sphere of Jackie through the kid gloves she wore to the Inaugural Ball, described in one account as "20 button white glacé kid gloves" which successfully avoided "wrinkle or downward sag." The gloves' perfection—no wrinkle, no sag—comes by virtue of the property called "glacé." A second route through which "glacé" and "Jackie" meet, in my imagination, is through the word "chignon." I think of Jackie's classic bouffant as a chignon: the word "chignon" (whose origin is "chain") recalls a kind of glazed cruller shaped like a twist (were they called "glazed twists" or "French twists"?).

Clip-on earrings: enameled, they resemble Chiclets. I can't remember any photos of Jackie wearing clip-on enameled earrings, and yet I associate icon Jackie with the sort of cheap clip-ons one could buy at Woolworth's or at a yard sale. The real Jackie wore expensive earrings (her Apollo 11 earrings, Ari's gift); she wore drop diamonds at occasions and openings, but for ordinary life no earrings at all. She preferred an unornamented look. Clip-on earrings, like Chiclets, are small, button-sized, edible-looking objects with a feminine air, treasures that I associate with an accessibly middle-class life, not with Jackie's upper-class milieu. Clip-on earrings recall the buttons on Jackie's Inauguration coat. I admire buttons because, inanimate but also secretly talkative (they speak to me, are speaking to me now), they live in the periphery of the outfit; one rarely identifies a coat or blouse by its buttons, and yet the buttons may be the outfit's central seduction. Buttons have a use—to fasten. In their modest taciturnity, buttons resemble clip-ons. Clip-ons avoid the pain associated with ear piercing; and yet clip-ons make the earlobe sore, and sometimes infected. The few times I've worn clip-ons I was surprised at the sharp pressure bordering on pain.

There you have it: a reduced list. Jicky, Chiclets, petits fours, clip-ons.

We may try to limit Jackie's significance. We may say that she belongs in one realm of culture but not another. We may agree that she belongs in "Popular Culture" but not in "Religion," that she belongs in "History" but not in "Celestial Bodies," that she belongs in "Washington, D.C." but not in "Hollywood." My experiment in synesthesia means to suggest that Jackie shouldn't be limited to one sense, one subject. She's more than sight, more than "Wife." Jackie enters culture disguised as political wife, as do-nothing celebrity, as beauty, as symbol of mourning. But then she moves on, translated into another element, another vocabulary. As odor may translate, for the synesthete, into color ("See Perfume"), so "Jackie" translates into "mourning," and then into other values, other rewards. Unstable, volatile, she has the power, as image, to go far, because she can't be pigeonholed. She's Jackie; but what is "Jackie"? If you follow her, in your imagination, she will take you miles away from your original destination.

I DON'T USUALLY consider Jackie a "white lady." But stop and note her whiteness. For a moment, say "white Jackie," and wonder to what degree icon Jackie's charm is the lure and gloss of looked-at yet invisible whiteness.

Was icon Jackie white? One straightforward answer: hell, yes. She was a prime exhibit in the whiteness museum. "White" describes not a color but a social position, a placement on the U.S. racial grid. Photos always portray her skin as pale; pallor documents her sanctity. The charmed nature of Jackie's First Lady reign rests on unstated whiteness. To accompany the photo of Jackie in her white gloves and gown stepping through white snow to the Inaugural gala, ready to enter her new life at the White House, a *Life* commemorative offers this white-inflected description: "The first flakes fell around noon on Inauguration eve, and by nighttime the White House was a winter palace. It was clear that Washington would have what no one had been dreaming of—a white Inaugural."

Was icon Jackie white? A second answer: almost, but not entirely. She was scandalously Catholic, hence not WASP; she married Irish. How narrow or how broad is the palette of whiteness? What shades of difference or ethnicity will white accommodate in 1960, in 1970? Frenchness keeps Jackie white, but she loses white sanctity when she marries swarthy Ari, the dark Greek, and moves to an island where her skin, too, darkens (jet-set tan). And yet she was already the daughter of Black Jack. He was called Black because of his year-round tan, his "sheik" exoticism, but it was an italicized, romantic blackness, not the same as occupying the social position of the "black."

Masquerading as the world's whitest lady, Jackie was First Lady in a moment of galvanic change in the racial politics of the United States. Despite JFK's ambivalent relation to civil rights, his era, if not always his policies, represented the first moment of genuine progress since so-called Reconstruction. Jackie emerges as icon at one of the first times in American history when whiteness, as such, might be noticed by whites—rather than taken for granted as privilege's unseen foundation. Paradoxically, when she was widowed, she wore mourning black; she occupies a widow triumvirate with Ethel Kennedy and Coretta Scott King, at least in such commemoratives as 1968's *United in Grief: Three Widows Share Their Sorrow*. (Betty Shabazz, widow of Malcolm X, is absent from this grief-struck tableau.) Sentimentalists may consider the murders of Kennedys and King as part of a single reactionary conspiracy: Oliver Stone's *JFK*, for example, indirectly argues that these three slain leaders were martyrs in the civil rights and anti-imperialist movements, making Jackie, I guess, a bit player in the diorama of African American sorrow and struggle. Certainly this view of Jackie was encouraged when Robert Kennedy persuaded her to attend Martin Luther King's funeral, where Jackie came in her capacity as grief expert, and where the meeting of Coretta and Jackie had great symbolic value, lending Coretta some of Jackie's glamour (turning Coretta into a black Jackie) and lending Jackie some of Coretta's moral force (turning Jackie into a white Coretta), or at least blurring the distinctions between the two assassinations and the two widows.

White Jackie became the Lady in Black when JFK was killed. Her sorrow contradicted her whiteness, as if whiteness and grief were incompatible. An article in a February 1964 *Ebony*, "The Lady in Black: U.S. Negroes look with nostalgia on former First Lady's White House reign," conflates, with the phrase "the lady in black," the black of Jackie's mourning clothes with the black of racial identity. This article suggests a bond between Jackie and many African Americans, asserting that black affection for Jackie "defies analysis. It merely exists." Why? First, because of her sorrow: widowed, she's "the lady in black." Second, because, as the *Ebony* article indicates, "her relationship with Negroes has always been free from that artificial cordiality that characterizes many white political figures' dealings with members of a racial minority group. Always gracious and poised, she would meet Negro guests the way they want to be met—like anyone else—with that same friendliness that endeared her to the world." *Ebony* claims that "more Negroes" were guests at the White House during her "reign" than throughout all the earlier history of the United States; she "simply includ[ed] Negroes on virtually every guest list she prepared," as she insisted that the honor guard accompanying JFK's casket be integrated. (According to Manchester, she said about JFK's assassination: "He didn't even have the satisfaction of being killed for civil rights. It's—it had to be some silly little Communist.") She was honorary chair of *Ebony*'s 1958 Fashion Fair; "she was loved by patois-speaking Louisiana Creoles

when she said, 'Moi, aussi, je suis d'origine française.' "
But what explains the "black affection" for Jackie is,
finally, her "toughness": "Watching Mrs. Kennedy stride
erect behind her dead husband's coffin, one teen-age
Negro girl exclaimed: 'Boy, is she tough!' " Why tough?
Because "she was able to hold her own next to a man as
illustrious as JFK." Maya Angelou, later, would call
Jackie "bodacious," another way of saying "tough."

Jackie's whiteness, though not discussed, grew more
differentiated and textured with time, as did Liz's. America's Two Queens: were they assuredly white? Liz's relation to whiteness had always been ambiguous: though
the roles that established her as an adult lead (including
A *Place in the Sun* and *Rhapsody*) cast her as a rich white
woman of leisure, like Jacqueline Bouvier, Liz's role in
Raintree County highlighted ambiguities in the construc-
tion of her whiteness. In *Raintree*, Liz imagines that she
is the daughter of a slave; from a fire in which her parents
died, Liz saved a doll with a half-melted face, symbol of
Liz's fear (or wishful fantasy) that she is racially "mixed."
Liz's racial marking grew more confused with *Cleopatra*;
her Queen of Egypt is white, I guess, or looks "white,"
but what race *is* Cleopatra? By this time, Liz had converted to Judaism, after marrying Eddie Fisher—this, in
the era of Sammy Davis, Jr.'s conversion to Judaism, and
Sammy's marriage to white May Britt. In my reading of
two decades of *Photoplay*, I've gathered that this era's
most magnetic scandals were the originally adulterous
relation of Liz and Burton, the marriage of Jackie and
Ari, and the "intermarriage" of Sammy Davis and May
Britt. A picture of Jackie and Caroline on the cover of
August 1962's *Photoplay* is juxtaposed with the headlines: MAY & SAMMY DAVIS: "WHY WE'RE ADOPTING

A BABY!" and LIZ BEGGING EDDIE: "COME BACK!"
Here, Jackie and Caroline supposedly represent domesticity and maternity at its whitest and finest, but the
convergence of Jackie with Sammy & May and with Liz
& Burton/Fisher suggests latent complexities in Jackie's
image. Isn't she, like Liz or May, in danger of migrat-
ing away from her impossibly white identity? The same
issue (March 1964) that includes A 12-PAGE SPECIAL
MEMENTO TO KEEP FOREVER: THE COURTSHIP OF
JACK AND JACKIE also features an article on WHAT
CHUBBY CHECKER MUST LEARN FROM SAMMY DAVIS
ABOUT MAKING MIXED MARRIAGE WORK; the
same issue (April 1964) that features Liz and Dick romp-
ing on its cover, and the headline, JACKIE'S LAST PROM-
ISE TO JACK—AND THE PLEDGE SHE MADE
FOR HER CHILDREN'S SAKE, also gives us an
article titled "WHY IS MOMMY WHITE?" SAMMY
DAVIS' ANSWER TO HIS SON. Adjacent scandals are not
necessarily parallel in meaning; but there's something to
learn from the contiguity, in the May 1963 *Photoplay*, for example, of the cover photo of Jackie with
Caroline on her lap (captioned WE FIND JACKIE'S
FORGOTTEN FAMILY) with HOW CRIPPLED IS LIZ
TAYLOR? ALL ABOUT HER LATEST ACCIDENT! and
MAY BRITT: "HOW SAMMY DAVIS CHANGED
ME AS A WOMAN." Just as Liz was subject to accidents
and weight gains and divorce, and May and Sammy
forded the new and difficult waters of "mixed marriage,"
so we were promised that Jackie had a "forgotten family,"
whose sanctity and racial/ethnic/national identity we
might never ascertain, because they were a forgotten
trauma, like the murder of Sebastian Venable that drives
Liz into dementia praecox in *Suddenly, Last Summer*.

As Liz converted to Judaism, so Jackie married a Greek and then, after his death, found a companion in Maurice Tempelsman, a Jew. They never married (his Orthodox wife wouldn't divorce him, the magazines tell us); but relish the dissonant denouement of Jackie with a Jew, of Jewish Jackie (mother of Caroline Kennedy *Schlossberg*)! Though ethnically marked as Catholic, she'd seem the epitome of a white woman whose whiteness was her transcendence, a whiteness that could not be seen but that afforded her privilege as well as purity; but the daughter of Black Jack confounds the platitudes and complacencies of invisible whiteness.

JACKIE'S "I"

I HAVE A COPY of the real Jackie's signature: the big, loopy "J" overcomes space, as if echoing "*Je*," the French "I." Imagine Jackie thinking of herself as an "I." Imagine Jackie speaking of herself in the first person. Imagine Jackie's interiority. To the person who contemplates Jackie, or who looks at pictures of her, she may seem to demonstrate a purely boundaried self, incapable of osmosis. No secret leaves her; no event has the power to stun her. She may seem, in fact, a model of the self-sufficient "I," fortressed, indomitable. Regardless of what we hear about her vulnerabilities or insecurities, she has, as icon, a branded identity, inescapable and only hers: she is Jackie, she has the right to use the first-person pronoun and say, "I am Jackie." This may mean we consider her pigheaded or bossy; or it may mean that we ascribe to her a Buddhist calm. Hypothesis: Jackie's "I" is stronger than and superior to other "I"s, including yours and mine. I don't mean the real Jacqueline Onassis's "I." I mean icon Jackie's "I." Icon Jackie has an "I" of stone or steel. She never becomes someone else; she never stops being Jackie. She is purely, simply herself. As such she may approach tautology ("I am I," "Jackie is Jackie"); tautology's threat is part of her poise. She has become Jackie O; she need go no farther.

This Jackie, with buttressed "I," is a Copernican

Jackie, center of the galaxy; everyone who's met her already recognizes who she is. Never anonymous, she is the "I" that others are dying to know. Everyone introduced to her is subordinated. Even Casals! Even Khrushchev! Even Liza Minnelli! Even Maria Tallchief! Whatever their accomplishments in art or diplomacy, these others must acknowledge Jackie's superior "I"-ness. The others have their own textures, individualities. Jackie has been polished to neutrality. Her edges say "Jackie," nothing more, and she has naught to do to prove she's Jackie.

This, of course, is my fantasy of icon Jackie's sufficiency. The power to induce this fantasy in others is Jackie's principal strength: she inspires us to become more solidly "I," as if in imitation of her. Identification with Jackie, or envy of Jackie, or contemplation of Jackie, engenders sensations of "I" in the spectator or fan. This process of gaining an "I" by contemplating Jackie is complicated, and I will try to explain it slowly.

Best to begin with an example: the rock song "Jackie Onassis" (1980) by Human Sexual Response. "I want to be Jackie Onassis" is the song's pounding refrain. The number's blandness—sung without emotion, by strung-out monotone singers, the words flat—made the desire to be Jackie Onassis seem a dull, ordinary desire. "I want to be Jackie Onassis. / I want to wear a pair of dark sunglasses." "Onassis" and "sunglasses" don't really rhyme. The poor rhyme makes the desire seem either trivial or doomed to fail. The song treats the desire to be Jackie Onassis as laughable, or already passé, or already so common that it can now be parodied. Or else the song is attempting to parody materialism, and overvaluation of celebrity; the song critiques a culture in which the desire to be Jackie Onassis is rampant. My response to the song, when I heard it in 1980, was divided: on the one hand, I too wanted to be Jackie Onassis, so I took the song as a straightforward celebration of this desire. On the other hand, I felt that the song was parodying my desire; that cool young people who listened to this music had healthy historical distance from the craving to be Jackie; that the urge to be Jackie was already part of a previous historical moment, and that this song congratulated those of us who'd successfully transcended that wish. As someone living between the two moments—wanting to be Jackie, also knowing that it was too late to want to be Jackie—I felt comforted *and* undermined by the song.

The title of Mrs. Mini Rhea's memoir, *I Was Jacqueline Kennedy's Dressmaker*, is a variant on the statement "I want to be Jackie Onassis." The declaration "I was Jacqueline Kennedy's dressmaker" implicitly says, "By having been Jackie's dressmaker, *before she was Jackie, before she'd become an icon,* I prove myself a superior being, or I prove myself an 'I,' worthy of writing a memoir." Compare "I was Jacqueline Kennedy's dressmaker" to "I was a teenage werewolf." Both describe recovery from a preceding state of emergency, a crisis that's also a status symbol; both statements imply a strong before/after axis, and suggest that the speaker has now moved on to the paradise of solid identity. But Jacqueline Kennedy's dressmaker isn't exactly a Jackie wannabe. In that category I'd place Jacqueline Susann, not simply because of her first name, or the fact that "Susann" seems an anagram of "Onassis," but also because, in the back-cover portrait of the paperback *Valley of the Dolls*, Jacqueline Susann in white satin evening gown slit up the sides seems striving to be more Jacqueline, to be more like *that other, classier Jacqueline*. This image of Jacqueline Susann has its own cult following: among aficionados of this sort of period piece, it's famous for representing a glamorous woman who is also not very successful at being glamorous—someone who poses as a role model for other Jackie wannabes but still falls short of the more famous Jacqueline. In this category of failed Jacquelines I place Jackie Collins and Jacqueline Bisset —stars who borrow luster from Jackie O but who *fail* at being Jackie.

Many of us spend our lives cruising the line between identities, hoping to cross it; after we cross it, we stay in the other territory as long as we can—a moment, an hour, a week—but then we are glad to return, refreshed, depleted, to our identities. We crave the sensation of losing our "I" location—but not for too long. If we lose the "I" forever we become psychotic, or we enter hell. Contemplating Jackie, I risk disappearance; but it's worth the risk, because the reward is earning glimpses of an "I" so large and central it usually travels under the incognito of "O."

Those of us who spend our lives straddling the fence between identities look for personalities—planets—who seem to represent *the opposite of me*; and to these others, these enigmas, we affix ourselves, hoping to dissolve the line between self and star. In a letter, Keats described this process of self-annihilation in the face of another's personality or aura; he described what it was like to have "no Identity" but to be "continually infor[ming] and filling some other Body"; he said, "When I am in a room with People if I ever am free from speculating on creations of my own brain, then not myself goes home to myself:

but the identity of every one in the room begins to press upon me [so] that I am in a very little time annihilated . . ." To paraphrase Keats: when I think of Jackie, then I am no longer home to myself, but Jackie's identity begins to press upon me so that I am in a very little time annihilated. Keats forgot to say: *and I love it!* The experience of annihilation offers a variegated, freaked joy, for at the cost of momentary vanishing, I get back my body as booby prize: if I step outside of my skin, and think of Jackie, then I'm rewarded by being able to live inside my skin with renewed attentiveness and presence. Jackie may shock me into nonexistence; but then, afterward, when the intoxication of not knowing who is "I" and who is "Jackie" dissipates, I'm *more* of an "I" than I was before, more Jackie-esque (more silent, more hermetically sealed). Contemplating Jackie, I'm asking her image a question: I'm asking her to slide into my consciousness and enlarge it; to colonize me; to undo my borders so that, afterward, they will resemble hers, shut as cells in a honeycomb.

Of course, any star or beloved can induce, in the "I," this sensation of annihilation and expansion, this dizzy impression of losing location by gaining a different "I," an "I" more glacial, complete, and adequate (Emily Dickinson described an experience of spiritual crisis as "The Adequate of Hell"—"Adequate" implying *entire unto itself*, as an aqueduct is equal to the water its walls contain). Any star may induce the "Adequate" sensation; but producing it is icon Jackie's entire job. She's undistracted by other duties. All she must do is symbolize the center of the universe and render you null, so you can then become a *"je,"* imitating "Jackie."

Jackie worship contains a fascistic undertone: it assumes that only Jackie is splendid, that only Jackie deserves adulation. One quickly grows sated with obeisance; and any required or rote obeisance—in the form of state power—is to be abhorred.

But Jackie worship isn't, finally, rote or required or patriotic or goal-oriented. It is a ceaseless spinning-in-place; it is deliriously noncompulsory. And it is instantaneous. The quickness with which you can fill your soul with Jackie is testimony to the icon's efficacy: she can do her job, which is to ionize you, irradiate you, inform you that she is an "I," that she is Jackie—she can do all this merely with a glance (*your* glance). You glance at her; you see that she is, indeed, Jackie; and her work is completed. Jackie looking like Jackie induces your surrender; and only if you surrender do you earn the right to say that you, too, like Jackie, are an "I."

IN A HAUNTING PICTURE, Jackie—the real Jackie Onassis—is flipping through magazines. Her hand reaches into the middle of a stack. On top is *Time*. Its cover features a gun, with the caption: "The Urban Guerillas." The real Jackie knew about guns and guerillas. The real Jackie also knew about representations, a forest, a grove, in which her image lived, fragrant and everlasting. In this photo she's striving for her usual sunglassed anonymity, and yet she also is trapped, bored perhaps, eager for reading materials to while away a plane flight (she's in Heathrow airport). Beside her are marshaled a row of mass-market paperbacks, each title seeming to explain Jackie the icon or at least to explain the culture in which icon Jackie circulated: *The Stud* (by Jackie Collins), *Room at the Top, The Rag Dolls, Pretty Maids All in a Row, Hotel, The Exhibitionist, The Au Pair Boy* . . . I cherish the infinitely human, infinitely pathetic tableau of Jackie, thrill-hungry or tired, cruising the mass-market confections, each paperback (*The Stud, Catch-22*) defining her era and the system of representations which holds her in delirious thrall.

Just as the real Jackie lived under the sway of media representations—relishing them as well as resisting them—so do I know icon Jackie only through media images; therefore my dream Jackie obeys the frazzled

Jackie among the magazines.

contours and tics of typeface and ad and headline and scoop.

Jackie's image appears beside advertisements; so do all news, all stars. But other stars or products or politicians eventually appear to us in a form more material than the ad; for example, we may see an ad for a movie starring Liz Taylor, or a perfume marketed by Liz, but it's possible to watch the movie and buy (or smell) the perfume, and thus obtain an illusion of an unmediated relation to Liz. But because Jackie herself never materializes; because Jackie, unlike a perfume or a movie, never crosses the border of print or photo to approach us, she retains the status of an ad. And therefore we may understand icon Jackie by perusing one of the fan magazines in which Jackie, recidivist, appeared and reappeared, and note the sort of products advertised amid the feature stories and photos. In a representative mid-1960s issue of *Movie Mirror*, the ads cater to housewives, dreamers, and drag queens—to anyone, particularly a woman, who is unsatisfied with her body or life, and therefore seeks marital aids, bust enlargers, diet secrets, negligees ("the undie world of Lili St. Cyr"), depilatories, star glossies, vanishing creams, inflatable female dolls, vibrators, correspondence courses, cellulite removers, harem jamas, "Shape-o-lette" Lycra spandex corsets, height-increase shoe pads, falsies, muumuus, sea monkeys, false fingernails, hormone creams, and wigs, including maxie wig, swept-back flipper, curly-cue s-t-r-e-t-ch wig, and a bippy tail that functions as braid, bun, twist, or dome. These seedy products won't produce the expected results; wigs and falsies can't deceive. The products promise physical transformations (weight loss, breast increase) that aren't easily obtainable; they promise class transformation as well as a renovated body. The relation between icon Jackie and these ads is not merely contiguity: she is not just *next to* ads, she herself functions *as* an ad. For what product is she the ad? For miraculous change of life, and the promise that we will survive—cross over, remain intact—during the breathtaking apocalyptic seam, the instant of conversion and switch-over. In Dallas, Jackie endured such a seam: she remained, miraculously, intact—but also she seemed reborn. She'd arrived at phosphorescent iconicity. Therefore Jackie advertises transformation and the survival of metamorphosis. The kind of transformation that Jackie promises is usually framed in terms of female attractiveness and domesticity, even though the allure of metamorphosis transcends the punishing culture of diets and makeovers.

Consider a recent issue of a tabloid that included on

its cover three headlines in juxtaposition, two referring
to female appearance, and one to Jackie:

FLATTEN YOUR BELLY
IN JUST THREE WEEKS!

For the first time anywhere!
JACKIE'S OWN
HEARTBREAKING
STORY OF DAY
KENNEDY
WAS SHOT

New 10-cent pill
makes varicose
veins disappear.

Looking quickly at the cover, the three separate stories
blend into one pitch: varicose veins, bellies, and Jackie's
widowhood form a single condition which the tabloid
reader possibly shares. Furthermore, the two features surrounding the "Jackie" scoop are not exactly stories: they
are advertisements for new products or techniques—an
exercise regime, a 10-cent pill. Not that readers imagined
Jackie had varicose veins or a big belly; rather, Jackie
epitomized an unreal woman *without* such stigmata.
Her "heartbreak" comes in other departments. The three
stories share futility, pathos: bellies won't be flattened,
varicose veins won't disappear, and Jackie, lockjawed carnival queen of the ephemeral and the indecipherable,
won't confess the heartbreaking story her glossy face, on
the cover, seems to hawk.

The cover was Jackie's proper home. She'd never occupy a subordinate slot. Because her picture always merited cover treatment, her face may seem to live on the cover, as if the cover were an actual and not merely representational space; she herself may seem to *be* a "cover," disguise or alibi. The stories inside rarely live up to the headline's promise: the cover is a tease. Therefore icon Jackie seems a come-on; because the stories won't reveal substantive facts, her face signifies promised, deferred revelation.

These cover photos of Jackie, traditionally cut from other contexts, are cropped to exclude everything but her face, hair, and body. Often the photo won't even include her body. Scissors make life hard for an icon; in a book of Jackie paper dolls, the reader/player is warned, "Do not cut out area between arm and body." Jackie's figure and face in magazines is a form of paper doll; but the artists haven't always been careful to keep Jackie intact. On the cover of *Movie Life*, beside the headline JACKIE: THIS IS MY SUMMER FOR LOVE, there looms Jackie in white above-the-elbow gloves and shoulderless blue formal gown and gold clutch purse, her hair a huge bouffant. Is this image a retouched photograph or a painting? She stands in no genuine space, but simply against the cover's lavender or mauve backdrop. Stranded there, she seems less awake but more aura-filled than if we could see her real surroundings, if we could know that, in the original photo, she'd been surrounded by paparazzi or she'd been window-shopping. These cut-and-paste techniques severely truncate our apprehension of icon Jackie: they render her isolated, autistic. For friends, she has only her own image, and the headlines to which she's juxtaposed. "This is my summer for love," she supposedly says. But, as usual, she's alone, drugged-looking, and arrested either by the confining process of being-turned-into-representation or by her elegant white above-the-elbow gloves, stiff as plaster of Paris casts.

Dada artists and other makers of collages (from Kurt Schwitters to Barbara Kruger) have exploited the techniques of journalistic and advertising cut-and-paste to express disjunction and to present arresting juxtapositions of materials usually segregated from each other (for example, elements of "high" and "low" culture). Because we've seen Jackie's image for over thirty years in cut-and-paste-style tabloids and movie magazines, it's no longer possible to divorce her from the beauties and ambiguities of typeface, of headlines, of cropping, and of unexpected juxtaposition. Jackie seems an inhabitant of a Dada realm where no laws of propriety or logic obtain. By now her face has the power to explain any headline; there is no typographic or narrative situation which her face cannot justify or modify.

These conventions of tabloid juxtaposition create the illusion of *fake (trumped-up) scandal*. And the scandal is announced in a burst, an exclamation—the "scoop." Jackie comes to us on the golden wings of "scoop": weekly she arrives in our consciousness with the exclamatory explosion of

Scoop!
Flesh Photos
of Jackie & Onassis
BIKINI
LOVERS
IN BROAD
DAYLIGHT!

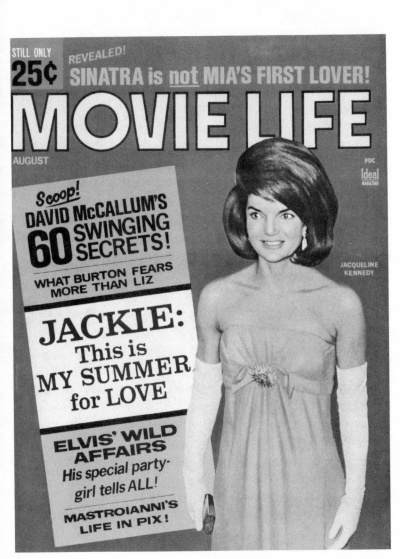

Jackie comes to us in all caps, surrounded by space-savers like ampersands. The ampersand—&—is the sign of illogical conjunction: Jackie & Onassis. And the excitement generated by such a headline may rest not only on its content ("bikini lovers") but on the ecstatic procedures of exclamation, of "scoop!" and of those ampersands and shorthand phrases ("flesh photos") that give the impression of rush, titillation, scandal—a piece of gossip so hot it explodes the frame of the magazine and the story. The scoop breaks open settled categories, confined rules of conduct (don't gain weight, don't commit adultery, don't desire); Jackie is so huge, so antipodal to ordinariness, that she may only be introduced to us via the magic, space-expanding "scoop!"—but the scoop is also the only forum in which Jackie is allowed to live, and so the very speed and breathlessness of the "scoop!" mechanism perpetuates Jackie's claustrophobia.

The headlines in which Jackie is incarcerated are often, when they're most exciting, vertical rather than horizontal; verticality expresses Jackie's scandalousness. The scoop about Jackie has been slimmed into an elongating bodysuit, sticklike and narrow as her own form; or else the scoop has been squeezed in at the last moment, so current is its burden; or else the best gossip (and gossip about Jackie is always "best gossip") must arrive at its own *tempo*, and the headline, by being arranged vertically, scores the words, spaces them out, provides a beat:

> HOW
> HE GOT
> JACKIE
> TO LOVE HIM!
> *Why Jackie wept*
> *when she told*

*the children
about their
new daddy.*

Since we're accustomed to reading horizontally, information that comes to us in vertical guise seems abnormal, extrasensory. The radicality and wildness of the vertical headline—its sudden emergence onto the page—parallels the technique of the paparazzo: as the photographer steals the moment of Jackie visibility, so the "scoop" steals a secret from Jackie's life. The gossip scoop brings us loot straight from Jackie's clutch purse.

In what kind of magazines and books did icon Jackie appear? Sometimes she materialized in magazines that lived on the border of soft porn. For example, a *Jackie Kennedy Onassis* souvenir booklet from the late 1960s was published by a company, "Collectors," that also issued *Peter Pecker, Oral Lust, Seduction of Suzy, Drugged Nurse, Queenie, Skirts, Whips Incorporated, Lesbian Foto-Reader, Adult/Lad Lovers, Punishment Journal, Chaplin vs. Chaplin*, and *True Love Stories of a Wayward Teenager*. In contrast to these lurid titles, children's books about Jackie ostensibly aimed to teach youngsters how to read, or to offer moral uplift. One children's biography of Jackie Kennedy Onassis ("A See and Read Beginning to Read Biography" by Patricia Miles Martin) includes as appendix an alphabetical list of "Key Words," which, read in isolation from any narrative of Jackie's life, show how icon Jackie comes to us as a set of coded, valuable vocables—nuggets of story and image that we can rearrange in our imaginations. Is there only one story to cobble together from this list of "Key Words," or could every reader, every fan, assemble a separate "Jackie" from this cabinet of givens?

actors
beauty
born
carriage
cheer
dead
decided
determined
dignity
divorced
dreamed
elephant
French
gift
gold
grace
guard
hitched
important
Italian
languages
married
mounted
musicians
paperweight
perfect
polished
President
queen
restored
secret
Senator
sleigh

Spanish
speaking
spoke
stirrup
studied

What does this bare list of words imply? That Jackie's life is sufficiently specific—and sufficiently recognizable from a distance—to be limned by an abstract series of particles; that Jackie's story is so generic that if you didn't know this list referred to JBKO, you'd never guess it from seeing the words alone; that Jackie, as icon, is reluctant to submit to the sentence, the clause; that Jackie, as icon, would rather be dreamily free-floating; that Jackie's relation to language is not simple, though the words used to describe her plots are suitable for ten-year-old readers. It's bizarre that there should be a children's bio about Jackie O, since her image epitomizes late 1960s salacious yet safe "adult" pleasures. And yet icon Jackie had the knack of inhabiting the border between porn and pedagogy, and shuttling between the two without blinking: the same picture of Jackie could be a lech's pinup, a patriotic talisman, and the picture that explained a baffling emergency headline.

The ability to rearrange Jackie has made it easy to fictionalize her. Many of us have perceived Jackie, in fact, as *that rich woman whose life, poor thing, we can so easily rearrange.* She appeared, disguised, in *The Widow* by Pierre Rey (1976), whose cover announces, "She was rich, beautiful, and alone . . . again!" She also appeared in *Lady of a Thousand Sorrows*, by Lee W. Mason (1977), whose plot is described, on the jacket, as follows: "Vivien Blanc Sarris must fight for her life. Her first husband, a famous politician slain in the Southwest; her second husband, one of the richest men in the world, dead in the south of France; her sister, a courtesan of royalty—none of them can protect her from inescapable danger now. Out of her past has come that final and terrible secret that may kill her. And in those last desperate days she must find the answer to a conspiracy of madness and evil." And she appears, splendidly, in Jacqueline Susann's posthumous *Dolores* (1976). Most of the book is ellipses. But the ellipses are themselves electric: they partake of breathless haste, of scandals the author hesitates to divulge, and of Jacqueline Susann's excited identification with Jackie O. In *Dolores*, the Jackie character ("Dolo") loves her fame and wants more of it. Dolo's attitude toward photographers: "She pretended to ignore them, but she didn't mind. Her publicity had been flagging lately . . . she had made the cover of only one movie magazine this month. . . ." And Dolo confesses, " 'I read all the fan magazines to keep up with my own publicity.' " To make sense of the novel, the reader must, every time the name "Dolo" appears, silently substitute it with "Jackie." But by the book's end, we finally believe in Dolo as an imaginative creation separate from Jackie O; Dolo, trustee of Jacqueline Susann's wish to be Jacqueline Onassis, proves that icon Jackie is *our desire for her*, that *Dolo equals Jackie* only if we want Jackie badly enough to seek her in *Dolores* and to make all the necessary transpositions. Susann even includes Jacqueline Onassis's name in the text, thereby proving that Dolo is *not* Jackie: Dolo thinks, in a rapturous moment of interior monologue, "Jacqueline Onassis was already established 'news' like Elizabeth Taylor. Now, *she*, Dolores Ryan, was the new glamour girl of the world." Through the mouthpiece of Dolo, Jacqueline Susann dreams of surmounting her idol; the reader dreams along with the author, imagining the existence of a Dolo who tops Jackie O. Consider every media photo of Jackie O as a representation of Dolo: Dolo is our "inner Jackie," the Jackie under our skin. Susann's own hostility toward Dolo is patent, however, and suggests what short shrift we give our inner Jackies. Dolo looks in the mirror: "She turned around . . . her fanny was getting a little loose . . . had it dropped . . . or was it her imagination?" Dolo's fanny is loose because she is purely imaginary; thus her connection to Jackie and to selfhood vacillates, droops, loosens. Like Jekyll spontaneously turning back into Hyde, sans potion, Dolo's imaginary identification with Jackie O is wearing out; atavism shows up first in the telltale sagging butt. As a consequence, Dolo has no pride and no sexuality. As she anticipates her wedding night to the Baron (the Ari character), poor Dolo thinks, "Oh God . . . tomorrow night this body would be his . . . to maul . . . to take. She could almost feel his lips slobbering on her." Dolo finally emerges not as glamour dominatrix, but as self-hating drudge.

Dolo represents an imaginary rapprochement between Jacqueline Susann and Jackie O; the fan magazines periodically staged similar reunions by inviting readers to comment on Jackie's conduct. After printing Reverend Ray's denunciation of Jackie (he accused her of behaving like a "pinup girl"), *Photoplay* asked its readers: "Has Jackie gone too far—or has Reverend Ray? Be the judge! VOTE NOW!" The two choices are: "The criticism of Jackie is fair" and "The criticism of Jackie is unfair." Another *Photoplay* poll asked readers if they thought Jackie should "(Check one) Devote her life exclusively to her children and the memory of her husband," or "Begin to date—privately or publicly—and eventually remarry," or "Marry right away." Later in the decade, a *Photoplay* poll allowed readers to choose Jackie's second wedding dress. Such polls created virtual Jackie, an interactive medium: one did not merely love, envy, or disapprove of Jackie, one voted on her conduct, as if the real Jackie, once apprised of the poll's result, would be moved to act in accordance with the consensus of *Photoplay* readers.

Beyond voting in Jackie Kennedy polls, the most interaction a reader could have with virtual Jackie was to compose a Jackie scrapbook, as the Michelle Pfeiffer character in *Love Field* does. The layout of a scrapbook, cut-and-pasted from clippings, mirrors the bricolage of the fanzines, and represents Jackie, therefore, as a dissonant mélange of photos and texts, never adding up to a consistent or true-to-life image.

The Jackie scrapbook, an act of homage, is a mimesis, or imitation, of a Hollywood fan magazine; it is not a mimesis of Jackie. The scrapbook is a melancholy genre; although it tries to perform a certain sympathetic magic, reanimating the scattered limbs and fragments of its subject, it knows it can't change the future or mend the past. And yet the surface rhythm of a scrapbook is jazzy juxtaposition, the pieces syncopated with a hectic optimism. The scrapbook hubristically proposes—like the horoscopes which are a staple of the fan magazine and which often include predictions about what the stars (including Jackie) will be doing in the New Year—to conjure a universe of certainties, in which even the tragedies occupy a predestined and therefore comprehensible slot. One unusual volume, *An Astroanalysis of Jacqueline*

Onassis (1970), by Marcia Moore and Mark Douglas, attempts to find the divine plan in Jackie's life. To do so, it must plot the horoscopes of every personage who influenced her—an odd bunch, including Maria Callas, Mary Jo Kopechne, and Sirhan Sirhan. For all its quackiness, this astroanalysis ultimately reveals a mission parallel to the scrapbook's: to *meet* Jackie. The authors say: "The selection of Jacqueline Onassis as the principal subject for this book was dictated less by the desire to augment 'the Jackie cult' than by the practical advantage of having an abundance of published source material which could be used to corroborate the basic horoscope of someone we have never met. Nevertheless, the fact that she is a beautiful and celebrated woman enlivened the task, and we are grateful to Jacqueline for her warm, magnetic personality which has made it a pleasure to know her in this vicarious way." How do the authors of the astroanalysis know that Jackie is warm?

Thus the media representations of icon Jackie convince us that we have befriended her; that she is warm to us; that the conventions of typeface, gossip scoop, photo cropping, irregular juxtaposition, and hyperbole in which her image and life story come clothed, express her personality. Her recurrence in headlines may strike us like repeated greetings from an old friend. Take, for example, the headline: JACKIE'S MIRACLE DREAM—"WE'LL MEET AGAIN!" Her miracle dream is that she'll meet JFK again. Jackie and JFK were always reuniting, for according to tabloids, JFK was not really dead, but was living on an island or a secluded estate, and was periodically visited by Jackie, who'd chat with him about old times. Apparently, they covered a lot of ground: conversations branched out to include talk about Marilyn and

Ari. The photo caption: "As a Secret Service agent stands guard, former First Lady Jackie Kennedy Onassis kneels at the side of the crippled ex-President." Jackie's reiteration in headlines, like déjà vu, or a flashback, blurs the line between reality and dream, between original event and reenactment; the media have staged a miracle dream in which Jackie and I—Jackie and you—meet again and again. If only we could coincide, and blend into one ("as the rose / Blendeth its odour with the violet," warbled Keats), then the meeting would not require restaging.

JACKIE AND APOCALYPSE

AT AN INAUGURAL GALA, JFK said, "Turn on the lights so they can see Jackie." Though her political importance to JFK lay in her identity as *seen* woman, her presence did not merely serve as decoration for JFK; symbolically, she stood close to the apocalypse over which JFK had actual control. As a nuclear weapon exploded over Bikini atoll was emblazoned with an image of Rita Hayworth, so did the U.S.'s Cold War, in its Kennedy phase, wear images of Jackie.

Historians may establish that JFK took Jackie's advice seriously, or that she had more knowledge of state matters than the press, at the time, conveyed. Regardless of whether or not Jackie had concrete political power, Jackie *as image* seemed the one who impeccably knew about the bomb, who disguised (from us) the bomb's truth and immanence, and who would make the bomb seem a beautiful, necessary addendum to our house. Was Jackie a bombshell? Jackie stood in relation to Cold War state power as Marilyn stood in relation to the Mob.

Mostly Jackie seemed not to know what was going on. That itself was comforting: if Jackie was innocent, and merely domestic, then perhaps JFK was in control. And yet, like the figure of the innocent child on the verge of corruption in Henry James's *What Maisie Knew*, Jackie's silence did not signify consent or confusion: rather, knowledge bruised the taciturn woman standing next to the President. What did Jackie know? Too much. If enforced separation from politics should have ensured Jackie's remoteness from apocalyptic knowledge (knowledge of how to set off the bomb, knowledge of how close we stood to annihilation), in fact her photogenic poise implied, as bomb shelters in American homes implied, that death and danger were deposited deeply within domesticity's foundation; that Jackie, as wife, as bombshell, had taken the Cold War to heart, and that she was being silent *on behalf of the state,* silent *because she knew too much to speak safely,* silent *because what lay beneath her "surface" beauty was classified information, dangerous if leaked.*

The danger of Jackie was contained by her silence and by photography's sure borders and boundaries: she'd never exceed the frame of the photo, she'd never actually enter your living room. Purely image, she could set off in the viewer a mock apocalypse (the "big bang" of realizing Jackie's supremacy, of realizing that "I" am annihilated because "Jackie" is superior); but all the emotions she set off in spectators fled from her in diaspora, and she herself, like a cartoon with impermeable outer edge, never exploded and never changed, remaining her own steady city-state, perfectly garrisoned.

Two anecdotes convey Jackie's paradoxical friendship with apocalypse. Allegedly she once said to the White House usher, "Mr. West, will you take me to the bomb shelter?" The line suggests Jackie's naïveté about apocalypse. She doesn't know where the bomb shelter is; she can't rely on JFK to show it to her, but turns to the usher; she doesn't ask to see the bomb-code-containing briefcase, but wants to see the shelter, where women and children hide from the havoc that men wreak. This anecdote demonstrates Jackie's ladylike, practical take on power and destruction: formally calling the usher "Mr. West," she inquires about apocalypse while seeming merely to ask about a housekeeping detail ("Mr. West, will you take me to the Blue Room?"). The bomb, and the bomb shelter, were parts of Jackie's White House; even if she had power only over the House, the presence of a bomb shelter inside her House shows apocalypse folded into the portfolio of her responsibilities and her exquisiteness. I daren't guess how much Jackie knew during the Cuban Missile Crisis (various accounts mention Jackie's curiosity about the "flow of power" and the Pentagon); but I intuit that crisis and missiles and apocalypse remained her symbolic companions, even if her physical and sartorial perfection seemed to banish danger.

A later anecdote: one of Ari's servants reportedly quipped about Jackie that "she looked like the kind of lady who would keep a manicure appointment on the morning of Armageddon." What does this mean? That Jackie O only cares about her appearance; that she's indifferent to apocalypse. Jackie *knows* that Armageddon is about to happen. How else could she be blamed for ignoring it? Privy to Armageddon's imminence, she doesn't care; she proceeds with her beauty business. The same stoicism and indomitability that earned plaudits in November 1963 gets reinterpreted, in this quip, as indifference to doom and danger. Is Jackie immune to annihilation? Will she be spared? She already knows about the bomb, but believes that it won't harm her, or else she reasons that amid catastrophe she needs to retain a grip on appearances. Assassination, Armageddon: Jackie stays manicured during catastrophic detonations. The quip indicts Jackie for shallowness: instead of trying to avert Armageddon (is this in her control?), she focuses on inessentials, such as personal grooming. Jackie's usefulness, as icon, is that she confuses the dogmatic opposition between inessentials and essentials; she summed up apocalypse's deferral (and its nearness), because she seemed always to keep up appearances, because she survived JFK's murder, and because she seemed the opposite of politics. "We're safe from the bomb, because Jackie's still here," we might think. Or, alternately, "Jackie looks glazed and composed because a prefiguring of apocalypse—the photographer's flash—arrests her; and because she knows she can't avert the explosion, she smiles and tries to hide from us her dire knowledge."

When Jackie Kennedy christened a Polaris submarine, in Groton, Connecticut, and whispered "Je te baptise le Lafayette," the news programs of the time did not entirely explain the purpose of the Polaris. Instead, they showed Jackie, in white gloves, shaking hands with the men who launched the ship. The red roses she holds and gives to the men foreshadow the red roses that she'll leave in the car after the assassination. The newscaster says, "With each handshake is born a story that will be told time and time again." The story of the Polaris becomes the story of Jackie's white-gloved hand: the story's repeatability ("told time and time again") belies the one-time horror of the bomb. The bomb drops once. Jackie drops into our lives again and again—through headlines, rumors, and sentimental keepsakes; her reiterability comforts, compared to the final singularity of the Polaris.

For Jackie's fortieth birthday, Ari gave her a pair of earrings to commemorate the Apollo 11 moon walk. JFK's imperially intergalactic ambitions: where do they end? As two moons, hanging from Jackie's earlobes. Jackie is like our own Armageddon earring: dear symbol, we wear her as decoration. What she symbolizes may be huge as the moon, or dangerous as atomic war; she's global, explosive, and cold. Worn in the form of a jeweled pendant, she rotates like a lit disco ball of mirrors above a dancing crowd. When we inhabit a memory of Jackie or contemplate her image, we're *wearing* her, as one wears a bauble; as her moon-walk earrings commemorate and neutralize an event fraught with imperial and eco-logically devastating ambitions, so do the explosions we've lived fifty years in mortal fear of (a fear we've repressed) find expression in a quiet icon like Jackie, whose indifference to this afternoon's Armageddon (she's too busy with her manicure) mimics our own denial.

JACKIE AND DURATION

HOW LONG DOES icon Jackie take? What is her image's duration? How does she affect our sense of time? Does she contract time, or suspend it?

Religious historian Mircea Eliade theorized two realms of duration—sacred and profane time. When we contemplate Jackie, we inhabit a species of sacred time, even if its contours are described by no recognized faith. When you inhabit sacred time, you're not merely living in a repetition, a mimicry, or a restaging of an origin. Rather, you're actually taking part in that first instant. For example, when a Catholic takes Communion, she's not eating a simulacrum or a mere symbol of Christ's body; she's actually consuming the Lord. To rephrase this scene in the secular terms of Jackie worship: when I contemplate a photo of Jackie, I'm not looking at just another representation of Jackie. Rather, the Jackie Moment is always the same instant, which patiently waits for me to revisit it.

It is difficult to speak about Jackie without resorting to a sort of private language based on words that she has used; I am so hermetically contained by the perimeters of Jackie contemplation that I can only point to Jackie, and interpret her, from within the circle of terms that originate with her. One example is the French word *durée*, even though I have no proof that she ever used it. Jackie once said, "I have an absolute mania now about learning to speak French perfectly"; I have an absolute mania about discovering the dimensions of Jackie's *durée*, and for placing Jackie worship and Jackie gossip within a French-tinged metaphysical and poetic scheme. I have an absolute mania for wondering how long Jackie's instant endures. Why the word *durée*? Because it sounds like the artist Gustave Doré, and thus it takes an abstract term that might hurt ("duration") or even evoke imprisonment (the "duration" of a prison sentence) and sugars it, turning it into a quixotic pleasure chamber, much as the secret presence of "Bouvier" within Jackie's official "Kennedy" character encourages me to believe that time, for Jackie, isn't linear, but that naughty and French aspects of her Bouvier years hide within the state-sanctioned Kennedy incarnation. Do I make myself clear? A second word with Jackie associations, this time a colloquial American word rather than a philosophically perfumed French word, is "clink." A fan magazine proposes that Jackie once said to Ron Galella, "I thought you finally got to the clink." Jackie's (imaginary?) use of the word "clink," which recalls the argot of gangsters, as heard in Warner Brothers movies from the 1930s (one can imagine Barbara Stanwyck derisively using the word "clink"), inspires me to suggest that Jackie, in photographs, occupies duration (*durée*) as if time were a *clink*. Jackie is locked within the moment's "clink" by the "click" of the photographer's camera.

To understand how Jackie is locked in a timeless instant's "clink," consider a photograph of Jackie, newly Mrs. Onassis, in a limo. There are countless similar pictures—variations on a theme. The proliferation of pictures of Jackie O in a limo arrests her in time; all the limo pictures take place in the same limbo moment. Therefore in retaliation against her cruel mistreatment at time's hands, she stops the spectator's clock. Time, when Jackie steps out of the limo, freezes. It's doubly frozen because Jackie's eyes are covered by bubble sunglasses, so she can't see the viewer; shades protect her from the instant's bright "click," as if the eye-endangered, or the blind, experience time's movement differently. I'm looking at a 1968 photo of Jackie O, and it's a poor reproduction. The poverty of the repro limits Jackie's temporal mobility; the black of her sunglasses blends with her black hair, the black limo windows, the black purse, and this cramped continuum of visual stimuli makes Jackie a victim of stopped time, but also herself a crafty agent of time's stopping.

Jackie, as icon, baffles chronology not simply because she seems, in photographs, arrested. She evades the clock and the calendar because we can't box her into a single historical moment, even though the "O" of her nickname strives to be a straitjacket. Either because of face lifts, or because of a fashion sense often praised as "timeless," or because of her preference for older men, Jackie often seemed the same age that she'd always been. Like most stars, an important aspect of her myth was visual stability: as Liz must always look like Liz in order to be Liz, so Jackie must look like Jackie in order to be Jackie. Dying at sixty-four, before age radically changed her, she never stopped looking familiar, and so the instant of Jackie recognition always seemed identical to last year's instant, and the year before's; the *durée* of Jackie O, then, was a room one reentered upon each resighting. Jackie O's time had never progressed; each revisitation of Jackie O was a return to the same, unchanged time zone, Jackie's O Zone, where it is always zero o'clock.

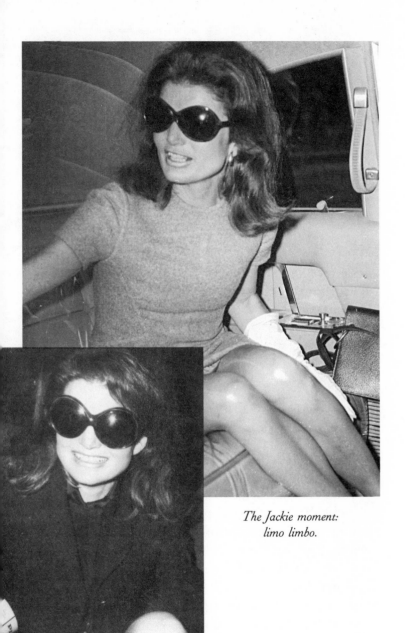

The Jackie moment:
limo limbo.

Inevitably a glance at Jackie is a backwards glance: she's retro. She became retro in 1963: *Life*, reporting on Jackie after the assassination, noted, "friends find her almost always in a reminiscent mood," and Billy Baldwin quotes Jackie as saying, "There's something so final and passé about it." She's positioned to the rear of us; to invoke "Jackie" or "Jackie O" was (until her death) at once to acknowledge an uncanny survivor, someone who'd managed to persist *to this day*, still contemporary, as it was to acknowledge a bygone actress in a vanished scene. Again, from the treasure chest of Jackie trivia, I draw out two quotations. The following couplet, from a poem by Jacqueline Bouvier (published in *One Special Summer*), seems to speak of her own position as a woman caught in limbo, an icon whose relation to dead Jack keeps her always provocatively stuck in a lapsed, vanished moment. In the poem, she

> *Danced a quadrille with the Jack of Spades*
> *Waltzed down the shadows of long arcades. . . .*

It's uncanny to hear Jackie speak of herself dancing with a card-game Jack (Black Jack? Jack Kennedy?), a quadrille happening in time but also apart from time (among the "shadows of long arcades," duration can't be too precisely measured). A second quotation: later in the decade, married to JFK, campaigning with him in Kenosha, Wisconsin, Jackie said, over a supermarket loudspeaker, "Just keep on with your shopping while I tell you about my husband, John F. Kennedy." It's likely that some shoppers didn't yet know who JFK was; if they paid any attention to the voice over the loudspeaker, it might have been because the voice seemed breathless, out of place

—having no relation to the aisles and the practicalities (Cheerios? Quaker Oats?) it floated over. I picture the shoppers keeping on with their shopping, while Jackie, not yet an icon, tells them about JFK. Why does this anecdote provoke in me a sense that Jackie occupied sacred or suspended time? Because she inhabits several degrees of time at the same instant, and these various, disjunct registers collide, making Jackie seem to exist in a temporal limbo. First, there's the time of the shoppers, who obey their own mundane and not-famous clocks. Second, there's the time of not-yet-famous Jackie, speaking to shoppers. Third, there's the *separation* between her voice over the intercom (as heard by shoppers) and her voice in her body, as she experiences it, a separation which initiates a split in time (microphone time versus actual bodily time). Fourth, retrospectively we know that Jackie would become the sort of legend who'd never make cameo appearances in Kenosha grocery stores; but here, magically, she's blessing shoppers of every era, blessing the activity—consumption—with which, as Jackie O, she'd be associated. Finally, there's *my* time, here, remembering Jackie, and noting that once she was located in time, in Kenosha, her voice on an intercom. Sacred? Only if a disruption in the fabric of experience is sacred—and if the figure who provokes that disruption, and who rides serenely and transcendentally over it, may be accorded a position of sacredness, because she has the freedom to exist in a specific, bounded moment, but also to soar above it, and inhabit other, far-flung instants.

All I know of Jackie are photographs and anecdotes; "Jackie" lives for me amid the long arcade of shadows formed by stories and images that prove nothing in particular and that have no inexorable hold on any single truth, but that combine willy-nilly. The main reason that Jackie rises above familiar, profane temporal dimensions is that we've moved on, in time, since 1963, but our image of Jackie hasn't entirely. When we plot our lifeline against hers, she seems fixed, while we accord ourselves mobility; this presupposition of her fixity allows us experimentally to arrest our own time clock, when we think of Jackie, as if this moment of sympathetic seizure or time arrest were homage; as if I were saying to her, "Jackie, because you're stuck in 1963, or because you're stuck in a photo, unable to leave the limo, unable to leave the 'clink' of Jackie O *durée*, I'll enter jail with you." I visit Jackie in November 1963's or the limo's clink, or any clink that a photo traps her in; I stop my own movement ahead in time because I want to experience life from her halted vantage point. The camera freezes her. I enter the frozen Jackie moment to befriend her and because that arrested instant looks familiar; I've lived in chronology but also apart from it, and "Jackie" is a technique for experimentally reformatting time, making it stop and then go. Jackie O seems to know more about time's vagaries than we do. Time's stopped on Skorpios (because we've never seen it), just as time's stopped on Air Force One, or in the White House, because there are no lifelike accounts of what went on in its rooms.

ALONG WITH SACRED TIME, there's sacred space. Jackie tears space asunder, as Moses parted the Red Sea. Space divides around her gaze and her form. Jackie cleaves space; trajectory, she moves forward into the photo's foreground, toward us. Other elements—landscape, JFK—recede. The speed and sureness with which she dominates a photo—moves forward as if *out* of its box —has the force of supplication.

In *Camera Lucida*, Roland Barthes speculates that each photograph holds a "studium" and a "punctum." The studium is the background. The punctum is that detail which rivets the viewer and announces itself as foreground; the punctum pricks the spectator, solicits sympathy, tenderness, fear. The punctum is that aspect of a photo to which we can't remain indifferent. Viewers might vary in their assessment of which detail constitutes a photo's punctum, for choosing the punctum is a subjective business.

But it's plausible to conjecture that in most photos including Jackie, she is the punctum; space organizes around her face. She pricks us because she's the most famous person in any photo, and so everything, compared to her, becomes background to her urgent foreground. She disorganizes the 2-D flatness of a photo; a photo becomes 3-D when it contains Jackie, because

Jackie pushes against the fourth wall. Or we push against it—push against the transparent window of the photo, hoping to become part of its festival.

Jackie's knack of hurtling forward out of a photo, rendering it 3-D, was noticed by Charles Spalding. Calling her an *"immense* woman, I mean, bigger than anyone knows,"* he suggested that one could measure her power in the visual sphere by replacing Jackie with someone else, in a photo of JFK and Jackie together, and noticing how JFK loses luster without his mate. Replace JFK, however, and Jackie still looks laden with aura. We're now accustomed to seeing Jackie without JFK, since she survived him, but even before 1963, photographs knew to compose themselves around her.

In photos of JFK and Jackie together, JFK often stares sideways into the distance, while Jackie looks directly at the viewer. JFK seems sleepy; notice the bags beneath his eyes. Jackie seems in a trance, too, but more *present* than JFK. History and ideals preoccupy the President, while tangibles of the present hour consume his wife. News footage registers the difference between Jackie's direct and JFK's indirect gaze; on TV's White House Tour, Jackie looks straight at the viewer, while JFK's eyes move skittishly around. She looks directly at him, too, while he seems almost to ignore her.

In a *Life* cover ("Jackie Kennedy: A Front Runner's Appealing Wife," August 24, 1959), Jackie in fuchsia lives in the upstage part of the picture, while Jack, blurred, in a dark suit, sits in the backward distance, already part of Jackie's historical drop cloth, as if he were merely a mural or rare fragment of wallpaper she were posed in front of. Or: on a souvenir ashtray picturing JFK and Jackie, she sits in the foreground, in a chair, while he stands behind it, his body tiny and foreshortened. Women are permitted bright colors; men of JFK's ilk wore dark suits. Therefore Jackie's clothes assist her forward movement in color photographs. And yet the same effect is apparent in black-and-white. Jackie's ability to upstage is more than just a consequence of lipstick and a pink dress; her domination of the photographic space seems a result of her personal charisma, her unusual face (with its wide-set eyes and cheekbones and dark helmet of hair), and of her commodification—so that, looking at photos including Jackie, we're caught in a vicious circle of *already recognizing Jackie*, a cycle that every new picture reinforces, encouraging us to murmur, "Oh, yes, there's Jackie again." JFK, too, is commodified, recognizable. But we know so much *less* about Jackie than about JFK, and a concern for such authoritative matters as *history* or *politics* can't legitimize our dishy curiosity about her. And so, in pictures, Jackie seems to match her commodity status, not exceed it; this tight fit between *real* Jackie and *icon* Jackie gives her an extra ability to hurtle forward, unimpeded by sag or lag. The other reason that Jackie dominates photos is that pictures of JFK and Jackie, when we look back at them after 1963, are rearranged by our knowledge of Jack's imminent death. Jackie's ability to upstage JFK in a photo becomes a figure for her feat of having transcended and outlived him.

I suppose it must be possible to look at a photo of JFK and Jackie together and value JFK more than Jackie— to perceive him as the punctum, the focal point. But I can't imagine such a sighting.

A photo which reveals Jackie at the climax of her ability to efface JFK was taken at Washington's Union Station, as JFK and Jackie arrived to greet Morocco's King Hassan.

The photo, in its incarnation as frontispiece to Mary Van Rensselaer Thayer's *Jacqueline Kennedy: The White House Years*, has been cropped, so that we see only Jackie and JFK. Jackie's enormous hat blocks most of his face. It might not even be JFK behind her; it could be any man in a suit, any man whose head Jackie's hat has the ingenuity and flair to erase. In the uncropped version of this photo, JFK (or the man who seems to be JFK) is talking with another man—some American official? When she's seen in the entire photo's context, Jackie seems mildly askew—set off, like a spinning top, on her own, slant orbit. Whether or not the photo's actually cropped, I crop it in my head, to remove everything but Jackie; I see Jackie always as if in close-up. Seized by her face, I ignore all peripherals. The history of Jackie as a visual phenomenon has been a movement toward the close-up, toward the cropped photo: everything near her has been neutralized, deprived of gravity. Even without the sympathetic fan's cooperating gaze, she made everything around her vanish.

In an Inauguration article on the new First Lady, *Time* noted that "her political role is mostly visual." (Reverse the statement: "her visual role is mostly political.") Of course JFK had the genuine power; Jackie released the fake fizz of a make-believe cocktail. And yet in photos she seems to declare spatial hierarchies invalid. By dominating her circumstances in the visual realm, she seems to rule in other spheres, too.

In a photo of Jackie in India, watching a cobra attack a mongoose, she's upstaged by the cobra and by the novel spectacle of her own terror. Or is it mock terror, a finishing-school feint? In jodhpurs, next to Lee in a print dress, Jackie looks deflated, ordinary. Does Jackie's

*Upstaging the President: Jackie's movement
toward the close-up.*

fear here, and the subsequent diminishment of her aura, suggest that Jackie's power in photos stems from our perception of her as fearless? Does her ability, when photographed, to seize the viewer rest on a misconception of Jackie as someone beyond fear and trembling? In any case, we've all been trained, by years of looking at Jackie in the media, to isolate her from her surroundings, and to imagine her as the center of all preoccupation, and to imagine her power to expand, enlarge. We look at her, then, as someone out-of-scale; a person unnaturally magnified. No circumstance or partner can diminish her.

Statement A: *I see Jackie*. But identification with Jackie increases apace, and I inch toward Statement B, a question: *What does Jackie see?* Looking at icon Jackie, I try to imagine *being* Jackie, looking *with her eyes* at the wide world of inexplicable, misty phenomena—whether cobras or kings. She moves into the photographic foreground because that's where her speedy gaze zooms. Even in a JFK funeral photo of Jackie behind a veil, her gaze travels outward, toward the middle distance. If Jackie cleaves space, and seems, like a superhero, to jump *out* of the photo, it's her gaze that's catapulting beyond the frame. If JFK seemed in pictures to be facing posterity, Jackie seems to be scrying the horizon for a beckoning transcendence, about to announce itself. Or else it seems she's just looking in a far-off mirror, and is entranced by what she sees.

JACKIE'S SUBLIMITY

EDMUND BURKE defined the sublime, in his *Philosophical Inquiry into the Origin of Our Ideas of the Sublime and Beautiful* (1757), as containing an admixture of terror. A sublime object or person or idea must be obscure: we must not know from whence it originates. A sublime phenomenon must be vaguely limned, invisible: God, or a goblin, is sublime, because we can't know when it has definitively entered the room. A sublime phenomenon must be dangerous: the ocean is sublime because we might drown in it. A sublimity must be powerful: it must have the strength to subdue us, even if we don't know we're being subdued. Sovereigns are sublime, because they inspire dread. Does the sublime bring pleasure? Yes: the joy of diminishment and self-annihilation. "If we rejoice, we rejoice with trembling," writes Burke. We "shudder" at the power of the sublime, which eclipses our small nature, and astonishes us. Earlier, I described Jackie in photographs as looking astonished, and suggested that we, perceiving her astonishment, mimic it. This astonishment is a prime characteristic of the sublime, as Burke writes: "The passion caused by the great and sublime in *nature*, when those causes operate most powerfully, is astonishment: and astonishment is that state of the soul in which all its motions are suspended with some degree of horror. In this case the mind is so entirely filled with its object that it cannot entertain any other. . . . Hence arises the great power of the sublime, that, far from being produced by them, it anticipates our reasonings and hurries us on by an irresistible force."

Jackie is not an object of nature. She is not an ocean or a canyon. Nor is she an art object, contrived to represent an ocean or a canyon. And yet, because we encounter her as *image*, she has the power of the object, and the natural phenomenon, to strike us with sensations of sublimity.

Icon Jackie induces effects of sublimity in spectators and contemplators—or she seems, herself, sublime—because in Dallas she became the seam linking two entirely detached temporal realms: the JFK administration and its afterward. One moment she was present with live JFK; the next moment, he was dead, and time had progressed, with only Jackie present to be liaison between the epochs. Jackie's sublimity resides in her position as presiding officer over this quick switch between day and night, between one world and the next. Equally sublime are the contrasts in *emotion* as well as in *period* that Jackie embodied: her ability to disguise shock and sorrow, and metamorphose these emotions into a waxen poise that itself seemed a form of glamour, made Jackie the home of impossible opposites. And when antitheses meet, in a single instant, in a single body, the clash provokes the sublime.

After Dallas, Jackie always had reason to be afraid. But because fear never showed on her face in photos, Jackie's trick of topping fear with a mask of beauty seemed sublime. We could imagine her secret fear, but always our conception of her terror was left hand to the right hand of her beauty.

Jackie's readiness to party, to be gay, to remarry, to lead a normal life: her ability to move on with existence seemed sublime, because it allowed the spectator to imagine Jackie making another improbable transition between moods usually portrayed as starkly opposite. Just as, in Dallas, she in one instant fell from clean wife to blood-stained widow, so after her official year of mourning ended she seemed to leap from mourner to swinger. A headline teased: REVEALED! NOW IT CAN BE TOLD! HOW JACKIE WENT FROM . . . MOURNER TO SWINGER. There was no interregnum, no transition. Mourner turned instantly into swinger; and our perception of emotional opposites (mourning, swinging) co-habiting one body, Jackie's, catalyzed sublimity.

Sublime, too, was Jackie's quick movement between echelons. Her presence in movie magazines was incongruous; her intrinsic royalty, when contrasted to the "sleazy" nature of *Screen Stories*, caused the spectator to shudder. Grand Jackie juxtaposed with mundane Dorothy Malone (DOROTHY MALONE—JACKIE KENNEDY: THE SECRET HEARTBREAK AND HAPPINESS THEY SHARE) meant that Jackie's magnitude was in partial eclipse, in hiding, and that it might suddenly reemerge, to ambush the dreamer, who thought, for a moment, that Jackie was as small as Dorothy Malone. The instability and unverifiability of Jackie's "greatness" made her more sublime than a solidly "great" lady could ever be: if she was always on the verge of trash, her greatness and superbness had repeated opportunities to rise to the surface and surprise the spectator, who might have forgotten Jackie's value. To be reminded of a dissipated value; to be stunned, again, by a luminousness that had seemed in permanent eclipse: these are sublime instants, even if they happen internally, and have no documented reality, but are merely progress reports in the ongoing relation between an abstract star and one of her numberless subjects.

Sublimity comes from our own eclipse at the hands of Jackie; our vanishing makes Jackie sublime. We vanish because we identify so strongly with her that she seems vested with greater substance than we ourselves possess. And we vanish because she seems more important—more famous, more beautiful, more historic—than we are. Why are we afraid when we contemplate Jackie? We are afraid because we've disappeared. We are afraid on her behalf: sympathetic fear. (Will Jackie be okay? Will Jackie be safe?) And we are afraid because the shape and stability of a personality are no longer self-evident; facing the enigma of Jackie, we can't know for certain what it means to be *here*, to reside in a present instant, to inhabit a body. Jackie's air of being *not here*, combined with a face and style we can't confuse with anyone else's, helps us realize that a person need not always be present to herself; that an identity may be an absence; that absence may be the beginning of glamour. Jackie is glamorous because she seems not thoroughly here. And if we must excuse ourselves from presence, too, in order to identify with Jackie's not-hereness, we will gladly do so, for glamour is the goal, and even taking the route of annihilation is worthwhile and pleasurable if the destination and reward is Jackie.

At the assassination, Jackie sprang to illicit life. Her sublimity began at the moment of JFK's murder. At that instant we identified with her (or in retrospect, reliving Dallas, we sympathize with her, and imagine the event from her point of view); the experience of identifying-with-Jackie-at-Dallas transported Jackie under our skin. Suddenly we felt her terror, as if it were ours; suddenly we saw the earlier, pre-assassination Jackie as forever remote from this new, bloodied, widowed Jackie. That no one, looking at prior photos of Jackie, would ever have been able to predict Dallas's extremity made "early Jackie" seem sublime, too, because "tragic Jackie" was always about to cast its shadow over her former tranquillity, and ruin it.

It's possible to identify with many public figures. But identification rarely happens as instantaneously, or as collectively, as on November 22, 1963, when "we" identified with Jackie, and therefore she migrated under our skin. Her dispersion among millions of bodies made her sublime, as did her resistance to this dispersion, her evident reluctance to be the subject of identification. Jackie's presence in our systems of thought and fantasy strikes me as sublime because Jackie, as a person, belonged in her own body, but she "chose," as icon, to travel beyond her skin into mine. Her ability to migrate becomes another foundation for identification and yearning; I imagine what it would be like to exit my body and move into someone else's thoughts. And I grow uncertain whether it is I who've migrated into icon Jackie or whether she has migrated into me.

Imagine being real Jackie, the bodily incarnation of icon Jackie, the place where photographers seek their proof of the icon's existence. Sublimity rests on identification with Jackie—imagining the icon's interior monologue; playing, again and again, the game of juxtaposing real Jackie and icon Jackie, to jolt oneself with the uncanny realization that some ghosts and some gods actually inhabit real bodies.

Jackie's sublimity, therefore, resides in the myth/reality contrast. She's a myth, yes, but she's also a real person. The swift flight from myth to reality hurts, like all sublime infusions; it hurts Jackie (who wanted, we imagine, to be real and not mythic), and it hurts us, because it hurts to shift our cognitive framework between levels of magnitude and truth, between "icon" and "real person." It hurts us (sympathetic pain) to imagine Jackie as an icon and then suddenly to recall, once more, that she is (was) real flesh and blood. The opposite hurts, too: imagining Jackie being lifted, against her will, into iconicity—feeling the glaze of fame, like frost, overtake her features. Even the real Jesus must have had similar growth pangs, as he felt his iconicity gather around him like oppressive ermine, making him invisible but also supra-visible, a resident inside any believer's soul. Jackie, like Jesus, is sublime because she can enter any head; because she can move, subcutaneously, into your psychic system, and you won't be able to find the puncture point, the vein she entered through.

JACKIE'S INFERNO

THE MAJOR MYTH that Jackie lived—the legend that inaugurated her sublimity—was the hell story. Passing through Dallas, she passed through inferno; and we each have our own ideas of hell, and could therefore understand Jackie's experience and register its extremity.

Jacqueline Onassis, in her essay on Diana Vreeland, quotes Vreeland discussing Sartre's *No Exit* and the problem of lost identity: " 'Do you remember at the end, those three characters are standing in a room? There is glaring light, no shadow, no place to ever be away.' She turned her head and placed her hand to shade her face. 'This forever, this is hell. And there is no mirror and you lose your face, you lose your self-image. When that is gone, that is hell. Some may think it vain to look into a mirror, but I consider it an identification of self.' " So Jacqueline Onassis and Diana Vreeland had a conversation about fame and loss of self, a conversation in which they justified vanity (or the love of clothes and appearances) by proposing that without a mirror, without narcissism, one is in hell. Being an icon perpetuated the hell of Dallas; to overcome hell, Jackie needed to look in a mirror. Jackie's glamour—her stylishness, her dependence on the realm of *mirrors*—was an assertion of self, against the annihilation represented by assassins and by what she allegedly called the public's "oppressive obsession" with her.

If Jackie passed through hell; if the space of the photograph, in which we still perceive Jackie, *is* hell, the inferno where real Jackie must live, oppressed by her own, unwanted iconicity; then Jackie is a Persephone, or a Eurydice, a woman who doesn't really belong in hell but dwells there as kidnapped victim or as pretty visitor. Will we be Jackie's Orpheus, singing her back to life? Or will we look back? Does excessive reminiscence moor Jackie where she doesn't want to be? Indeed, perhaps our nostalgia dooms Jackie; limits her mobility; keeps her embedded in oppressive, identityless darkness.

Jackie had a relationship with the Furies, which makes her wild and profound. Doom came to her, in Dallas, and it may have seemed retribution for hubris.

While we acknowledged the horror of having one's husband murdered before one's own eyes and the world's, Jackie's presence near bloodshed seemed, if scrutinized from a fey distance, sublime. The tragic credentials she thenceforth held, She Who Passed Through Hell, made her seem an elect, if pitiful, being. No one would willingly endure what she endured; but having done so accorded her a tragic stature. She wouldn't be an icon if she hadn't passed through hell, and survived the trip, and never described, afterward, what hell looked like, or whether it resembled other mansions and situations she'd encountered. One assumes that even an event as unprecedented as JFK's murder gave Jackie déjà vu—as if she'd been prepared, by some early sorrow we'd never thoroughly know, for his martyrdom.

Jackie climbed on the trunk of the car, looking for a piece of the President's skull. She climbed *backward*. We look back at Jackie in Dallas and establish her iconicity and sublimity thereby. There's a metaphoric equivalence between our retrospective glances toward Jackie in 1963 and Jackie's own movement onto the back of the car, an instant obsessively replayed. Symbolically, aren't we climbing with her on the trunk of the car? Aren't we trying to retrieve some shard? Because Jackie herself could not remember climbing backward, that moment has become a figure for *the failure to remember, the failure to retrieve.* Jackie couldn't retrieve the memory of the incident; Jackie couldn't retrieve JFK's life; we can't retrieve Jackie, who seems always as lost to us as JFK was lost to her.

But there's a second sense in which Jackie looked back. First, she climbed back on the car's rear deck, and second, she looked back into the car at JFK, slumped in his seat. As *Life*'s commemorative volume puts it: "In desperation Mrs. Kennedy turned to look back at her stricken husband."

Jackie is caught, in photos, in the hopeless posture of looking back. One feels terribly sorry for Jackie, not only because JFK has been shot but because she's caught motionless in a photo of that dreadful moment, as if the photograph, by arresting her in the instant of horror, magnified it. Jackie's hell, therefore, isn't just Dallas, or assassination, but being sentenced, for life, within the frames of the Zapruder footage.

Inferno is a temporal disturbance. At least, in Dante's *Inferno* the dead remain conscious, in pain, and they repeat, forever, semblances (or ironic reversals) of their sins. "Dallas," or "November 22, 1963," or "Jackie's Ordeal," or "JFK's Murder," or "What Jackie Went Through": whatever grave phrase I use, that moment disturbed the time line, because the assassination instant (via Jackie's *reaction*) remains alive. Our wish to plumb the depths of what Jackie felt or didn't feel, what Jackie was looking for on the back of the car, ensures that this instant retains an afterlife.

Jackie reportedly remembered the "very neat" expression on JFK's face after he was shot. We can't remember JFK's expression; we weren't in the car. But we can remember Jackie's "neat" movement onto the rear deck of the car. It's "neat" because it is definitive, incomprehensible, and uncommunicative. We may not care about JFK; we may not care about American sovereignty. But we still want to know what Jackie was looking for; or, rather, we want to insert ourselves into a moment excerpted from the flow of time. What makes this assassination instant "infernal" isn't just its tragic dimension; it's the moment's detachability from forward-moving time, and Jackie's position as the backward-crawling woman locked in this instant's cage. Years pass, and still November 22, 1963, retains its ripeness, its willingness to be interpreted. The moment is flexible and capacious and infinitely extensible because it's a frozen instant with a living woman captured inside it, like a woman in hell, compulsively repeating a task without meaning. The task Jackie repeats is to crawl on the trunk of the car and then to look back at JFK, to crawl on the trunk of the car and then to look back at JFK . . . When we rescrutinize this instant, under the guise of trying to figure out who killed JFK, we're actually participating in Jackie's inferno, by resubjecting the prisoner to her set task, a mirror of our own. We look backward; so does Jackie. Neither of us will solve anything. The limo speeds up, and time moves on, but icon Jackie will never leave this instant's fiery perimeter.

We repeat a movement, or a task, or a ceremony, if

we want to figure out who is responsible for a crime. The crime was JFK's murder. Who did it? Seeking the perpetrator, we repeat the Zapruder footage; we reexamine the moment of Jackie climbing backward. Jackie worship is itself a ceremonial, repeated task. Climbing backward onto the trunk of the car, we are trying to retrieve a piece of our consciousness. The world's "oppressive obsession" with Jackie is a ritual repetition of a single crime, *our* crime, not Jackie's: the crime of wanting to exit a vehicle, the crime of wanting to be rid of one's President, or one's husband, or one's father, or one's life. Or simply the crime of wanting to flee one's identity. We repeat icon Jackie to make sure she's stuck in her identity. Meanwhile our own identities, while we watch Jackie, may enjoy radical flux and discontinuity. We flee the limo again and again; we're alone now, without the President, and we're stupefied but renewed. Our life as icon has begun.

JACKIE AS DIVA

NOW THAT I'VE TRAVELED with Jackie through hell, I'll confess it: I love to imagine her supremacy over her enemies and detractors—even over her husbands. She was called "Durga, Goddess of Power," when she traveled in 1962 to India, and she is my Goddess of Power. Jackie biographies confirm (true? false?) an image of Jackie's covert will to power, of Jackie as diva: ruthless, imperial. Hairdresser Jean-Louis called her "a bit impossible." I want to hear about Jackie's impossibility not so that I can impugn her for it but so that I can celebrate her for it. Knowledge of Jackie's behind-the-scenes intractability counteracts the sanctified, saccharine myth. Her supremacy may have been simulacral: she had a camp relation to power—that is, she didn't have real sovereignty, only an appearance of it. And the appearance seemed so convincing, it almost seduced us into forgetting that power is sometimes terrifyingly genuine. For the reader of gossip scoops, icon Jackie's power *is* genuine. As image, she always gets her way, and we let her live under our skin because we take vicarious satisfaction in hearing about her petty triumphs and excesses, which she has earned the right to enjoy, having passed through inferno.

Jackie reigned from an early age; schoolgirl friends nicknamed her "Jacqueline Borgia." Of Jackie as First

Lady, *Variety* declared, JACKIE IS UNDISPUTED TOP FEMME IN WORLD. No one dares dispute that Jackie is Top; the rest of the world must play Bottom. In icon Jackie's closet S/M drama, she rules, like Diana Rigg in *The Avengers*, with feline sinuosity. Her sovereignty proceeds from fashion smarts. She makes the Best-Dressed List, surpassing Rose; she calls Lady Bird (behind her back) a "pork chop." The other First Ladies and Kennedy women serve as her undistinguished backdrop; they're drab and dull so that Jackie can shine. Recall, again, the picture of Jackie on the porch of the Kennedy Hyannis Port house: exotically beautiful, she seems not only a finer "specimen" than Jean and Ethel et al., but a possible subversive who's infiltrated the clan to destroy it. As Christina Onassis later (allegedly) said of her stepmother: "What amazes me is that she survives while everybody around her drops. She's dangerous, she's deadly. She has decimated at least two families—the Kennedys and mine. If I never see her again as long as I live it will be too soon." Jackie didn't attend Christina's funeral. Do you blame Jackie?

Christina's astonishing comment comes from C. David Heymann's gossipy but unreflective *A Woman Named Jackie*. From such biographies it's possible to confirm Jackie's "Durga" identity. Remember, any evidence that Jackie was "bad" (selfish, ruthless, catty) can be transvalued by the Jackie fan into evidence of Jackie's goodness (resilience, fierceness, drollness).

Jackie called Rose a "dinosaur" and a "dimwit." Jackie would "visibly cringe" while the Kennedy clan cavorted. Janet tried to get Jackie to change her hairstyle before the Inauguration, but Rosemary the stylist said, "The new First Lady's mind, as well as her sweeping chignon, were set." Wrote Jackie, in a memo, about the nanny: "Maud Shaw won't need much in her room. Just find a wicker wastebasket for her banana peels and a little table for her false teeth at night. . . ." It's important that Jackie be a wit, if we support her Borgia tendencies. In the White House, Jackie demanded new towels three times a day. Of the Girl Scouts, the Muscular Dystrophy Association, the Association for the Prevention of Cruelty to Animals, and the Commission for the Blind and Physically Handicapped, Jackie allegedly said, "Give them to Lady Bird." Jackie was adept at the so-called PBO: the polite brushoff. Jackie referred to her Fine Arts Commission as "my Politburo." Greedy for donations, she wrote, in a note, "I hope that if you ever see Mrs. Warren, you will light a fire under her—as there she is sitting in Newport— with so many houses filled with pretty things and she hasn't even produced one tiny thing" (i.e., she hasn't donated a single bibelot to Jackie's White House). Jackie enjoyed receiving leaders in the White House after Jack's death, according to her (jealous?) cousin John Davis: "Finally she was running the White House. She loved being the center of attraction with all the world's dignitaries coming to pay homage to her." She was furious that LBJ called her "sweetheart" on the phone. Said one informant, according to Heymann, "As for publicity, Jackie loved it. Couldn't get enough of it." Some Whitney woman called Jackie a "publicity maven." Truman Capote, ever unreliable, said that Bunny Mellon has "lasted" as a friend of Jackie only "because she's terrified of Jackie." He called Nancy Tuckerman Jackie's "indentured slave." Jackie had the power to stop conversation in any room she entered, simply by entering it. Jackie never took second helpings at dinner parties, and others were ashamed, in her presence, to do so. At first Jackie wouldn't fly Olympic airplanes because they reeked of feta. Jackie, however, wanted to keep rabbits with her in First Class. At a dinner party, Jackie silently "stared into space all evening." Jackie asked for a discount at Bonwit Teller's because she gave the store such good publicity. Her doctor advised Jackie to "stay put" at Ari's deathbed, because "the whole world is watching," but Jackie flew back to New York anyway. When Sophia Loren and Jackie rode the same elevator, once, at Doubleday, Jackie seemed jealous that Sophia upstaged her. Do you believe it? Do you believe that Jackie agreed to play a cameo role (as a "modern witch converted to Christianity") in a Pier Carpi film?

Borrowed gossip incites my desire for a Jackie who can snub, shop, flee, bitch, play; a Jackie not above petty rivalry with Sophia Loren or Joan Kennedy; a Jackie who loves her own publicity, and clips photos of herself from magazines to place in a scrapbook; a Jackie who "knew just what costumes to wear, just what light she looked best in"; a Jackie whose "fantastic" snobbishness trips my light fantastic and ensures her the supreme seat. Sublime, to get international credit for being unselfish and soft-spoken, and then, behind the world's back, harbor an egotism of murderous intensity. In the fantasy of icon Jackie as Durga, Goddess of Power, she can wreck or salvage any party, simply by skipping it, or attending it; she wears white gloves and by doing so implies that the women who lack the taste to wear white gloves are slobs. Somewhere in icon Jackie a fat slob is locked, waiting to be released. Or somewhere in the fat slob, a Jackie O beats its diaphanous wings.

In order to explain the pleasure I take in myths of

Jacqueline Borgia, I need to unveil the concept of the so-called "block lady"—my private phrase for the ladies who were my neighbors when I was a child on an ordinary suburban middle-class tract-house cul-de-sac. I am closer to a block lady than I am to Jackie. I experience the allure of Jackie from the block lady's point of view. I perceive Jackie as the kind of woman who can put a block lady to shame. Icon Jackie is on God's Best-Dressed List and the block lady wears sloppy flip-flops. "Block lady" is shorthand for my earliest desire to transcend what I myopically imagined were the grim circumstances of my youth. And yet I loved the block ladies; I may have scorned their cigarettes and their braying phlegm-laced laughs, but I secretly adored them for seeming, also, on a generous continuum with stars like Liz and Jackie. These block ladies didn't have real jobs; as far as I could tell, they lived to gossip, smoke, drink, and wear muumuus. Muumuus held an inverse glamour; my vocation would be to perform that magical reversal, to *invert* the block lady's paraphernalia (polyester stretch pants) into the apparatus of a Jackie, and simultaneously to invert ethereal Jackie into a block lady, fated to endure (and to enjoy!) endless baked-bean bingo evenings. This was my life, too, and I wanted the power to flip it; I realized I could best reverse my premises and foundations by helping the block lady (in my imagination) realize her secret affinity with Jackie/Liz, and by teasing the lineaments of the block lady out from Liz/Jackie's glamorous opacity.

Jackie triumphs because her style is aristocratic. And yet her "high-class" status is only a vehicle for intangible spiritual victory. Jackie rules and ascends to nirvana not just because she's rich and refined but because we think she *deserves* to win—because we've thrown our own id's capital behind her, and imagine that beneath her glamour there rests a sad grimy alterity, a previous incarnation of sour-smelling muumuus. In an earlier life, Jackie was dowdy. She's come back, in the body of Jacqueline Borgia, to conquer her old enemies. You can't refuse such a fairy-tale character her destined victory. She's "Top Femme," and her "top" position is delightful because she seems not to care. She pretends indifference to fame and supremacy. Meanwhile she achieves, through her blasé composure, perpetual glory. Her injunction "Do not look at me" means that look we will.

As I pen this sober interpretation of icon Jackie, I imagine that two other books are being written, somewhere in the world. One book is the true biographical account of lovely Jackie: how she raised her children right, treated her men right; how she suffered, how she stoically endured. The other book is the life of Jacqueline Borgia: how she bitched; how she wasted money; how she demolished her enemies. I want to read both.

IT'S TEMPTING to play the "what if" game with Jackie's life: to imagine alternative scenarios. About Jackie, it's difficult to distinguish rumor from fact; thus, hypothetical narratives and outcomes haunt the Jackie contemplator. From incomplete fables, possibilities flower. Her life seems simultaneously to have followed a foretold path and to have been subject at every moment to revision and whim. At any time she might have leapt into a different identity, a rockier or rosier destiny.

Most pressing are the assassination "what ifs." The real Jackie was tormented by thoughts of how she might have averted the catastrophe. And so I wonder, as if on her behalf: What if she'd insisted the bubbletop be lowered over the car? What if she hadn't accompanied him to Dallas? What if she'd asked him to turn around? What if he'd survived and been reelected? Would they have divorced? Would his affairs have become public knowledge? Would Jackie have become as iconic, with JFK still alive to overshadow her?

Bouvier "what ifs" also haunt the Jackie-contemplating imagination. What if Jackie hadn't married Jack? What if she'd stayed single, or married her first fiancé, the investment banker? What if she'd accepted the *Vogue* Prix de Paris and worked in France? What if Jackie had turned out like Little Edie? What if Jackie had become a painter or journalist? What if Lee had become more famous than Jackie, and Jackie had never outgrown that stupefied look she wore until she learned how to maneuver her own charisma?

Then there are Aristotle "what ifs": What if Jackie hadn't married him? What if he'd married Maria? What if he'd been nicer to Jackie, or if he'd divorced her, as, apparently, he'd planned (via Roy Cohn)? The Ari "what ifs" are less compelling.

Maternal "what ifs": What if Jackie hadn't suffered a miscarriage, a stillbirth? If Jackie'd had more kids, would she have been too busy to be an icon? If baby Patrick hadn't died in August 1963, would Jack have escaped assassination? Most "what ifs" involve magical thinking, a hope that causality's domino chain can be interrupted. (For example, if JFK hadn't been killed, then maybe no one would have shot Bobby.)

The "what if" game reveals several working principles. It demands that we believe in destiny, and that we take Jackie's life to be overdetermined, so that if one variable were altered, the entire sequence would reconfigure. On the other hand, the game assumes that Jackie's life, though foreknown, is also random and loose, and therefore open to change at every turn. The game assumes that Jackie is a victim of her destiny, and needs to be rescued from it by our imaginative restructuring of events; we may wish to reconceive Jackie's life so that she would never have married Jack, so that, instead, perhaps, she'd have married the cute sketching instructor she's photographed beside in Venice (reproduced in *One Special Summer*). Maybe once upon a time, before politics and fatality descended on Jackie, she'd been free to express arty impulses, and flirt with bohemian men as outré and alluring as she. By imagining that Jackie's destiny is malleable, we may convince ourselves that we can affect our own fates, that we, too, with proper effort, could lift ourselves from compromise and dolor.

Rearranging Jackie's life from afar—what if Jackie hadn't married Jack? what if Jack hadn't been killed? what if Jackie had consented to give interviews? what if Jackie had written her memoirs, confessing all?—disturbs the time line and deprives events of solid absoluteness. Icon Jackie comes to us as a set of tableaux that seem tragically fixed yet also seductively alterable; choosing to alter them in imagination, we perform a devastatingly magical act, taking away time's rude sequence, pretending that history can be, through whim and wish, respliced, and that wherever there are uncertainties in the story of Jackie, pieces missing, events and motives we'll never know, we can replace enigmas with scenarios of how different Jackie's life *might have been*, if the gods, for a moment, had countenanced a betrayal of the already scripted sequence of events.

It is a pleasure, through imaginative voodoo, to redo Jackie's life. She has become not a true historical character but a fetish. Ultimately we fool around with fetishes if we want to conceal our own decline and diminishment. We sense that Jackie's life obeys an upward movement —she climbs toward success—and yet the "success" is tinged by tragedy; and in order to rewrite fears of our own decay, fears that we, unlike Jackie, totter on the verge of annihilation, we pretend that Jackie's life, though it's already unfolded, still might be changed, might be rethought and reorganized around new, imaginary events. (What if Jackie hadn't married Jack? What if Jack hadn't cheated on Jackie? What if Jack hadn't been shot? What if Jackie hadn't cared so much about money? What if Jackie had enjoyed her fame? What if Jackie's fame had faded?) We rearrange Jackie's life to avoid noticing our own plight. Said Jackie's cousin, Bouvier Beale (according to C. David Heymann), "If Jackie hadn't married the Irishman, we all could have sunk into shabby gentility, and nobody would have been the wiser." A long-ago Miss America said, "If only I looked like Jackie!" Both hypotheses, both *ifs*—if Jackie hadn't married the Irishman, if only I looked like Jackie—assert the speaker's diminished, depleted status. Each wishful conjecture conceals a *then*, a finer outcome: If only Jackie hadn't married Jack, *then my own life would be miraculously secure*. If only Jack hadn't been shot, *then the intergalactic political family would still be in place, and Jackie would be happy, and I too would be happy*. What if Jackie had told Jack to go to hell? What if, after she was photographed for the cover of *Life*, sailing with Jack ("Senator Kennedy Goes A-Courting"), she'd left him? *Then no one would have known that she might have become an icon, and she would have endured the loneliness of unacknowledged majesty*. Wishing different scenarios for Jackie's past, like playing the lottery, or heeding horoscopes, betrays a lack of trust in agency, and a belief that at a certain charmed instant in every life, choice is possible, but that after this moment has elapsed, one's fate is forever sealed. Dreaming about how Jackie's life might have been different is a disciplined meditation. Playing "what if" with the facts of Jackie's life, we "dwell in Possibility — / A fairer House than Prose," to quote Emily Dickinson. It's a delight, and a subversion of fact—against whose tyranny we need to expend every interpretive wile—to toss out evidence and gorge on the improbable.

BRINGING UP JACKIE

HOW DOES ICON JACKIE function in lay conversations? In what interpersonal verbal situations does she emerge? What does it mean to "cite" Jackie, to drop her name, to bring her up? (Is hers a *dropped* name, or a name one brings *up*? Which way: up? down?)

One may bring up Jackie in order to say "poor Jackie." This must have been especially common between November 1963 and October 1968. But even afterward one might have brought up Jackie to signify respect for her sorrow's immensity. Now, after Jackie's death, this has become the dominant mode: one mentions Jackie in order to pity her, to express grief, or to elegize. This is a *sympathetic* citation of Jackie.

One may bring up Jackie in order to condemn her lifestyle or her taste (excesses, lapses). One expresses scorn about Jackie in order to vaunt one's own moral supremacy. This is a *scornful* citation of Jackie. Most citations of Jackie fall either in the sympathetic or in the scornful category.

Another, less frequently noted, verbal use of Jackie is to elevate or lower the conversational tone. To mention Jackie in the middle of a serious conversation is to lighten it. To mention Jackie in the middle of a men's conversation is to feminize it. Et cetera. Jackie may be summoned, as conversational aid, in order to torque

266

discourse—to move it up, down, left, right. Most often the name "Jackie," particularly if cited as "Jackie O," will stop a conversation. There's nothing much to say after Jackie has been mentioned. The very word seems to curb thought.

Therefore the name "Jackie," in discourse, functions as a joke: a release of steam, a statement of will or desire. Jokes express uncontainable social and psychological forces; jokes put a cap on these forces, but also obliquely vent them. One may make a "bad taste" joke about Dallas; or one may make a joke about Jackie's alleged "bad taste." Any Jackie joke is in bad taste. And Jackie O, a one-liner, a name that, once dropped, stops thought and conversation, or incites knowing laughter, or poignant recollection, works as a joke: either it provokes a reaction or it fails, goes flat. There's a connection between *Jackie* and *joke*: as with all jokes and slips of the tongue, a reference to Jackie functions as a defense or a displacement. When Jackie is mentioned, one should listen for what agendas and meanings are being concealed. An allusion to Jackie is rarely on the surface what it purports to be, for Jackie is a screen.

One may mention Jackie, in conversation, to root oneself historically: to express a relation to a year, a period. This use of Jackie articulates one's position in contemporary history. It's a way of saying "I was there," or "I am here." A temporal reference, Jackie fits into our conversations much as does the weather, or Watergate: to remind us that we are stuck here, and to express an oblique opinion about that rootedness. One mentions Jackie as one mentions the assassination: to initiate a time line. "Jackie" is a period reference, vividly accessible now, perhaps less so in the future. But "Jackie" will doubtless function variously in the speech of different generations: if you're older than Jackie, you'll have one attitude; if you're younger, another. And if you weren't even born until 1970, your attitude toward Jackie obsession may be sheer confusion.

One may mention Jackie in order to elicit Tall Tales, or to tell a Tall Tale oneself. Bringing up Jackie, one may be bragging about having seen her in person. Mentioning Jackie draws fables out from the woodwork. The ultimate use of Jackie in conversation is to make a claim of personal contiguity or intimacy: to say, "I knew Jackie." Like a wonder of the world, or a historical freak, Jackie is mentioned as a feat or marvel sighted. As in: *I was present during the Great Earthquake*. Or: *I worked with Jackie at Doubleday*. Think of the people, the world over, claiming Jackie knowledge!

One mentions Jackie in order to tease or stun. For "Jackie," as a concept or icon, has shock value. She shocks because she's associated with lurid, bloody scenes; with greed; with sorrow; with erotomania and anhedonia; with conspicuousness; with invisibility. Saying "Jackie O" fills the mouth with laughing gas. Can the mouth saying "Jackie O" not provoke? Was the nickname "Jackie O" coined for a purpose other than to titillate and sensationalize? Hear its explosiveness: "Jackie O." For posterity I need to make perfectly clear that in my day we actually referred to Jacqueline Kennedy Onassis as "Jackie O." This was not a rare affectation; for at least two decades it was common currency among many classes. And it was, on a mild, mild level, a shocking expletive. It interrupted the flow of polite life with a pretend hiccup.

To drop "Jackie" into a conversation is to let out a melancholy note with no fixed implication. It's never clear what "Jackie" means, and so you can let the word fly, you can let "Jackie O" go into speech without circumspection or forethought. Not much may come from the reference. It will create a minor eddy and then disappear. That disappearance is melancholy, too; mournful, that the name "Jackie" can't drive a conversation forever, that its force to provoke must dissipate, if only because there is rarely a ground for Jackie cogitation, only for speculation and fantasy.

"Jackie" is currency: one spends it, expecting reward or exchange value. The price of a conversation goes up when Jackie is mentioned—for a moment. "Jackie" inspires fantasies of fraudulent wealth. Then the value of the reference drops again.

One mentions Jackie to make a political point without seeming to do so. To bring up Jackie isn't to talk overt politics, so there's room for many political statements, none bearing the mark of praxis.

One mentions Jackie to celebrate her, or to celebrate the idea of a personage this illustrious and vague, or to celebrate some value or attribute she supposedly stands for, like beauty, class, mourning, or the past. The category doesn't need explaining; to allude to a realm ("style") by mentioning this specific symbol ("Jackie") allows the subject to evade inspection. Thus one mentions Jackie in order to mystify, or because the mood of mystification is itself alluring, and one wishes to spend more time immersed in it. Bringing up Jackie postpones clarity.

One can't discuss Jackie; one can only mention her. She can only function as the explosion *into* a conversation, not the conversation's steady, droning pulse.

To say "Jackie" is to pose her as a question, to ask,

"*Why* Jackie?" To mention mysterious Jackie is to initiate the task (impossible) of figuring her out.

With whom do you wish to share Jackie in conversation? We speak about Jackie collectively because we want to acknowledge that we're alive, or that we were alive at a certain moment. We want to speak about that aliveness, and have no way except this route of near-muteness, "Jackie." We mention Jackie to each other and we pause, never clear where the reference will go, whether it will blossom into an answer, into the false certitude of biography or autobiography, or into the deception of a gaze—in which case we'll have turned away from speaking about Jackie, and we'll have resorted just to pointing at a photo, saying, "Look, there's Jackie." We'll have fled back from speech into sight. But if we want to return Jackie into speech, where she never, as icon, seems to wish to go, we need to present her to someone else; we need to share her in conversation. She exists, as icon, to be consumed communally; in pairs, in circles, in crowds. I mention Jackie mostly because I want to be assured that I inhabit the same universe as other people; that I am not alone on a distant shore. Jackie glues me to this world—most effectively when I can find a way to mention her name or her attributes, when I can find a pretext, however frail, to introduce her into a conversation, even at the risk of non sequitur, bathos, and incoherence.

JACKIE'S

REPLACEABILITY

AS A FIGURE with a halo, or with a scarlet "O," icon Jackie is ruefully generic—rueful because I'd like to imagine that she is irreplaceable, that no other star or symbol could galvanize emotion as she could. And yet the tides of worship move on; other goddesses will take up her slack.

One of Jackie's original and primary functions was as national (or international) fetish: because JFK was killed, a populace needed Jackie to stand in for his absence. If JFK's death was a sort of national castration, then Jackie was where the nation could look instead, as a means of looking away from Jack's loss. Because November 22, 1963, represented an interruption in history, a ripping open, a cut, a wound, obsessive attention to Jackie deflected the national gaze from the missing place, the rupture. That "Jackie" is itself also a man's name made it easier to see slim, contained, and silent Jackie as a replacement Jack. Part of the fascination Jackie inspired—the elated and surprised sense that Jackie was uncannily *still here*—emerged from the knowledge that Jack was not; to look at pretty Jackie was, indirectly, to look at murdered Jack, or to feel, in one's heart, a sensation that a *replacement* was occurring: Jackie was standing in for Jack, Jackie's silence was standing in for the muteness of Jack's corpse. Because Jackie was never just herself, but carried vibrations of Jack's absence, it will be possible for other figures to carry Jackie's vibrations—for her legend to diffuse itself in tributaries, to migrate into objects with which she was associated, places and buildings and causes, and for other stars, other silences, to preoccupy us in her stead.

In sum: since the allure of Jackie was itself a conglomeration of borrowed auras; since Jackie's uncanniness came, in part, from our sense that she was a scene of migrations and displacements (she'd borrowed Jack's aura, the gleam of movie stars, and even the cachet of commonness, the sense—subversive—that ordinary people, such as "block ladies," had Jackie potential, and that Jackie was simply a commonplace person turned inside out, surreally magnified); since Jackie glittered because other scenes and other bodies had migrated into her, then it will be possible for Jackie's aura, which seems now properly and eternally her possession, to migrate *away* from her, into other stars and other monuments.

About aura, we have amnesia; the aura of antique stars, of bygone potentates, seems dim now, fictive and hypothetical. It's hard to get worked up now about Shirley Temple, or the Duchess of Windsor, except as a nostalgia item. Will Jackie suffer a similar fate? Was Jackie a flash in the pan, even if the flash lasted over thirty years and the pan was America? I suggest that Jackie will be remembered not so much for what she *was* but for what she invoked and catalyzed; the emotions she evoked, however, are destined to travel elsewhere. For a time she served as sphinx who helped us stage-manage chaos. The chaos remains, and needs stage-managing; for which we must turn now to other divinities.

Even during the life of icon Jackie, she was replaceable;

because she was silent, and because, in her silence, she seemed endlessly attentive *and* endlessly dismissive (depending on your mood, you could imagine either that her gaze was riveted on you or that she was staring into deep space, turning you into apparition), her patient tolerance for the surrounding blankness meant that you could replace Jackie with another figure of divine oblivion. She was as oblivious to the particulars of your fate as the Virgin Mary or the Buddha. Either you believed that she knew who you were, and dispersed benedictions on you; or else you believed that she didn't know what she was blessing, and that she wasn't really in a position to bless—only that the iconic nature of her photographs made her seem to be eliciting and rewarding worship. Letitia Baldrige, who traveled with Jackie to India in 1962, commented: "I gave the helpful staff of servants in my house a picture of Mrs. Kennedy, and I was startled to see that back in their living compound, the Christian-Hindu worlds had been beautifully melded together by the First Lady. Three pictures were mounted on the crude walls, each with a burning votive candle in front. One depicted a Hindu god, one was of the Virgin Mary, and the third was the photograph of Jacqueline Kennedy." Jackie's fitness to reign in a "crude" servant shrine, beside the Madonna and a Hindu divinity, proves that once you are set up for worship, it doesn't matter exactly what or whom you worship. Or else Jackie earned her place in pantheistic stratospheres because of her *extreme* beauty (large face, large smile, large hairdo); it's easier to lose yourself while adoring a wide head.

We call Jacqueline Kennedy Onassis "Jackie" because we want to establish familiarity, we want this aloof symbol to be ours. "Jacqueline" would have been a more appropriate name for this goddess: it would have implied Frenchness, aristocracy. Instead, everyone called her, from the start, "Jackie." Forward, impertinent, when we used the nickname we were saucily approaching the shrine. Saying "Jackie" was to step, boldly, uninvited, into the radius of her gaze; to claim a direct relation.

Fascinations fade. The question remains whether an icon's half-life may be reversed; whether, in fact, the process of canonization for Jackie has only begun; whether more episodes, and more uses, of icon Jackie, wait to be invented. There are countless different Jackies. Jackie may silently say more about difference than she says about sameness, even if her image seems to stay the same, in picture after picture; even if it may seem that everyone feels the same sentiments about Jackie. Probably my Jackie is different from yours. Probably you and I love different Jackies.

MANHATTAN AND OTHER
JACKIE MEMORIALS

MEMORIALS AND SOUVENIRS remain to embody Jackie and to serve as crypts and wonderlands. Even when real Jackie was alive, one couldn't approach her. To most of us she had no location, except in the media. One visited Jackie by visiting a newsstand. Now that Jackie is dead, and the fantasy of meeting the real Jackie has died, too, I have, instead, Jackie memorials, tangible monuments and habitations, places I can visit, legitimately, in a decent search for aura and memory.

About her grave at Arlington, there is nothing to say, except what one says about graves. The consolation of a grave is that it wants you to visit it. Now Jackie's grave holds Lourdes power: it heals. A tabloid headline announces: DOCTORS BAFFLED AS HUNDREDS GET WELL—INSTANTLY! JACKIE KENNEDY'S GRAVE HEALS THE SICK! Said a visitor from North Carolina, "It's a miracle! I touched her tombstone—& my pain vanished." A doctor muses: "A powerful curative force is emanating from that grave." A drug addict from New Orleans was cured of her addiction: "When I got there I felt my craving for heroin leave me." Odd, that Jackie, our drug, should now, after death, undo addiction. Her cool gaze has always been a healing stare, for those of us who'd known how to excavate photos and immobilities for their undercover miracles.

Arlington, though miraculous, is a governmental monument; there, Jackie has been assimilated into national narrative. For unassimilated Jackie one must visit other memorials.

Sites devoted to the memory of JFK are also obliquely Jackie's: the JFK International Airport, the Kennedy Center; boulevards, schools, plazas. And the JFK Memorial Library, Jackie's project, at Columbia Point in Boston: it poses as a research center, austere and useful, and yet it embodies Jackie's desire for Jack. She was instrumental in the museum's planning; she helped choose the architect, I. M. Pei. It is her building—her major public address to Jack. A letter to him, in stone, it conveys her constancy, her status as survivor and keeper of the flame. It says, "I have done my duty to your memory." It also says, "I respect your loneliness and solitude, which I share." Situated on a spar of land, far from Boston's hub, this isolated, visionary mausoleum communicates the themes of solitary voyage. Rarely do troubled marriages attempt to cohere in the form of a public monument: visiting the JFK Memorial Library, one apprehends Jackie's version of her marriage to Jack, although, until her death, she was nowhere commemorated in it. (Now she's subject of a small exhibit, including a gown and a video loop.) The museum superficially subordinates her; virtually no pictures of her are sold in the gift shop. The memorial is *by* Jackie but not *about* Jackie. And yet, visiting it, I feel I am trespassing on Jackie's property: delectable, authorized transgression.

The White House is a Jackie memorial. Others live there now; others reign. But it was once Jackie's, and although Pat Nixon took down the bronze plaque commemorating that IN THIS ROOM LIVED JOHN FITZ-

GERALD KENNEDY WITH HIS WIFE JACQUELINE, the White House tangibly proves that Jackie once had legitimate custody over our affection. After she left the White House it became prurient or intrusive to care about Jackie; but when she lived in the White House, Jackie obsession was patriotic.

Now Hammersmith Farm, the house in Newport, Rhode Island, where Jackie spent summers in her adolescence, is a museum (hyperbolically called a "Summer White House") run by a firm named Camelot Gardens. If you've spent time looking at photographs of Jackie's wedding, then Hammersmith (where the wedding reception was held) will offer material coordinates for what seemed phantom events. See the balcony over which Jackie tossed her bouquet. See the riding ring where Jackie and the Kennedy brothers posed for the famous photograph. See Jackie's bedroom, with twin beds, tiled-floor bathroom, and a window overlooking Narragansett Bay. On Jackie's bookshelf, I noticed a paperback copy of Sylvia Plath's *The Bell Jar*; published in the mid-1960s, this book obviously postdates Jackie's tenure at Hammersmith Farm. And so the decor in this room, or at least the books on its shelves, must not be authentically Jackie's. See, however, the veritable fixtures of affluence, including buttons, in each room, labeled "M" and "P," to call the maid and the pantry. See, downstairs in the study, photographs of Jackie and her children—pictures that Janet Auchincloss actually pinned to this bulletin board? Compared to other visitable Newport mansions, Hammersmith looks rather plain. The absence of the rococo proves Jackie's or Janet's "good taste." The museum wishes to advertise lavishness (the docent bragged about Mrs. Auchincloss's extravagant and fastidious flower arrangements) and yet it also seems just an "ordinary" mansion, like the houses in which classic M-G-M movies were filmed. When I visited Hammersmith (it was August 1993), Jackie was still alive. She owned her aura then; it hadn't yet traveled into inanimate sites, like Hammersmith. I looked out the window in her bedroom, saw Narragansett Bay, and wondered whether that view had fostered a contemplative and spacious adolescence, or whether Jackie's evolving personality had been, in other ways, cramped. The docent said, as we climbed the stairs, "I'll meet you down the hall in Jackie's room!" Downstairs, the docent had called her "Mrs. Onassis" or "Jacqueline Kennedy Onassis." The act of ascending the Hammersmith stairs transported the docent into the inner circle of Jackie's affection. I remember wondering whether the docent had met Jackie, and whether the chance to meet Jackie was one of the job's perks. I imagined the docent having long conversations about "Mrs. Onassis" with the woman who sold tickets to Hammersmith, and also, perhaps, with the gardener, who tried to maintain the property at a floral pitch in keeping with Mrs. Auchincloss's high standard.

My favorite Jackie monument is Manhattan. Legitimately I pass sundry buildings associated with Jackie, and think "Jackie." Manhattan is too large and complex to symbolize just one person. But she is not just one person; she is a system of correspondences and intersections, parallels and perpendiculars, like Manhattan's grid.

Manhattan Jackie memorials include her apartment building, 1040 Fifth Avenue, and the entire block on which it sits, and its side streets, and the blocks of Fifth Avenue surrounding it, the blocks on which one may feel 1040's imminence. ("We're almost at Jackie's place!")

Central Park, because Jackie frolicked in it, and had a view of it, is Jackie's. The reservoir has been named Jacqueline Kennedy Onassis Reservoir. I would have given her all of Fifth Avenue, or at least "Museum Mile"; I would have called it "Jackie's Mile." Grand Central is a Jackie monument; she helped to save it from destruction, and so, the day after her death, visitors signed a memorial book in the station to pay their respects. Grand Central, symbol of mob scenes ("it's as crowded as Grand Central Station" signifies unwanted hubbub and traffic), is an odd memorial for a reclusive woman; and yet Grand Central, scene of chance intersections and fortuitous love matches (like the old Penn Station, where Judy Garland and Robert Walker rendezvous in *The Clock*), has become Jackie's. Walking beneath Grand Central's starry ceiling, I feel strangely connected to Jackie, even if she rarely rode trains. The feeling of connection isn't new; I've felt linked to Jackie for most of my life. But the link's legitimacy is new. Because her work in saving Grand Central has proved Jackie *the invisible benefactress of Manhattan's weal*, I sense Jackie's presence amid Grand Central's crowd, as if even the act of *commuting* has become a figure for Jackie as transportation artist, initiator of hysterical/sublime transports. Distance from other strangers—travelers, transients, police—embodies one's distance from Jackie; or else Jackie draws together Grand Central's mobs into a silent, Saharan embrace.

Every Manhattan store or church or cultural center that Jackie visited now resonates as a Jackie memorial: the stretch of Park Avenue where her funeral was held; the Pierre, where Ari had a suite; the Carlyle, where she stayed as First Lady, and while she was waiting to move into 1040 Fifth Avenue; Kenneth's, and Van Cleef &

Arpels, and Tiffany's, and "21," and the Cooper-Hewitt, and the New York Public Library at Forty-second Street, and La Côte Basque . . .

Jackie has turned places of commerce into shrines. Stores (Bergdorf Goodman's, for example) are now *places where Jackie once experienced desire*. Never forget the story of the lucky shopper trying on a "green cashmere sweater set" in Bloomingdale's, a stranger to whom Jackie said, "You should take them, they go with your eyes." To this day, Jackie blesses purchases: "Just keep on with your shopping," her image seems to whisper.

Sunlight in Manhattan speaks of Jackie, if only because in her anonymous "Talk of the Town" piece she described the Upper East Side in bright sunlight: "Accompanied by Mr. Katz, we left the Metropolitan and walked up the Park side of Fifth Avenue in bright sunlight. We stopped at the corner of Ninety-fourth Street and looked across at the façade of what is still known as Audubon House, a six-story Georgian building of red brick, with shiny black shutters. Lovely it is." Jackie knew buildings, addresses, façades, sunlight, shutters: walking down Fifth Avenue in bright sunlight is my Jackie memorial, even if I sully the memorial by speaking about it.

I consider the transplanted Temple of Dendur in the Metropolitan Museum of Art to be Jackie's mystic property, not only because she indirectly facilitated its transfer to the Met, and because she attended parties held at the Temple, but because one can see 1040 Fifth Avenue from inside the glass-enclosed museum wing devoted to the Temple, and therefore, I assume, Jackie could see (with the aid of a telescope?) from her Fifth Avenue penthouse down to the Temple. I must turn to rather obscure aesthetic and holy venues like the Temple of

Dendur to worship Jackie because the feelings of remorse and elation that icons like Jackie evoke do not hold a position of value in our public life. Where—except for here, in these sentences, or silently, at the Temple of Dendur—can I remark on Jackie's significance, on her tendency to ripple into unseen, undusted corners of one's life?

Certain Manhattan institutions bear a relation to Jackie: the New York City Ballet, for one. For another, the media, particularly trade book publishing. Doubleday is a Jackie site; but because a wide range of publishing figures had professional dealings with Jackie, and because, symbolically, *Jackie as book editor* invested Manhattan's publishing industry with a certain glamour, a glamour shared by such figures as *The New Yorker*'s Tina Brown, accordingly the New York book world, or the New York media in general, contains Jackie aura. The media reacted with such uniform intensity to Jackie's death not merely because they wished to describe public grief, but because icon Jackie was a media creation, and so the media were mourning their own child, their own high-toned product. Often memorialized was not Jackie's life, but her life as it appeared in the media. Many magazines—*The New Yorker, Vogue, Harper's Bazaar, Town and Country, House Beautiful*—tried to express or invent a connection between Jackie and the periodical's secret history. *Life*, for example, reported in its special commemorative issue: Jackie "met recently with Petranek and David Friend, LIFE's director of photography, to show them a new collection of photographs. She was very thin, they report, but seemed vibrant and vital. She served her visitors lunch, showed them the photographs, then quietly took her leave. Two days later she checked into New York Hospital. Six weeks after that she was dead. Her last business appointment was the meeting with LIFE." Thus Jackie, as icon, had come full circle; Jackie's "last meeting with LIFE" might as well have been a warm-up for meeting her maker. The media mourned Jackie not only because they wished to remember her, and loved her (can the media *love*?), but because Jackie herself, as editor, was part of the media, and shed luster on the enterprise, making its practitioners feel that the process of commodifying glamour was itself glamorous. Jackie loved books; when John Jr. spoke to reporters after her death, he said that she died surrounded by her books. New York's book industry remains surrounded by Jackie's memory, an embrace that enables Manhattan's "book people" to feel that the process of book production is itself iconic, that books are people, and that the difference between a "celebrity" and a "book" is minimal (celebrities write books, celebrities *are* books).

Icon Jackie has migrated not only into Manhattan, and into Manhattan's media, but into modes of action, of thought, and of gesture. Imitators of "the Jackie look" have, for thirty years, absorbed her glamour. Now that Jackie is dead, those who wear Jackie-style sunglasses, or scarves, or A-line skirts, or stacked heels, or bouffants, or who speak like Jackie, or who value what they imagine Jackie valued (privacy, heroism, antiques) are keepers of the Jackie flame; Jackie's mode has died only to be reborn in their bodies. Imitation of Jackie, once a form of borrowing, or envy, or love, now has become a style of memorial; to imitate Jackie is to mourn her, and to imagine that her attitude toward the world has been exported into the emulator's body. Looking at the ocean, or reading a book, or putting on sunglasses: these generic acts are now invested with Jackie's presence. It may be enough just to pick up a book to feel like Jackie. It may be enough just to put on dark sunglasses, while staring out at the bright Atlantic, to feel that Jackie's introspection has become your own.

Contemplation and *self-containment* are Jackie's legacies, or hauntings. Engaging in contemplation, silently, I feel that I am recapitulating Jackie; or that I am responding to her presence; or that I am haunted by her. Putting on a pillbox hat is one way to memorialize Jackie. Visiting Arlington is another. But engaging, at length, in "sessions of sweet silent thought" may be, too, a full-strength Jackie memorial. A woman whose introspection no one had any inkling of, a woman who seemed, therefore, to live without self-reflection, is now a patron saint of introspection. Jackie haunts us when we silently consider our position, when we, self-consciously, *locate* ourself against a cultural or historical landscape. The act of silent self-positioning (call it *interior posing*), not without its modicum of resistance and defiance, is a Jackie effect; when you compose yourself inwardly, even without saying a word you perpetuate Jackie. The body that positions itself, that reflects on its place and its predicament, is a Jackie museum; not Arlington, not Hammersmith, but *the body that knows where it stands* is the fittest Jackie memorial, however anonymous and unmarked. To know oneself; to make a list; to breathe; to walk; to put on sunglasses; to swim; to reflect; to sleep; to read; to watch; to be watched; to enjoy gusts, or guests; to adjust one's windblown hair—these are all Jackie activities, and by performing them, you become, if you wish, one of Jackie's inheritors and curators, transforming a media icon into a magical lesson in embodiment, your teacher in the art of training your "I" to feel like an "I."

It has been my duty (a task both welcome and arduous) to describe Jackie emulation; to describe the imaginary effects of an icon; to demonstrate, through speech, the allure of a certain silence. I didn't want to be sentimental. The point was to speak clearly and at some length about the effects of an icon whose powers seemed misunderstood, even maligned; a star who had the uncanny ability to penetrate every pore of one's skin, without saying a word, without clamoring for attention; a luminary who epitomized the system of celebrity and yet, because she remained seemingly detached from hers, portrayed elevation (or illumination) as an elixir available to all, and who made it seem that the path to celebrity (or the path to *centrality*) was to render oneself anonymous.

Now the work of interpretation is over, and the pleasure of imitation begins. Even if I never bring up Jackie again, Jackie will have influenced me, infiltrated me. Even if I don't say "I'm imitating Jackie," or "I miss Jackie," or "I wish I'd met Jackie," or "I feel as if I've met Jackie," I will be enacting Jackie. I *do* miss Jackie, most of all because she is part of me; she lent herself to transposition, and to perverse uses. It may sound paradoxical to say "I miss Jackie"; it implies that, for me, she was once *truly here*. Was she ever entirely here? If I'm here, conscious enough of theater and syntax to give voice to these reflections, then it's because Jackie, once here, still animates me, still draws me out.

Is the Jackie moment over? No. Jackie's monumental presence continues to accept worship. Anywhere you look, a photo of her bouffant magnificence awaits your tribute. Flashbulbs still arrest her as she emerges from the darkness of the limo; her face is still glazed against the attention she can't want but must silently accept. Some people thought her moment was 1963. Others thought it 1968. Others claimed her moment ended with the 1960s. Others would say that her moment lasted no longer than the "click" of the camera's shutter. I'd say, though, that Jackie's moment remains available, unfinished; that Jackie's moment reopens or recommences whenever you consider her; that every moment you imitate Jackie, or stage your own emergence into imaginary limelight or into the clarity of self-knowledge, then the Jackie moment rebegins, proving itself a running show, too popular to close. Someone once called Jackie "spacy." If she was spacy, bless her for it. Only a spacy icon has the space for every worshipper. Jackie's spacious duration is still expanding, still permitting imaginary voyage, still providing buoyancy and steam and wind for any flight or cruise the contemplator wants to take. Jackie will never condemn a dreamer's transports. Her motto is motion.

Select Bibliography

For my sense of icon Jackie, I remain most indebted to magazines, tabloids, and ephemera, especially back issues of *Photoplay* and *Life*, and to documentary news footage. For biographical details, I have particularly relied on C. David Heymann's *A Woman Named Jackie* and Kitty Kelley's *Jackie Oh!*; of unusual interest were Mary Van Rensselaer Thayer's *Jacqueline Kennedy: The White House Years*, Mary Barelli Gallagher's *My Life with Jacqueline Kennedy*, and Mini Rhea's *I Was Jacqueline Kennedy's Dressmaker*.

Bair, Marjorie, *Jacqueline Kennedy in the White House* (New York: Paperback Library, 1963).

Baldrige, Letitia, *Of Diamonds and Diplomats* (Boston: Houghton Mifflin, 1968).

Baldwin, Billy, *Billy Baldwin Remembers* (New York and London: Harcourt Brace Jovanovich, 1974).

Barthes, Roland, *Camera Lucida: Reflections on Photography*, trans. Richard Howard (New York: Hill and Wang, 1981).

Birmingham, Stephen, *Jacqueline Bouvier Kennedy Onassis* (New York: Grosset & Dunlap, 1978).

Bouvier, Jacqueline and Lee, *One Special Summer* (New York: Delacorte, 1974).

Bouvier, Kathleen, *To Jack, with Love: Black Jack Bouvier, A Remembrance* (New York: Zebra Books, 1979).

Bowman, Catherine, *1-800-HOT-RIBS* (Salt Lake City: Gibbs Smith, 1993).

Bradlee, Benjamin C., *Conversations with Kennedy* (New York: W. W. Norton, 1975).

Brady, Frank, *Onassis: An Extravagant Life* (Englewood Cliffs, N.J.: Prentice-Hall, 1977).

Bryant, Traphes, with Frances Spatz Leighton, *Dog Days at the White House:*

The Outrageous Memoirs of the Presidential Kennel Keeper (New York: Macmillan, 1975).

Buck, Pearl S., *The Kennedy Women: A Personal Appraisal* (New York: Cowles, 1970).

Cafarakis, Christian, with Jacques Harvey, *The Fabulous Onassis: His Life and Loves*, trans. John Minahan (New York: William Morrow, 1972).

Capote, Truman, *Answered Prayers: The Unfinished Novel* (New York: Random House, 1987).

Carpozi, George, *Jackie & Ari: For Love or Money?* (New York: Lancer Books, 1968).

Colacello, Bob, *Holy Terror: Andy Warhol Close Up* (New York: Harper-Collins, 1990).

David, Lester, and Jhan Robbins, *Richard and Elizabeth* (New York: Ballantine, 1977).

Dyer, Richard, *Heavenly Bodies: Film Stars and Society* (New York: St. Martin's Press, 1986).

Evans, Peter, *Ari: The Life and Times of Aristotle Socrates Onassis* (New York: Summit Books, 1986).

Four Days: The Historical Record of the Death of President Kennedy, Nov. 22–25, 1963, compiled by UPI and *American Heritage* magazine (American Heritage Publishing Co., 1964).

Fraser, Nicholas, Philip Jacobson, Mark Ottaway, and Lewis Chester, *Aristotle Onassis* (Philadelphia and New York: J. B. Lippincott, 1977).

Fuss, Diana, "Freud's Fallen Women: Identification, Desire, and 'A Case of Homosexuality in a Woman,' " *Yale Journal of Criticism*, Vol. 6, No. 1 (Spring 1993): 1–23.

Galella, Ron, *Jacqueline* (New York: Sheed and Ward, 1974).

Gallagher, Mary Barelli, ed. Frances Spatz Leighton, *My Life with Jacqueline Kennedy* (New York: David McKay, 1969).

Griffin, Susan, *A Chorus of Stones: The Private Life of War* (New York: Doubleday, 1992).

Grobel, Lawrence, *Conversations with Capote* (New York: New American Library, 1985).

Hainley, Bruce, "Special Guest Star, Paul Lynde," *Yale Journal of Criticism*, Vol. 7, No. 2 (Fall 1994): 51–84.

Hall, Gordon Langley, and Ann Pinchot, *Jacqueline Kennedy: A Biography* (New York: Frederick Fell, 1964).

Heller, Deanne and David, *Jacqueline Kennedy: The Warmly Human Life*

Story of the Woman All Americans Have Taken to Their Hearts (Derby, Conn.: Monarch Books, 1963).

Heymann, C. David, *A Woman Named Jackie* (New York: Lyle Stuart, 1989).

Horgan, Paul, *Tracings: A Book of Partial Portraits* (New York: Farrar, Straus and Giroux, 1993).

Jackson, Michael, intro. by Jacqueline Onassis, *Moonwalk* (New York: Doubleday, 1988).

Jovich, John B., ed., *Reflections on JFK's Assassination: 250 Famous Americans Remember November 22, 1963* (Kensington, Md.: Woodbine House, 1988).

Kelley, Kitty, *Elizabeth Taylor: The Last Star* (New York: Dell, 1982).

———, *Jackie Oh!* (New York: Ballantine Books, 1978).

Klapthor, Margaret Brown, *The First Ladies* (Washington, D.C.: White House Historical Association with cooperation of National Geographic Society, 1975).

Klein, Richard, *Cigarettes Are Sublime* (Durham, N.C.: Duke University Press, 1993).

Kunhardt, Philip B., Jr., *LIFE in Camelot: The Kennedy Years* (Boston: Little, Brown, 1988).

Lincoln, Evelyn, *My Twelve Years with John F. Kennedy* (New York: Bantam, 1965).

Lowe, Jacques, *JFK Remembered: An Intimate Portrait by His Personal Photographer* (New York: Random House, 1993).

Mailer, Norman, *The Idol and the Octopus* (New York: Dell, 1968).

Manchester, William, *Portrait of a President: John F. Kennedy in Profile*, rev. ed. (Boston: Little, Brown, 1967).

———, *The Death of a President* (New York: Harper & Row, 1967).

Martin, Patricia Miles, illustrations by Paul Frame, *Jacqueline Kennedy Onassis* (New York: G. P. Putnam's Sons, 1969).

Martin, Ralph G., *A Hero for Our Time: An Intimate Story of the Kennedy Years* (New York: Fawcett Crest, 1983).

McShine, Kynaston, ed., *Andy Warhol: A Retrospective* (New York: Museum of Modern Art, 1989).

Meyer, Richard, "Warhol's Clones," *Yale Journal of Criticism*, Vol. 7, No. 1 (Spring 1994): 79–109.

Moore, Marcia, and Mark Douglas, *An Astroanalysis of Jacqueline Onassis* (York, Me.: Arcane Publications, 1970).

Onassis, Jacqueline, ed. and intro., *The Firebird and Other Russian Fairy Tales*, illustrations by Boris Zvorykin (New York: Viking, 1978).

———, ed., intro. by Audrey Kennett, designed by Bryan Holme, *In the Russian Style* (New York: Viking, 1976).

———, "A Visit to the High Priestess of Vanity Fair" (New York: Metropolitan Museum of Art, 1977).

———, "Being Present," *The New Yorker*, January 13, 1975: 26–28.

Pollard, Eve, *Jackie* (London: Macdonald Unit 75, 1969).

Ponge, Francis, *Soap*, trans. Lane Dunlop (London: Jonathan Cape, 1969).

Rhea, Mini, with Frances Spatz Leighton, *I Was Jacqueline Kennedy's Dressmaker* (New York: Fleet Publishing, 1962).

Ronell, Avital, *Crack Wars: Literature—Addiction—Mania* (Lincoln: University of Nebraska Press, 1992).

Shaw, Maud, *White House Nanny: My Years with Caroline and John Kennedy, Jr.* (New York: Signet, 1966).

Shulman, Irving, *"JACKIE!": The Exploitation of a First Lady* (New York: Pocket Books, 1971).

Smith, Duncan, *The Age of Oil* (New York: Slate Press, 1987).

Sontag, Susan, *On Photography* (New York: Farrar, Straus and Giroux, 1977).

Sparks, Fred, *The $20,000,000 Honeymoon: Jackie and Ari's First Year* (New York: Bernard Geis Associates, World Publishing, 1970).

Stafford, Jean, *A Mother in History* (New York: Pharos Books, 1992).

Susann, Jacqueline, *Dolores* (New York: William Morrow, 1976).

Taylor, Elizabeth, *Elizabeth Taylor* (New York: Harper & Row, 1965).

Thayer, Mary Van Rensselaer, *Jacqueline Bouvier Kennedy* (Garden City, N.Y.: Doubleday, 1961).

———, *Jacqueline Kennedy: The White House Years* (Boston: Little, Brown, 1971).

Thomas, Helen, *Dateline: White House* (New York: Macmillan, 1975).

Vermilye, Jerry, and Mark Ricci, *The Films of Elizabeth Taylor* (New York: Citadel, 1989).

Vreeland, Diana, with Christopher Hemphill, *Allure* (New York: Doubleday, 1980).

Warhol, Andy, and Bob Colacello, *Andy Warhol's Exposures* (New York: Andy Warhol Books/Grosset & Dunlap, 1979).

Weinberg, Jonathan, " 'Boy Crazy': Carl Van Vechten's Queer Collection," *Yale Journal of Criticism*, Vol. 7, No. 2 (Fall 1994): 25–49.

West, J. B., with Mary Lynn Kotz, *Upstairs at the White House: My Life* with the *First Ladies* (New York: Coward, McCann & Geoghegan, 1973).

Wicke, Jennifer, *Advertising Fictions: Literature, Advertisement, and Social Reading* (New York: Columbia University Press, 1988).

Wills, Garry, *The Kennedy Imprisonment: A Meditation on Power* (Boston: Little, Brown, 1982).

Wolff, Perry, *A Tour of the White House with Mrs. John F. Kennedy* (Garden City, N.Y.: Doubleday, 1962).